*The Biblical Seminar*
*50*

# SATAN —
# THE PRODIGAL SON?

# SATAN

## THE PRODIGAL SON?

# A Family Problem in the Bible

*Kirsten Nielsen*

Sheffield Academic Press

Original title: *Satan—den fortabte søn*
© Forlaget ANIS, Frederiksberg Alle 10A, 1820
Frederiksberg C, Denmark, and Kirsten Nielsen, 1991

English translation Copyright © 1998 Sheffield Academic Press

Published by Sheffield Academic Press Ltd
Mansion House
19 Kingfield Road
Sheffield S11 9AS
England

Printed on acid-free paper in Great Britain
by Cromwell Press
Melksham, Wiltshire

British Library Cataloguing in Publication Data
A catalogue record for this book is available from the British Library

ISBN 1-85075-820-4

CONTENTS

# PREFACE

In my case an interest in demonology dates back some way. It began in the mid-sixties when, as a student, I was called upon to choose my special subject. My choice was the representations of the devil in late Judaism. This arose from my surprise that Satan, who plays a very limited part in the Old Testament, appears so frequently in the apocryphal and pseud-epigraphic texts. Where did these representations of the devil originate? Was the background to be found in biblical material, or must we look to an influence from other religions?

I was then already convinced that the background was primarily to be sought within Judaism itself. I therefore tried by religio-historical means to outline the development of representations of the devil throughout the Old Testament and in the non-canonical texts.

In the long run, however, it did not suffice for me to uncover the progress of history. Theological questions intruded, and my subsequent work on 'There is Hope for a Tree: The Tree as Metaphor in Isaiah' directly suggested that I should examine the representations of Satan from the viewpoint that descriptions of Satan must be read figuratively, always considering what the link is between God and Satan. Demonology cannot be separated from theology.

In Spring 1989 I had an opportunity to study for three months at Durham University, and I decided to concentrate my studies in 'Theology and Literature' on the biblical texts referring to Satan. During my time at Durham, I turned my attention to recent discussion in the field of literature, and mainly as a result of this I was inspired to read certain texts in a wider intertextuality. I am very grateful to Dr David Jasper for inspiring dis-cussion and for useful referrals to recent research in literary theory.

I was able in 1991 to publish the book 'Satan—den fortabte søn?' (Satan—the Prodigal Son?) largely because, shortly before this, I had spent six months as a visiting professor at Christian-Albrechts-Universität in Kiel. Here I was given the peace necessary for work, and an opportunity to try out my ideas on a group of German students. Their receptiveness to new perspectives when they read the text increased my confidence that my analyses might also be of use to others. I wish therefore to thank the theological faculty at Kiel for the loan of interested students and for access to an efficient library.

Support from the Aarhus University Research Fund has made it possible for a revised edition of my Danish book to be translated into English. I therefore wish to thank the Fund for its support and the publishers for undertaking to publish this English version.

The sensitivity for the Danish and English languages shown by Christine and Frederick Crowley, the translators of my book, has made it possible for them to express my ideas in a form both recognizable and pleasant. I would like to thank them both for yet another example of efficient and enjoyable cooperation.

Finally, I thank my husband Leif Nielsen most sincerely for his constant support and encouragement during the project and the periods abroad that this made necessary.

Kirsten Nielsen
Aarhus 1996

ABBREVIATIONS

| | |
|---|---|
| *BASOR* | *Bulletin of the American Schools of Oriental Research* |
| BKAT | Biblischer Kommentar: Altes Testament |
| *BZ* | *Biblische Zeitschrift* |
| BZAW | Beihefte zur *ZAW* |
| *ExpTim* | *Expository Times* |
| *JAOS* | *Journal of the American Oriental Society* |
| JSOTSup | *Journal for the Study of the Old Testament*, Supplement Series |
| *NTS* | *New Testament Studies* |
| OTL | Old Testament Library |
| *SBFLA* | *Studii biblici franciscani liber annuus* |
| *SEÅ* | *Svensk exegetisk årsbok* |
| *ST* | *Studia theologica* |
| *TF* | *Theologische Forschung* |
| *THAT* | Ernst Jenni and Claus Westermann (eds.), *Theologisches Handwörterbuch zum Alten Testament* (Munich: Chr. Kaiser, 1971–76) |
| *ThWAT* | G.J. Botterweck and H. Ringgren (eds.), *Theologisches Wörterbuch zum Alten Testament* |
| TOTC | Tyndale Old Testament Commentaries |
| *TWNT* | G. Kittel and G. Friedrich (eds.), *Theologisches Wörterbuch zum Neuen Testament* (11 vols.; Stuttgart, Kohlhammer, 1932–79) |
| *TZ* | *Theologische Zeitschrift* |
| *VT* | *Vetus Testamentun* |
| ZAW | *Zeitschrift für alttestamentliche Wissenschaft* |
| ZNW | *Zeitschrift für neutestamentliche Wissenschaft* |

# INTRODUCTION

Once upon a time there was a man who had two sons. This is how many stories begin, among them the story we call the Parable of the Prodigal Son. The subject is familiar, and we as listeners have certain expectations in regard to such a story. We know that relationships between two brothers often give rise to difficulties. We expect brothers to be different in their natures but alike in the desire to become their father's favourite. Only one of them can attain this, and what the story tries to recount is therefore the rivalry between the pair of them.

When the brothers meet we anxiously await the outcome. Is it a Cain and Abel story, an Esau and Jacob story? Is it the story of the jealous older brothers in their relations with the favourite son Joseph? Who is blessed and who is accursed? Is the younger given preference over the older, as Isaac is over Ishmael, Ephraim over Manasseh? And what fate awaits the one who is passed over?

That stories about a father and his two sons are so frequent is of course because they tell of well-known conflicts. We have all tried to win the love of a father or a mother, and we know how bitter it is when attention concentrates around another sibling. Mutual rivalry and reciprocal jealousy are among the conflicts of childhood. If they are not fought out within the nuclear family they arise in the playground and in the classroom, and later on history repeats itself at the workplace or the leisure centre.

We need stories that can analyse our own experience. That these stories are indeed so widespread is not merely because we can see ourselves directly reflected in them and recognize our own feelings; it is also because the image of the close and yet complicated relationship between a father and his two sons gives us good food for thought. This we can use as a key to interpret other phenomena in life, when we must acknowledge that two things can at the same time be so alike and yet so different.

One of the images which has played an important part in biblical tradition is indeed that of the father and his sons. My contention is that this image has also been employed to interpret the relationship between good and evil, between God and Satan.

It would not be surprising for a theologian to base his or her argument on the image of a father and his son if the subject were the New Testament story of Jesus of Nazareth. The father–son image is the central metaphor in Christology, the root metaphor from which other metaphors grow. The situation is wholly different if—as is my intention—one concerns oneself with demonology, the biblical representations of evil. In this context, few will expect to be presented with an image of a father and his sons.

If it were necessary to suggest suitable metaphors, they would have to be metaphors which emphasize the difference between God and the demonic world, metaphors taken from war or from jurisprudence. One needs only call to mind the Book of Revelation's description of the angel seizing the dragon, the old serpent, who is the Devil and Satan, binding him and throwing him into the bottomless pit before the final vanquishment. For then must the devil be cast into the lake of fire where the beast and the false prophet were also, and where there is torment day and night for ever and ever (cf. Rev. 20).

This description of the devil's punishment accords with what we normally consider to be the Bible's view of evil. And for good reason, since it was images such as this which came to play the major role in our tradition.[1] But if we take a closer look it comes to light that the biblical texts contain various ideas and offer various models of thought.

In the Christian church images which emphasized the difference between God and Satan triumphed, and as a consequence we have often repressed those traditions which assert the close proximity of the creator to that part of creation which we can describe as Satan's work. But the question arises, whether we may have thereby deprived ourselves of the opportunity to think discerningly and realistically about the relationship between good and evil.

1. In her book, *The Origin of Satan* (Harmondsworth: Penguin Books, 1996), Elaine Pagel has thoroughly analysed the role of the Satan figure in the New Testament and early Christianity as an identification model for 'the others', including in particular the Jews. As a step in the Christian communities' attempt to create their own identity in contrast to their surroundings, they stressed the cosmic struggle between God and Satan, and interpreted their own struggle as a part of this. The greater the social conflicts, the more clearly was Satan accentuated as the adversary. Elaine Pagel's book thus concerns the dualistic features in the Christian tradition. But what I want to do is to concentrate on its monistic features.

Our daily experience indeed suggests that good and evil are often so approximate to one another that it can be difficult to draw a clear distinction. Good intentions have evil consequences, and evil intentions have good consequences. Perhaps the relationship between God and Satan is not so straightforward that we can see them simply as diametrical opposites? Perhaps we still need the Old Testament's emphasis that God is a God who creates light and darkness, so that we do not forget that good and evil are linked to one another and mutually condition one another?

In other words, there is a need to be reminded of the monistic aspects of the Judaeo-Christian tradition at a time when dualism is intruding into all possible fields with its tempting clarity, its logical simplicity and its despairing ability to rigidify everything in binary systems and orderly fronts. And there is a need for images that maintain proximity and difference at a time when opposing trends manifest themselves in new religions in an eagerness for universality and an urge towards the universal abolition of differences.

In this situation, those who work each day on biblical texts have an obligation to assemble and present the essential knowledge of how the Bible's authors saw the relationship between good and evil. One way is to investigate the imagery used at the time. Our culture has taken over and developed a great deal of this, but important aspects may have been lost or repressed along the way.

The revival of such suppressed images calls for a broad reading not only of the biblical texts but also of texts not included in the canon. This concerns primarily the apocryphal and pseudepigraphic texts from around the beginning of our era.

More often than not the non-canonic texts are kept separate when we are dealing with theology, and are left to special religio-historical analyses. We thus lose a vital source for understanding the ideas that are accepted as belonging to the canon, since it is indeed by looking at what was not included, what was marginalized and what was completely excluded at the time that we can arrive at a proper understanding of why certain images are given such limited space in the biblical texts while others have become so central. Such a process also forces us to consider whether, in our own theology, we should have continued this tendency to marginalize, reject and exclude images which are undoubtedly biblical but are simply not taken seriously at present.

If we are to work with biblical texts, therefore, we must see them in the context of the literature and history in which they were created. My text readings can best be referred to as literary analyses. The texts are interpreted not merely in the direct context in which they are to be found but also in their thematic connection with other texts about a father and his sons. Such an analysis will be in principle limitless, since the Bible consists of an immensely complex network of texts. I can therefore present in this book only a restricted abstract. But my hope is that those who by reading it become aware of the significance of thinking in terms of the image of a father and his sons will themselves wish to investigate its use in other texts.

The intention is not to give a religio-historical account of which perceptions have been derived from which sources at certain times in history, but to demonstrate how different texts reflect one another and reciprocally interpret one another within the overall biblical context.

I have chosen to call attention to an image suppressed in our tradition not because I intend thereby to begin a new form of image suppression in which, for example, the war metaphor is kept away from theology. What is crucial is the assertion that where God is concerned we cannot be content with a single image. Far too often have we spoken thoughtlessly about the biblical image of God, as if God could be depicted once and for all by using a single linguistic term. And this is despite the fact that the Creed does not consist of one image but of a narrative about God's acts of redemption as Father, Son and Holy Ghost.

The image of a father and his sons is not the only image the Bible uses when it wishes to speak of the relationship between God and Satan; it is one among many. What I here present by way of material and discussion is not therefore a proposal for a 'new dogmatics', with the image of the father and the two sons as the central metaphor; neither do I wish to monopolize a single image. I wish rather to call attention to one of the images that has not played a central part in our theological and ecclesiastical tradition in order to highlight the danger of simplified models. My work should therefore be read as a—in my opinion necessary—contribution to the continuing discussion of the biblical tradition to which not only exegetes but also systematic theologians are pledged.

In this context, I would certainly like to see the narrative of a father and his two sons discussed by those who are concerned with pastoral care in their daily work. It is indeed here that we experience time and again the decisiveness of our image of reality and the importance to us of seeing the Bible as an opportunity for change. The father–son image presents an opportunity for something new to happen, something unexpected and surprising. Today need not be the same as yesterday, and tomorrow is rich in new possibilities. But nevertheless our image of reality often becomes rigid, standing in the way of change.

In his studies of pastoral care, the American theologian Donald Capps [2] emphasizes the opportunity for change created by the biblical texts. The Bible is a book of surprises, an astonishing book. The same point is made in the preface to the collection of sermons by the Danish scholar Knud Hansen, '—og glædelig er hver en dag' (—and full of joy is every day).[3] Bishop Helge Skov rounds this off with the following recollection, which tells us briefly and concisely something about the preacher Knud Hansen and something about the texts on which he has worked throughout his life:

> I remember an evening when, before leaving after a convivial party, Knud Hansen raised his hands over the company and gave the following pontifical salute: 'The Lord bless you and surprise you!'.

2. D. Capps, *Biblical Approaches to Pastoral Counselling* (Philadelphia: Westminster Press, 1981), and D. Capps, 'The Bible's Role in Pastoral Care and Counselling: Four Basic Principles', in L. Aden and H. Ellens (eds.), *The Church and Pastoral Care* (Grand Rapids: Baker Book House, 1988).

3. K. Hansen, *—og glædelig er hver en dag* (—and full of joy is every day, Sermons) (Hadsten: Forlaget Mimer, 1990).

Chapter 1

## WHY AND IN WHAT WAY SHOULD WE CONCERN OURSELVES WITH SATAN TODAY?

> The intention of this book is not only to jeer at the devil and flout him but to offer ways of thinking and speaking about him (or it) that might deprive the devil of any respect from Christians and give the glory to God.

The British university lecturer Nigel G. Wright uses these words to indicate the intention of his book *The Fair Face of Evil: Putting the Power of Darkness in its Place*.[1] It is useful to keep this declaration of intent in mind when entering the field of the evil one, or evil. What Wright draws to our attention is in fact that not merely do we need a language if we are to think and speak of what the Bible, for example, refers to as Satan or the devil, but also that theology's duty is to speak in a certain way; that is, so that God is praised and not Satan.

Perhaps the latter point should be taken for granted; but there are some indications that present-day interest in demonology and satanism often leads to Satan and not God being regarded as the Lord of Man and thus worthy of adoration.

What should also be taken for granted is that we must speak of the devil in such a way that we do not end in obscurantism. The advances of science in the Age of Enlightenment form the basis of modern society, with its desire to seek scientific facts and to exploit the awareness attained for the benefit of mankind. No one among us is justified in renouncing the blessings that science has brought about. It has often thrown light on facts which in the past were explained simply by a reference to demonic powers, with consequent persecutions of various kinds for scapegoats. The trials of witches are just one example of the consequences of an uncritical use of Satan's name to explain crises and misfortunes.

If we theologians are to concern ourselves with the demonic powers,

---

1. N.G. Wright, *The Fair Face of Evil: Putting the Power of Darkness in its Place* (London: Marshall Pickering, 1989), p. 15.

we must bear in mind this dual objective. It is indeed as a science that theology must concern itself with the demonic powers. Devil concepts must be analysed on the same lines as other religious concepts, and by using the same methods as other text-sciences. Furthermore, no questions are excluded from the outset in such an investigation. But as theologians we do not analyse concepts of the devil in isolation, as if they were significant in themselves. They should be seen in their interaction with the texts' concepts of God, since what we say about God will have consequences for what we say about Satan, and what we say about Satan affects our way of speaking of God.

History's alarming examples make it understandable, but not excusable, that Satan has been given a modest place in recent theology. It is scarcely surprising that opinion-forming theologians such as Rudolf Bultmann contributed to the avoidance of serious involvement in the New Testament concepts of the devil by the majority of preachers and theologians in our part of the world. Or, rather, these theologians thought they were giving serious consideration to the devil by consciously demythologizing the self-same concepts. Indeed, as Bultmann put it, 'No-one can use the electric light and the radio or the discoveries of modern medicine and at the same time believe in the New Testament world of spirits and miracles.'[2]

Such an attitude did not necessarily indicate that the New Testament's references to demons were considered meaningless. What was demanded was a modern exegesis in which demon obsession is considered in terms of the area of experience today assigned to psychology and psychiatry.

Whatever sympathy one may have for good intentions, we should not overlook that if we consistently demythologize the Christian message by translating it into modern usage we lose the biblical texts' way of referring to evil. And thereby we lose far more than is realized by many of those who advocate and echo demythologization.

It is apparent from a number of standard works on demonology that it has recently become general to avoid speaking of the devil in a Christian context. A good example is Herbert Haag's large book on demonism published in 1974.[3]

---

2. R. Bultmann, *Kerygma and Myth* (ed. H.W. Bartsch; London: SPCK, 1953), p. 5.

3. H. Haag, *Teufelsglaube: Mit Beiträgen von Katharina Elliger, Bernhard Lang und Meinrad Limbeck* (Belief in the Devil: With Contributions from Katharina Elliger, Bernhard Lang and Meinrad Limbeck) (Tübingen: Katzmann, 1974).

Herbert Haag begins with a general discussion of the background to the belief in demons and devils. Haag considers that the need and the attempt to explain the existence of evil is as old as mankind itself. But the way of expounding this has changed. In the past it was believed that demons and evil spirits were the cause of wickedness and misfortune. This kind of explanation is now rejected, and instead we use our scientific awareness. Or to put it more directly: Haag considers that belief in demonic powers belongs to the olden days among 'uninformed' people who have no awareness of true (scientific) relationships.

Haag also mentions that he himself published a brief paper in 1969 which he called 'Farewell to the Devil'.[4] Several people took the opportunity to tell him it was somewhat superfluous to say that modern people could not believe in the devil; nor did they need to in order to be Christians. The paper nevertheless attracted enormous attention and gave rise to a series of counter-attacks, *inter alia* from Rome. This violent reaction took Herbert Haag completely by surprise, but it forced him to write his book on demonism in which he tries to substantiate his assertion that Christians of today are not obliged to believe in the biblical statements about the devil, demons and evil spirits. According to Haag, these concepts belong to the Bible's marginal phenomena, to the mythological material we can easily do without.

Whereas Haag represents a clear example of a modern theologian's distaste for these so-called marginal phenomena, Nigel Wright (see above) is a committed advocate of the view that theologians must take this matter seriously. But how, as a theologian, can one take demonology seriously? For me, as an exegete, the first step must be an exhaustive discussion of how the biblical statements referring to Satan are in that event to be read so as to be meaningful to a modern Christian interpretation of existence.

This takes us back to the question of the language we are to use if we are to speak credibly of evil in today's world.

### *Speaking about the Devil and Speaking about God*

I have pointed out above that logical demythologization means distancing ourselves from the New Testament's own way of speaking of the devil. But this is not all, since if we renounce the language in which we speak of the devil we also renounce the language that speaks of God. And the

---

4. H. Haag, 'Abschied vom Teufel' ('Farewell to the Devil') in H. Küng (ed.), *Theologische Meditationen* (Zürich/Einsiedeln/Köln: Benziger, 1969).

crucial point is this: if we change the New Testament's way of speaking of the devil this will have implications for the way we speak of God.

No one who reads the New Testament can be in any doubt that the devil is referred to here with the greatest seriousness. God allowed his son to be born into the world in order to destroy the works of the devil. It is indeed in extension of this that in the Danish National Church the renunciation of the devil is included in the Creed: To acknowledge the faith means to begin by renouncing the devil and all his works and all his ways. If we no longer believe that the devil is a real power in the world, we must, as Nigel Wright puts it, find another reason for the coming into the world of the Son of God.[5]

Another British theologian, Michael Green, expresses the same viewpoint by asserting as follows: 'You cannot simply write him [the devil] out of the human story and then imagine that the story is basically unchanged.'[6]

This view has been sharply criticized. Many consider that this gives the devil too large a role in the story of redemption. Although Nigel Wright must agree that Green is correct in his fundamental attitude, one senses a healthy anxiety that a theology which takes Satan seriously might confer on him greater praise than he deserves.

One of the points to which Nigel Wright objects is the very question of choice of words. What words can we use when we speak of evil? Are we to speak personally of the evil one, or are we to speak impersonally about evil? It is worth noting here that Nigel Wright does not use the personal name Satan in the title of his book. Wright speaks of 'the fair face of evil', 'fair' suggesting both light and good, in the same way as in the subtitle he speaks of 'the power of darkness'. The reader must then consider whether the word 'face' is used to indicate that evil can be talked about in the way we talk about human beings, or that the word 'face' merely indicates the surface of something.

Wright himself does not conceal that he wishes to discourage the tendency to magnify the devil to the detriment of God. Satan must not be a subject for belief but for lack of belief or non-belief. For this reason he considers it questionable to speak of the devil as a person. This personifies the devil and gives him a dignity he has not deserved. We should rather

5. Wright, *The Fair Face of Evil*, p. 21.

6. M. Green, *I Believe in Satan's Downfall* (London: Hodder & Stoughton, 1981, republished in 1988), p. 20.

think of the devil as a non-person or a sub-person; we should rather refer to the devil by speaking of 'it', thinks Nigel Wright.[7]

Another consideration is that 'personal' language indicates some restrictions which form part of being a person but which do not apply to the devil. For example, the devil cannot be restricted to being in one specific place at a time. Wherever there are people, the power of darkness is also present. Wright would therefore prefer us to avoid 'personal' language.

Nevertheless, when he finally concludes that we cannot do without using personal language this is because Jesus spoke of the devil as a personal power. But in addition person-orientated language has the advantage, says Wright, of making it possible to see the powers of evil as intelligent. And one thing we should not do is to underestimate the opponent's intelligence.

### We Must Speak in Images of both God and Satan

What interests me most in Wright's book is the problem of finding an adequate language. What I mean by this is that Wright must be supplemented by more fundamental consideration of how God and Satan are spoken of in the Bible.

Wright seems to find it difficult to accept that the Bible uses both non-personal and personal language about the devil. To my mind, this is absolutely necessary. This in fact makes it clear to everyone that the language used is metaphoric. In the same way that it is possible to speak of God only in images, so is it possible to speak of the devil only in images.

The Bible when it uses images of God takes them from many places. God is described in the image of a person: as father, mother, warrior and shepherd, to name but a few characteristic images. The world of the elements is also included. We encounter descriptions of God as fire, God as water, God as air, God as a rock.

God is like the burning bush which blazes but is not consumed, says Exodus 3. God is like a life-giving fountain, says the prophet Jeremiah. And he adds that this is the very fountain which Israel left in order to dig cisterns for itself which crack and cannot hold water (Jer. 2.13). God is like the wind, God's breath rushing across the valley with the dead bones and creating new life (Ezek. 37.9). And God is like firm rocky ground, God alone is my rock and my salvation (Ps. 62.7).

Not enough can be said about God if only one area of experience is

7. Wright, *The Fair Face of Evil*, pp. 28-32.

employed. Indeed, in addition to the world of persons and the four elements, the animal world must be included before we can arrive at a language for speaking of God. Then, like the prophet Hosea, one must speak of God as the young lion which goes prowling in search of prey in the house of Juda, destroying and carrying off so that no one can rescue it (Hos. 5.14).

When we wish to speak of God, therefore, we cannot use literal speech. The image of God as father has certainly often been misunderstood as literal speech. But here the Old Testament, with its complex use of images, acts as a good guide, since probably no one would identify God with fire, water, air and earth, or with such different animals as a lion prowling in search of prey and an eagle which, according to Deut. 32.11, bears its young on its pinions; not to mention Hosea's frightening image of God as a sickness going to the marrow: 'But I am like maggots to Ephraim, like rottenness to the house of Juda' (Hos. 5.12). Images such as these may well surprise and shock. They do not accord with our customary concepts. But at least they make it clear to us readers that what is said about God is said in images. And this we perhaps detect more readily when God is described by the image of a destructive illness than when we hear tell of a loving father.

The same is true of the language we use of the devil. Everything said about the devil must be figurative. And of the devil we must speak both impersonally, as we speak of powers, and personally, as when we speak of Satan. Neither should we forget the images of the old dragon or the wily serpent. These images and images taken from the four elements must be included if we are to refer adequately to life's destructive powers.

That I emphasize this so strongly is because I wish to refute the misunderstanding that what the Bible calls the devil or Satan is merely a well-known phenomenon, like a certain form of psychical deviation for example. The American film *The Exorcist* was a clear example of such a putting down of the devil. But the status awarded to the devil by the Bible cannot be restricted to phenomena which form part of the individual psyche. The Bible includes the devil in the salvation narrative in a vital form. The devil must therefore be understood as a power factor going beyond what we understand as psychical phenomena.

### *What, then, Is an Image?*

To define briefly the characteristics of a literal image we may say that it identifies uniformities, while at the same time maintaining differences. If it were concerned merely with differences, and asserted that in God's case matters are not like this, and not like that, and not like the other, then the value of the language as a source of information would be extremely limited. If the images were to identify uniformities only, the result would be that God and his creation would become identical; and that is blasphemy. God and his creation cannot be made to be identical to one another. But what images can do and try to do is to maintain the tension between uniformity and difference while speaking of similarity.[8]

A German theologian once said that the crucial theological question is this: How can God, who is not of this world, make himself known to the world? For the Old Testament writers it was crucial to speak of God without transgressing the prohibition of images, which was indeed intended to ensure that God was not identified with the world. They knew that God is not of this world; but they also knew that God has repeatedly made himself known in the fortresses of Zion. And by imagery they have found a way to speak adequately of God.

When we employ images from this world, we speak of what is different on the basis of what is known, but without rendering them identical with one another. Imagery does not claim to speak exhaustively, and therefore never intends to set limits to who or what God is. Imagery would be useless if this were so, when what is referred to is the inviolable and incomparable God. By using images the biblical writers can maintain uniformity and difference simultaneously. They can assert that God both reveals himself and conceals himself.

By using imagery, therefore, we can strike a balance between the two extremes. One extreme is blasphemy, where God is identified with the world which he himself has created; but this is to mock God by making him too small. The other extreme is tautology, where one can only say that God is God, or that God is wholly different, something of which one can say nothing and should therefore keep silent. If we understand the imagery correctly, we must reject both fundamentalism's consistent and literal reading, which forgets that images also are different from what they describe, and tautological 'philosophism', which in its anxiety to say that there is similarity between God and the known world refrains from speaking plentifully about God, thereby in reality making the revelation empty.

A correct understanding of imagery does not, however, prevent other abuses. Recent theological debate repeatedly emphasizes the all-important

8. A detailed definition of what is meant by imagery is to be found in K. Nielsen, *There is Hope for a Tree: The Tree as Metaphor in Isaiah* (JSOTSup, 65; Sheffield: JSOT Press, 1989), pp. 42-67.

significance of language. This is justified, since without language our surrounding world would be wholly different. Indeed, it is only through language that it becomes our surrounding world. But danger may lie in the unceasing concentration on speaking about God. Listening to contemporary preaching or reading recent contributions to the prevailing discussion sometimes gives the impression that speaking of God itself replaces God, so that God becomes identical with language. God can be tied to the language to such an extent that the limits of language become God's limits, and God's existence becomes merely a linguistic existence. This leads to a narrowing down of God's activity and actuality that is contrary to the purpose of speaking about God, which is to create space for God in the world. And this leads to a serious misunderstanding of the central message of the New Testament. The New Testament does not claim that God became word, but the opposite: the word became flesh and dwelt among us.

### Which Images are Usable?

How then can we now speak of God and the devil without ending up in the abuses which theologians before us have justly wished to avoid? An initial precondition is of course that we see it as important that the devil is indeed concerned both in theological studies and Christian preaching. This means that the correct procedure is to render the powers of evil visible instead of trying to operate a conspiracy of silence against them. Modern psychologists can contribute here with a series of investigations into what such repression leads to, and how important it is to find words for that which is evil. The use over generations of the Old Testament's lamentations in private devotional life shows that we need to give a language to sorrow, pain and suffering, not only as an unarticulated cry but as a prayer to God. These very psalms have the ability to express what modern people are inclined to conceal: doubt, anxiety and anger. Although anger may take the form of a direct accusation against God it must be heard. For even then the worshipper knows he is in the hands of God.

The crux of the matter is, therefore, not to keep silent but to speak. And here the biblical texts offer us both personal images and non-personal images where evil is concerned. We must therefore consider briefly the theological points regarding evil to be found in personal and non-personal speech.

Nigel Wright rightly drew to our attention that personal speech makes it possible to emphasize the intelligence lying behind evil, that the work of the Creator is not merely random or incomplete. When we speak of evil in personal images and refer to 'the evil one', we can stress the peril—the conscious will behind the evil actions. Whereas personal speech reminds us of the will behind the evil, non-personal speech can stress the all-pervading nature of evil. For the same applies to evil as to darkness, which repeatedly pushes itself forward and drives away light.

If we choose an image from the everyday world to describe the relationship between good and evil, for example light and darkness, the contrast between the two becomes clear. We may ask what light and darkness have to do with one another, and thus the dissimilarity easily becomes absolute. Our perceptions are locked into a sharp contrast, whose consequence is dualism. If, on the other hand, personal images are also used, we can speak of the interaction between these powers in a way which shows that not everything has been said by merely contrasting the two with one another. They depend upon one another, indeed they condition one another like a pair of twins.

Any reader of the New Testament knows that formulations often occur in which God and the power of evil are opposed to one another as enemies. Think, for example, of John's use of the light–darkness metaphor, and of Revelation where the struggle motif is played out as in few other places in the Bible. But such contrasts are not universal. And if we turn for a moment to the Old Testament it will be seen that we encounter here ideas which indicate a much closer proximity between God and evil.

In Deutero-Isaiah, where we meet monism formulated in a characteristic manner, God refers to himself by using the words: 'I am the Lord, there is no other. I form light and create darkness, make weal and create woe, I the Lord do all things' (Isa. 45.6-7). Here the contrasts, light and darkness, are gathered under the same creator. The creator has formed both parts as the potter creates his vessels. There is thus not only a difference between light and darkness; there is also a proximity. Deutero-Isaiah and the exile period found consolation in this, for they were still in the Almighty's hands although surrounded by darkness and not light.

The image of the God-creator can unite the elementary phenomena we often see as contrasts. But this can become more refined when the image is taken from people's intercourse with one another in everyday life, images we recognize from family life and its often complicated relationships.

Let us briefly turn to Job, and thus to one of the texts which will play a central part in what follows. Job, ch. 1, says that one day God gathered his sons in heaven, and among God's sons was Satan. Then follows the description of God's favourite among men, the righteous Job. Could any father wish for a better son than this Job? God certainly does not hide the closeness of this creation to the heart of its creator. The father's preference for one of the sons in fact immediately causes the son Satan, who feels passed over, to react and to speak evil of the spoilt younger brother. Two sons of the same father, and yet so different.

God is not only like a potter who shapes various vessels. God is not only he who creates light and darkness. God is like a father who has both light sons and dark sons, and like a father who, although he has his favourite, never denies his fatherhood to any one of them.

### What Is the Task of Theology and Preaching Today?

What are the conclusions, then, we can draw from this? For the moment, only the following: as theologians, we must once again take seriously what the Bible has to say about evil powers. We must again discuss the type of language used. We must analyse the possibilities inherent in the various images in order to discuss the power of evil with commitment. And in interdisciplinary fellowship we must try to identify the consequences for theology and preaching which this work will occasion. We achieve nothing by keeping silent at a time when so many others are discussing Satan and all his works. Neither can we be content to repeat the biblical stories in the traditional language without critical reflection on their significance and the consequences that follow therefrom. But above all we must avoid the danger which consists in believing that we can speak of Satan without at the same time clarifying to ourselves what we say about God.

But to clarify to ourselves the relationship between speaking of God and speaking of Satan also means that we must discuss the distribution of power between the two. Christian discourse about Satan should neither underestimate nor overestimate Satan's power. I fully agree here with C.S. Lewis, who in the preface to his book of 1942, *The Screwtape Letters*[9] stresses that there are 'two equal and opposite errors into which our race can fall about the devils. One is to disbelieve in their existence. The other is to believe, and to feel an excessive and unhealthy interest in them. They themselves are equally pleased by both errors and hail a materialist or a magician with the same delight!'

9. C.S. Lewis, *The Screwtape Letters* (Glasgow: Collins, Fount Paperbacks, 1942), p. 9.

Chapter 2

## LITERARY ANALYSIS OF IMAGERY TEXTS

The text analyses I wish to present below can best be described as literary analyses of imagery texts. Since no text reading is free of preconditions, I must briefly explain the methodological considerations that underlie my method of reading.

An important part of the inspiration stems from what may be called recent text theories within the field of literature. Let us begin with a characteristic viewpoint taken from the poetics of Harold Bloom, the American literary critic. Bloom emphasizes here that his interest lies in the poets who fight to the death with cogency and persistence against their great predecessors. Bloom himself expresses this as follows: 'My concern is only with strong poets, major figures with the persistence to wrestle with their strong precursors even to the death.' [1] Any work of poetry is a misreading of an earlier work, a kind of murder of a great predecessor, thinks Bloom. By destroying an earlier text the artist creates not only his own text but himself as an artist.

This approach is fruitful. It draws attention to a phenomenon which is well known in biblical research, although Bloom's formulations bring it to a head to such a degree that one wants to resume the search for the texts which are deconstructed by a work of art such as the Book of Job. Or, to use imagery, what kind of Jacob-and-the-angel battle is being fought?

Biblical texts are part of a long tradition, and are a step in an unremitting deconstruction of earlier texts. But the deconstruction is at the same time a reconstruction. From the first text the next is created, in turn giving nourishment to new texts. In analysing the Book of Job, therefore, we cannot be content to ask about the book's great predecessors. We must

1. H. Bloom, *The Anxiety of Influence: A Theory of Poetry* (Oxford: Oxford University Press, 1973), p. 5.

also consider who has since wrestled with the narrative about Yahweh, Satan and Job.

Such a procedure is not in fact new. On the one hand biblical researchers have been concerned for generations with the lines of connection between individual texts, and on the other hand most modern editions of the Bible are provided with cross-references which help to show the reader how the biblical authors reuse other passages in the Bible.

But it will soon become apparent that in the literary analysis we cannot content ourselves with these references alone, for whereas the cross-references catalogue mainly a uniformity of wording between different texts we must in our context be prepared for the re-use to manifest itself also in transformations of themes and chains of events. In such a case there need be nothing in the usage itself to divulge the connection. It may be that no actual quotation is concerned but a re-use of a basic structure which controls the sequence of the text. And what I here refer to as structure will often prove to be a central image with a well-known narrative sequence.

Where, therefore, I refer in the following to the texts' intertextuality and speak of a number of recent discussions of the text-concept, this will be on the basis that the biblical tradition has come into existence from continued re-use of older texts. And where, with Bloom, we speak of a struggle even to the death to overcome the strong predecessor it is still to the point that the struggle is life-giving, that the deconstruction is productive.

Bloom speaks of the poets' struggle to find themselves by murdering their predecessors. Such parricide demands, of course, that there are both sons and fathers, artists of strong will and character. But is it really possible for present-day exegetes to consider a clear authorial influence upon the transmitted texts? For example, can one speak unconcernedly about the author of the Book of Job? On the one hand our knowledge of the history of tradition indicates a far more complicated process of creation than that which normally lies behind the creation of, for example, a modern poem, and on the other hand the tendency of modern literary criticism is towards a total down-grading of the author's influence upon the text.

On the whole, the textual concept itself has been the subject of a radical debate in recent years[2] which must be taken into consideration if one

2. A clear introduction to some of the developments of theory under discussion is to be found in the following works: T. Eagleton, *Literary Theory: An Introduction* (Oxford: Basil Blackwell, 1983); T.R. Wright, *Theology and*

wishes to work with methodical awareness on a text such as the Book of
Job. Before analysing the relationship between Yahweh, Satan and Job,
therefore, we must discuss the methodical basis of the analysis.

### The Textual Concept in Recent Literary Research

Earlier research believed that it could express itself with relative certainty
about the meaning of the text. That is, the meaning was defined as the
significance the author wished to pass on to his listeners or readers. But
recent research has shown that this is far too narrow a definition. The natural
assumption that the meaning comes into existence when the reader en-
counters, via the text, the author's intention no longer follows so naturally.

There are many reasons for this, and we shall merely concern ourselves
with a few of the more important. The author is often a highly inaccessible
entity about whom we know only what we believe we can derive from
the text. In many cases, therefore, it will be more proper to keep to the
text, instead of trying to reconstruct the unknown author's intention in
what he has written. And even should we be in the fortunate position that
the author's identity is well known and that information about his external
circumstances and ideological attitude is abundant, it is nevertheless
questionable to assert that the text contains precisely what its author
intended (intentional fallacy),[3] let alone to assert that the text really conveys
what the author himself believes it to say.

In recent textual analyses, therefore, the author plays a very limited part;
indeed, some consider him as a 'dead' relative to his text.[4]

The unambiguousness of the text has also been extensively called into

*Literature* (Oxford: Basil Blackwell, 1988); W.A. Kort, *Story, Text, and
Scripture: Literary Interests in Biblical Narrative* (University Park: Pennsyl-
vania State University Press, 1988), and S.A. Handelman, *The Slayers of
Moses: The Emergence of Rabbinic Interpretation in Modern Literary Theory*
(Albany: State University of New York Press, 1982).

3. Cf. for example Terry Eagleton's critique of E.D. Hirsch in Eagleton,
*Literary Theory*, pp. 67-74, and one of the classics of English literary theory:
R. Wellek and A. Warren, *Theory of Literature* (New York and London: A
Harvest/HJB Book, 3rd edn, 1977), pp. 41-42, 147-48. Cf. the term 'intentional
fallacy' in W.K. Wimsatt, Jr and M.C. Beardsley, 'The Intentional Fallacy', in
*The Verbal Icon: Studies in the Meaning of Poetry* (Lexington, KY: University
of Kentucky Press, 1954).

4. Cf. for example S. Prickett, *Words and the Word: Language, Poetics
and Biblical Interpretation* (Cambridge: Cambridge University Press, 1988),
p. 26.

question. Text readings and analyses of recent years have revealed
language's ambiguity and its appeal to the reader to become involved in
a continuous interpretation of the text. In extenuation of the 'death penalty'
on the text's author, the inquisitorial question followed: 'Does a text exist
at all?'[5] Can one speak of a text with a definite meaning which presents
itself to the reader, or is the text's meaning whatever each individual reads
into it and so gets out of it? And if the latter is the case, can we then
speak of *the* meaning? Are there not an infinite number of meanings which
are equally valid? Is it not therefore the exegete's lot continually to arrive
too late at transient meanings in an eternal race through network after
network, so that the exegete ends in Derrida's deconstruction?[6]

## *The Intertextuality of Biblical Texts*

This brief outline of the postmodern situation for exegetes and literary
annotators may appear utterly daunting, but it should come as no surprise
to biblical researchers that the authors of the texts we wish to interpret
are largely inaccessible, that the texts are ambiguous and that readers'
response is diverse. But it will probably come as a surprise to some that
precisely by giving serious consideration to this ambiguity and not limiting
the text's potential meanings we show respect for the text as a text. Werner
G. Jeanrond draws attention to this as follows:

> ... to do justice to the text does not entail that one must exclude a pluralism

5. A very illuminating and entertaining discussion of this is to be found in
Stanley Fish's book *Is There a Text in This Class? The Authority of Interpretative Communities* (Cambridge, MA: Harvard University Press, 1980),
pp. 303-21, who reassures his readers, however, by saying that although the
texts are ambiguous, interpretation is always in specific situations which create
the framework for the understanding that makes communication possible.

6. As regards the deconstruction phenomenon, refer primarily to Jacques
Derrida's own works. Among recent introductions to deconstruction, refer to:
C. Norris, Deconstruction and the Interests of Theory (London: Routledge,
rev. edn, 1991); R. Young (ed.), *Untying the Text: A Post-Structuralist Reader*
(London: Routledge & Kegan Paul, 1987); and D. Jasper, *The Study of
Literature and Religion: An Introduction* (London: Macmillan, 1989). While
many have stressed Derrida's destructive activity, Clarence Walhout indicates
the positive aspect. Deconstruction represents a constant challenge to a change
of culture, and thus a confirmation of mankind's freedom and creative abilities.
Cf. C. Walhout, 'Texts and Actions', in R. Lundin, A.C. Thiselton and C.
Walhout, *The Responsibility of Hermeneutics* (Exeter: Paternoster Press, 1985),
p. 38.

of readings. In fact, precisely the opposite is the case: we require a reading pluralism in order, as far as possible, to do justice to the text, something which a single reading perspective of itself can never guarantee.[7]

That these are the exegete's conditions is to be seen with all desirable clarity from the biblical texts' own genesis and their subsequent history of effect. The Old Testament is a work of tradition. It has been created in a prolonged process of interpretation and reinterpretation and has itself occasioned an abundance of comments, not only within the canon itself but also in the form of independent commentaries. Whoever seeks to interpret such a work must therefore also have a sense of its many meanings; this, after all, is part of the exegete's working conditions.

What we must today face as exegetes is not, therefore, that the exegetic analyses presented up to the present are generally incorrect but that they are inadequate. We have contented ourselves too readily with an analysis of part of the whole, and have published part-analyses pretending to be complete analyses. We have worked with far too narrow a text-concept because we have too often neglected the intertextuality.

In the entire way in which commentary after commentary envelops the core text, the Jewish Talmud is also a clear illustration of the exegete's working conditions.[8] One is aware of this in recent literary theory, and it is indeed worth noting that the rabbinic exegesis is included as an example of a more satisfying method of text-reading. In her fascinating book on the influence of the rabbinic interpretation on modern literary theory, Susan A. Handelman gives a convincing picture of this feature.

> The Rabbinic world is, to use a contemporary term, one of *intertextuality*. Texts echo, interact, and interpenetrate. In the world of the text, rigid temporal and spatial distinctions collapse. The elements of the text are treated as much as objective reality for its students as empirical facts are by scientific observers ... The Talmud is also not simply the record of the discussions and interpretations of the sages, but is a reconstruction by later students and generations. It has, hence, a form unlike any other literature. The reconstruction presents itself as a mélange of voices from different times and countries brought together within the perimeters of the text. The

---

7. W.G. Jeanrond, *Text and Interpretation as Categories of Theological Thinking* (Dublin: Gill and Macmillan, 1988), p. 135. Cf. also pp. 105-14, 'Aspects of a Theory of Reading' and note the absence of the author in the considerations. The subject is clearly 'the dialectic between text and reader', p. 106.

8. Cf. Handelman, *The Slayers of Moses*, pp. 42-50 with the reproduction of a page from the Talmud, p. 48.

style is often freely associative and laconic. It is not at all a flowing prose, and to those not familiar with its special vocabulary it is cryptic.[9]

If one reads recent text-interpreters, one has the impression that the above characteristic is pertinent not only to the Talmud but to many more of the so-called classic works, which are indeed distinguished by a strong resistance to easy and automatic interpretation.[10]

A crucial step on the road towards total abolition of 'the meaningful text' is taken by the advocates of deconstruction. They not only demonstrate, as does Ferdinand de Saussure, the arbitrary relationship between the sign (*signifiant*) and the sign's meaning (*signifié*), but reject that any meaning is present in the sign.

> A sign or word is defined as much by what it does *not* mean as by what it does mean, so that meaning is as much absent as present. Meaning can never be nailed down, can never be quite grasped, is always, in a sense *deferred*.[11]

David Jasper here repeats a central point in Jacques Derrida, a point which causes metaphor-researchers to recall recent research's strong emphasis on the diversity's significance to the metaphor's function. What distinguishes the metaphor's way of creating meaning from literal speech's way of creating meaning is the very fact that the metaphor builds on difference. Without difference there is no metaphor.[12]

In the light of this, it may appear that only one of the three original participants in the interpretation process—author, text and reader—has 'survived' The author's intention in the work is rejected as irrelevant or directly misleading, and the text's meaning is called into question to a degree where absence of meaning appears to be more characteristic than its presence. There remains the reader or the exegete who, as text-producer, must realize that the commentary he or she evolves has an absence of meaning to the same extent as all other texts, and that his or her intentions in recording a text about texts are without meaning, or at least without any specific meaning.

9. Handelman, *The Slayers of Moses*, pp. 48-49.
10. Cf. Jeanrond, *Text and Interpretation*, p. 118.
11. Cf. Jasper, *The Study of Literature*, p. 119.
12. Cf., e.g., Paul Ricoeur's definition in 'The Metaphorical Process as Cognition, Imagination, and Feeling', in S. Sacks (ed.), *On Metaphor* (Chicago: University of Chicago Press, 1979), p. 146. Cf. also K. Nielsen, *There is Hope for a Tree: The Tree as Metaphor in Isaiah* (JSOTSup, 65; Sheffield: JSOT Press, 1989), pp. 52-53 and 62-66.

In such a situation there are two possible strategies: either to impose silence upon oneself, or to fight back with the only possible weapon: the heretical language. But if we choose the latter path, it must be considered whether the nihilism that may result from the theoretical discussion of recent years can be turned into something positive. Can we deconstruct the deconstruction and get something constructive out of it?

The sketch presented of the interpreter's working conditions has indicated the ambiguity of the language and the interweaving of individual texts into networks of meaning. But the fact that a word, an expression, or a narrative contains several potential meanings does not signify that *all* these are realized in the concrete situations in which they are used.[13] Werner G. Jeanrond presents the following suggestion:

> I suggest ... that we might more aptly distinguish between 'possible' and 'realised' sense of a text. The possible sense consists accordingly in a number of meanings out of which the reader in the act of reading constructs a real text sense. The quantity of meaning of a text is however to be received only through acts of reading, and never independently of them.[14]

In the same way that a sentence is always used in concrete situations and contexts,[15] and thereby obtains its meaning, so are narratives used in concrete situations and read as text, not in any, possible, intertextuality but in that which at the relevant time, in the specific environment and in the specific situation is found to accord best with the text.

We as readers are not independent of our own times and of the environment in which we find ourselves. We belong from the outset to one or more groups, 'interpretative communities',[16] and we therefore perceive within specific frameworks of understanding. A text is always read through other texts on the basis of certain expectations which will either be met or disappointed but are always present, and therefore contribute to the restriction of the number of potential meanings.

That the author is usually anonymous or absent (or, in parts of a process of analysis, should be kept out of the analysis) does not mean that the author has been unable to help the reader to follow the intentions he or

---

13. Cf. Nielsen, *There is Hope*, pp. 20-21.

14. Jeanrond, *Text and Interpretation*, p. 80.

15. Cf. Fish, *Is There a Text*, pp. 307, 310. Cf. also Jeanrond's emphasis that we always encounter the language used, not 'langue', a view he shares with Paul Ricoeur. Jeanrond, *Text and Interpretation*, pp. 47-48.

16. Kort, *Story, Text, and Scripture*, p. 129, who takes the term from Fish, *Is There a Text*, p. 14.

she has had in writing the text. If we accept that any text is always a contribution to a dialogue with one or more earlier texts, or is an attempt to disarm an earlier text,[17] we obtain indirectly through the text information about the intertextuality in which it should be read, if we wish to read the text in terms of the author's intentions but without necessarily allowing ourselves to be restricted by them in our reading.

If one consciously chooses to read in opposition to the author's intentions, one can arrive at most exciting results (cf. for example the ideology-critical reading of popular literature) of great significance to an understanding of the author's psyche and socio-economic situation, indeed of the whole society of which the author forms a part and which he reflects through his work. But this involves a conscious analysis of a number of elements outside the text, which can be revealed with the aid of the text.

Such reading is in principle no different from the historical-critical analyses which try to derive historical and geographical information from an Old Testament prophet's preaching, and whose value closely accords with the limited but legitimate objective of the analysis.

The author's help for the reader consists not only in positive 'hints' in regard to earlier text (texts) with which he struggles. The 'gaps' the author has equipped the text with and which compel the reader to reply may also lead the reader in a certain direction, for example to an earlier text.[18]

Despite the emphasis in recent years on the author's absence and the texts' ambiguity, we must insist that communication is possible. There is, it is true, no direct discussion between an author-person and a reader-person. What the reader relates to are texts in the plural, those actually available, the texts the reader possesses in his pre-understanding, the texts the author intends to be read/thought of as the context. The reader is helped in various ways to understand the text, and thereby to build up a new text in his own mind.

17. Cf. Eagleton, *Literary Theory*, p. 183, and Handelman, *The Slayers of Moses*, p. 182.

Cf. also Harold Bloom's description of the author's work as a power struggle in which the younger deliberately misinterprets the precursor. 'Let us give up the failed enterprise of seeking to "understand" any single poem as an entity in itself. Let us pursue instead the quest of learning to read any poem as its poet's deliberate misinterpretation *as a poet* of a precursor poem or of poetry in general.' Bloom, *The Anxiety of Influence*, p. 43.

18. Cf. Jeanrond, *Text and Interpretation*, p. 109, and M. Sternberg, *The Poetics of Biblical Narrative: Ideological Literature and the Drama of Reading* (Bloomington: Indiana University Press, 1985), pp. 186-229.

What we have so far said about text reading has mostly concerned the internal relationships in a text and the relationships between the texts. But this does not mean that texts are only inter-referential. It has certainly been maintained for decades that literary texts refer to nothing but themselves,[19] but this applies only in the sense that there is no direct connection between language and the world. For any text there are two levels; the first is where the meaning arises—the textual level—and the other is where the meaning is applied to reality and the text's significance is created.

Paul Ricoeur has energetically maintained—in opposition to, *inter alia*, Claude Lévi-Strauss and Jacques Derrida—that there is something outside the text to which the text refers.[20] That the text refers to reality does not mean that the text is photographing this, but rather that the text throws up a proposal for understanding reality, and thereby constitutes reality for the reader.[21] The biblical texts thus constitute, through their narratives, the history of Israel which is part of the Jewish and Christian communities' history.

### Exegetic Consequences

What, now, are the consequences of this for the practice of exegetics? It must above all be pointed out that what I can submit below on the relationship between God and Satan in the Book of Job and in a number of biblical and inter-testamentary texts in no way exhausts the significance of these texts. Any interpretation is always inconclusive and open to further interpretation, depending upon the *intertextuality* in which the text is read.

The analysis is based on the most copious of the Old Testament texts in which Satan appears, the Book of Job. This should make it possible to avoid an unintentional confinement of the Satan image, and it should

19. Cf. Wellek and Warren, *Theory of Literature*, pp. 25-28.

20. Cf. L.M. Poland, *Literary Criticism and Biblical Hermeneutics: A Critique of Formalist Approaches* (Chico, CA: Scholars Press, 1985), pp. 169-70. Cf. also Wright, *Theology and Literature*, p. 40: 'It is not enough for Ricoeur to explore the internal relations of a piece of writing: "To understand a text is to follow its movements from sense to reference: from what it says to what it talks about"'; The Ricoeur quotation is from P. Ricoeur, *Interpretation Theory: Discourse and the Surplus of Meaning* (Fort Worth: Texan Christian University Press, 1976), p. 89.

21. Cf. D. Tracy, *Plurality and Ambiguity: Hermeneutics, Religion, Hope* (San Francisco: Harper & Row, 1987), p. 48, and Nielsen, *There is Hope*, p. 60.

become easier to reveal the contexts, networks of significance, on whose basis Satan is to be interpreted. The texts selected will be considered as possible transformations of one another (dialogue partners/combatants).

But having said this it must be added that the texts to be discussed are to a large extent expressed in *imagery*, which increases the possibility that each of them is incorporated in a number of networks of significance, whereby the analysis becomes more complicated and receives more light and shade.

It must also be remembered that the aim of the analysis is to reveal *the texts' polysemy*, at the same time clarifying which *meaning potentials* must be expected to have been realized in which context, that is in the specific interpretative and use situation.

That biblical texts are included in different contexts—perceived both as other texts in the literature of the time and as the specific interpretative situations—also means that the analyses must deal with chronological and historical matters. That we accept the current situation of scientific theory with the above-mentioned definitions and limitations means indeed that the exegete must include knowledge of the world in which the texts are interpreted.

The methods we use must correspond to the methods referred to as historio-critical. The difference is merely that I wish to work using an extended concept of the contexts, and to give more respect to the polysemy as a quality of the texts. Indeed, I do not see this as a fault to be concealed as quickly as possible by an unambiguous commentary which excludes several possible interpretations.

That the texts' mutual chronology and separate genesis must also be considered (although such considerations in our context will be given a modest place) is because a purely synchronous way of reading may result in unnecessary misunderstandings. Biblical texts have been created over a long time-scale, during which various transcribers and editors have added their comments. If we ignore this and read the text as if it were the finished text of one author, a later addition may have an utterly disturbing effect on the meaning or give the impression that the author knowingly wishes to express himself in paradox.

To avoid this we must use exegetic means that have proved themselves over many generations. The changed situation in regard to scientific theory has led to new theories as concerns what texts are and what they are not and what interpretation consists of, but this has not rendered the well-known tool superfluous. It is hoped that the debate has in fact influenced those using the tool towards greater care in regard to the texts, and thus

towards greater caution in projecting ready-made opinions onto them, so
that we transform the texts to fit our own image.

A crucial feature of any interpretation is indeed the possibility of keeping
such a distance from the text that one can assess it both positively and
negatively. The reader must be ready to allow his formerly favourite texts
to be corrected by a new text, and likewise for the new text to be evaluated
in comparison with earlier texts. And this suggests another characteristic
of the present debate on interpretation.

Theorists such as David Tracy emphasize that we move beyond the iso-
lated linguistic analysis which structuralism and deconstruction represent.

> In technical terms, this may be described as the movement from language
> as use (step one), to language as object (step two), to language as discourse
> (step three).[22]

And thereby we are sent from the language into history and society where
the debate is in progress, well aware of the postmodern conditions. But
by indicating our participation in a specific culture and history and our
participation in this by way of discussion, David Tracy approximates this
to proceeding to the question of responsibility in the discussion.

In the light of the premises of deconstruction, both the responsible reader
and the responsible author appear to fade. But it is precisely to this that
Werner G. Jeanrond replies. On the basis of, *inter alia*, the interpretation
models of Paul Ricoeur and David Tracy he prepares a dynamic model
in which the meaning comes into being as an interaction between text and
reader, and in which it becomes possible to maintain the critical distance
from the text which makes the reader morally responsible without permit-
ting him to fall under the control of the text or his personal whims.

> My thesis therefore runs as follows: no concept of understanding can lay
> claim to adequacy unless it includes right from the start a dimension of
> criticism regarding both the matter (Sache) of the text and the situation in
> which the interpretation takes place ... In this way interpretation is deter-
> mined in a threefold manner: through the dimensions of understanding,
> explanation and assessment.[23]

---

22. Tracy, *Plurality and Ambiguity*, p. 48, and Nielsen, *There is Hope*, p. 60.
23. Jeanrond, *Text and Interpretation*, p. 65. Cf. also p. 125 on the reader's
responsibility. Cf. also A.C. Thiselton's article, 'Reader-Response Hermeneutics', pp. 112-13, where 'interpretative responsibility' is referred to as an
important and constructive hermeneutic category, and the question of the text's
possible meaning is changed to the question, 'whether we can take it to mean
this *responsibly*' (in Lundin, Thiselton and Walhout, *The Responsibility*).

In other words, what the debate has opened up is the ethical aspect in the use of the language and thereby the necessity of considering the language user's responsibility. Although it has become clear that the language is totally at the mercy of the user, but that the user is himself part of this linguistic world, we must maintain that the responsibility for use rests with people and not in impersonal language structures.[24]

Without this assumption, any interpretation will lose value as a contribution to the continuous discussion. By its nature, an exegetic work will be a dated, temporary, unfinished, partial contribution. Recording it arrests the mobility which—it is hoped—is to be found in the exegete's mind and the process which has taken place during its preparation. But the very openness of the language to new interpretation, the undermining action of ambiguity and diversity, will make what is presented a contribution to discussion, open to new contributions, new questions and new answers.

The exegete's responsibility consists therefore in willingness to discuss the matter on the basis of his own text, as well as willingness to revise his own text on the basis of the discussion. What must be demanded of today's exegetes is not only that we know our trade, whatever the school we have been brought up in, but that we must also be able to discuss the ethical consequences of the methods we use.

The texts we are considering are part of our own culture as identification texts and function in the religious institutions as the basis of true preaching. The truth in this context is not an available entity which exists independently of universities' research and the religious institutions' use of research. It is also not immaterial, therefore, whether the exegete chooses to work on the basis of methods which open up discussion of what is truth, or methods whose primary task is to demarcate a text's possible meanings and to codify a single interpretation as the truth.

In writing about Satan today, therefore, one must be aware that the exegetic results will form part of the constant power struggle about the right to interpret the Bible. In this situation, someone will probably consider it less than responsible to choose the very topic 'Satan—the Prodigal Son?' as the basic theme. Is there not a far greater need for a strong and clear renunciation of the devil and all his works and all his ways?

There can be no doubt that there is a need to reject the demonic powers

---

24. That David Tracy refers to discussion as fundamental to the understanding of language and a vital element in any culture also means that language and personal responsibility belong together. Cf. Tracy's preface in *Plurality and Ambiguity*, p. ix.

of the world, but for me the crucial question remains whether we should content ourselves with proclaiming a renunciation of evil, as if we knew once and for all who Satan is. But we will understand who Satan is only by continuous discussion of who God is. The object of this book is, therefore, to encourage this responsible discussion of God and Satan.

Chapter 3

METAPHORS AND CLUSTERS OF METAPHORS:
THE FATHER–SON IMAGE AS A ROOT METAPHOR

Any text analysis must have an eye for the ambiguity of individual words and statements and for the dependence of the meaning upon the context. Yet it must be stressed that this aspect becomes of particular relevance when we are reading texts expressed in imagery or containing various forms of image.

The Book of Job is an example of such a text, not only from the aspect that, in the dialogues, Job and his friends use single metaphors to express views but from the aspect that the fundamental conflict in the book is expressed metaphorically as a dispute between a father and his two sons. I am also of the opinion that in reading the Book of Job and its inter-textuality there are some texts we must include because the author struggles against them or is later attacked by them, narratives about the relationship between a father and his sons.

We can speak of God only in images. If we speak of God's sons, this also must be in images,[1] that is, the image of a family used of God and his relationship to others. When the Old Testament uses the image of a family certain associations are aroused in the perceptive reader. At the time of the Old Testament, the family was primarily perceived as a hierarchically constructed group with the father as its head. The family image connoted relationship and authority,[2] and this image had many possibilities. It could give rise to widely differing narratives. Perhaps happy circumstances were involved, where the sons, or at least one of them, live up to the demands

1. Cf. the terminology in K. Nielsen, *There is Hope for a Tree: The Tree as Metaphor in Isiah* (JSOTSup, 65; Sheffield: JSOT Press, 1989), pp. 42-66, and the description of imagery's function on pp. 65-66.

2. Cf. M. Bossman, 'Images of God in the Letters of Paul', *BTB* 18 (1988), pp. 71-74, and B.J. Malina, *The New Testament World: Insights from Cultural Anthropology* (London: SCM Press, 1983), pp. 94-121.

presented by the role as son and the father lives up to the responsibility which falls to him; relationships perhaps marked by strife and deceit.

These negative aspects also form part of the family image, and in ancient Israel they led, for example, to scrupulous legislation in regard to the distribution of inheritance between sons. Deut. 21.15-17, for example, describes the situation where a man might wish to give the eldest son less than his due share. If, indeed, a man has two wives, one of whom he loves and the other he disregards, and the first-born is the son of the disregarded wife, the law provides that the rights of primogeniture belong to the first-born. As the first-born, a son is entitled to double of everything, because he is the first fruit of the father's manhood.

The father is not permitted, therefore, to follow his own feelings and wishes and place the youngest before the eldest. One senses behind this law that many a father has felt a particular attachment to the son of his old age (and his young mother), and did not necessarily wish to consider his eldest for the extra part of the inheritance to which he was entitled. We have only to think of Jacob's love for Rachel's sons, Joseph and Benjamin.

In any event, very strong relationships will often be at stake. There may be good reason here to bear in mind that whereas we in the Western world of today associate particularly close emotional affections with the relationship between spouses, such affections were at the time primarily associated with the brother–sister relationship and with that between mother and son or father and son.[3]

As we shall see later, biblical literature is by no means unacquainted with narratives of the type: 'There was a man who had two sons.' The father–son image is a good and fertile soil for narratives, but because the role of father involves diverse relationships the father image can produce other forms of image.

Authority and solicitude belong to the father role. The father has begotten the sons, who are dependent upon him and who owe him respect and love. In return, he provides for their needs and protects them from external threats and dangers. In his studies of Mesopotamian history of religion,

---

3. Bruce J. Malina has shown the importance of the relationship between parents and children and between siblings at the time of the New Testament compared with what we are used to in the modern Western world. 'The affection we expect as a mark of the husband and wife relationship is normally a mark of brother-sister and mother-son relationships.' Malina, *The New Testament World*, p. 98.

Thorkild Jacobsen has shown that different god-images have been dominant in different periods. In the second millennium BCE, the parent-image
is central and makes it possible to express the relationship between man
and his God in highly varied terms:

> Normally, the image of the god in relation to his worshipper is quite a
> different one, that of master and slave. Even the most powerful king was
> a slave in relation to the god of his city and country; only in relation to
> his own personal god was he, to quote a standard phrase, 'the man, son
> of his god.' In considering this concept more closely we may distinguish
> some of the various strands that make it up. First, its physical aspect: the
> father as engenderer of the child; the mother as giving birth to it. Second,
> the provider aspect: the father as the provider for his family. Third, the
> protector and intercessor aspect. Fourth, the claim parents have upon their
> children for honour and obedience.[4]

The father role is thus reminiscent of the creator's role in relation to the
creation, the king's in relation to the people, the judge's in relation to the
accused, to mention just a few of the best known god images in biblical
tradition. Taken together, these images may be considered as a metaphor
cluster with its root in the father image. This father image may then be
referred to as a root metaphor.[5]

4. Cf. T. Jacobsen, *The Treasures of Darkness: A History of Mesopotamian
Religion* (New Haven: Yale University Press, 1976), p. 158.
5. Cf. the use of this concept in P.A. Porter, *Metaphors and Monsters: A
Literary-Critical Study of Daniel 7 and 8* (Toronto: Dr Paul A. Porter, 1985),
pp. 33-42. In his examination of the Book of Daniel, chs. 7–8, Porter reaches
the point that the root metaphor that gathers the metaphors into a cluster is the
shepherd image. This is the image that creates the connection between the other
images:
'Our thesis is that the root metaphor "shepherd" has generated the following
external metaphors informing Daniel 7 and 8: (1) The herd leader is the
SHEPHERD of the flock; (2) The military leader is the SHEPHERD of the
warriors; (3) The warrior is the (destructive) SHEPHERD of the enemy; (4)
The ruler is the SHEPHERD of the nation; (5) God/Michael is the SHEPHERD
of the angels; (6) The ruler is the SHEPHERD of the temple; (7) God is the
SHEPHERD of truth; (8) The judge is the SHEPHERD of the oppressed; (9)
The predator is the (destructive) SHEPHERD of the oppressed; (10) The man
is the SHEPHERD of the animals; (11) The storm god is the SHEPHERD of
the flock; (12) God is the SHEPHERD of Israel.
'Evidence for these external metaphors will be found primarily in the OT
lamentation literature, which, we shall argue, provides an important source
of the animal imagery of Daniel 7 and 8', p. 61. Cf. also the conclusion on
p. 121.

Sallie McFague gives such vital significance to a religion's root metaphor that she can say

> ... if the root-metaphor of a religion is lost, so is the religion: one does
> not have the same religion without its basic model.[6]

If we think of the Christian tradition in this context, we must say that the
image of God as father is a root metaphor of this kind. Jesus' reference
to God as his father cannot be removed from the New Testament texts
without changing their meaning. The same religion cannot be preserved
if the basic thought-model is removed. Jesus' words, that he and the father
are one, cannot simply be paraphrased by using another image or translated
into a non-figurative statement. A root metaphor does not stand in isolation;
it gathers other metaphors around it and thereby creates and organizes the
network of meaning which forms the religion's cognitive content.

If we are to examine Satan's role in the Old Testament, therefore, we
must also expect that it may be necessary to include images other than
the image of a father and his sons. In a juridical context, the Satan role
could for example have been adopted by the accuser, and it is then the
relationship between the accuser and the judge that must be of interest to
us, cf. the description of Satan in Zech. 3.1-7.[7] Similarly, the image of
the creator will make it natural to seek Satan images among the highest
creations, which do not necessarily belong to the human race (cf. e.g., Job
40.19).[8]

If we then ask why indeed the parent image came to play such a large
role in Mesopotamia in the second millennium BCE, Thorkild Jacobsen,
having briefly indicated personal religion's paradoxical confidence that
the cosmos cares for the individual, answers as follows:

---

Cf. also T.N.D. Mettinger, *In Search of God: The Meaning and Message of
the Everlasting Names* (Philadelphia: Fortress Press, 1988), where Mettinger
singles out the king as root metaphor, and T.N.D. Mettinger, 'The Study of the
Gottesbild: Problems and Suggestions', *SEÅ* 54 (1989), pp. 135–45 [138-43],
where Mettinger, in his examination of the God-images in the Old Testament,
indicates two different root metaphors: the Covenant (the Northern Kingdom's
traditions and the deuteronomistic movement's theology) and the king (the
pre-exile Judah's official theology).

6. S. McFague, *Metaphorical Theology: Models of God in Religious Language* (Philadelphia: Fortress Press, 1982), p. 110. In this section, McFague
relies on David Tracy and Paul Ricoeur in particular.

7. Cf. more specifically pp. 132-35.

8. Cf. more specifically pp. 80-82.

Furthermore, the inner 'form' or 'metaphor' of the parent, of 'father' and 'mother' under which the personal god came to be seen, does more: it serves as a psychologically possible bridge to the great and terrifyingly awesome cosmic powers. For it is within human experience that even the highest, greatest and most terrifying personages in society have a mild, human, and approachable side in their relations to their children ... There is a stage in childhood when parents are all-powerful and divine to the child. The child (to grow up) has eventually to adjust to the disturbing realization that parents are after all only other human beings with human limitations. But in this case such adjustment was excluded. The divine parents were, and had to remain divine.[9]

### The Metaphor's Function in the Field of Tension between Similarity and Dissimilarity

The basis of the text analyses is the assertion that the description of Satan must be understood metaphorically and in close association with the God-images. In the same way as the canonic and non-canonic authors attempted to express their experience of God by means of different images and names, they tried to express their experience of other aspects of their reality by means of different images and names.

The use of names such as Yahweh, Michael, Uriel, Gabriel, Raphael, Satan, Belial/Beliar and Azazel shows that one of the ideas about reality is that beyond the people of this world there are also 'persons' in a heavenly world, or rather that realities exist which can be referred to in personal images and named as persons are named. These realities are not restricted by the limits that apply to people, and they must therefore be referred to by images other than personal images, for example by animal images or images from the elementary world.[10] In our context the main emphasis will be on personal images, and therein on the father–son image.

9. Cf. Jacobsen, *The Treasures*, p. 161. In extension of Thorkild Jacobsen's analysis of relationships in the Mesopotamian area, there is reason to refer to the analyses Rainer Albertz has presented in his book, *Weltschöpfung und Menschenschöpfung: Untersucht bei Deuterojesaja, Hiob und in den Psalmen* (Creation of the World and Creation of Mankind: Investigated in Deutero-Isaiah, Job and the Psalms) (Calwer Theologische Monographien, 3; Stuttgart: Calwer Verlag, 1974), where he emphasizes the dualism in the Israelite God image: God as cosmos creator and as creator of the individual person, a view we shall return to later, cf. pp. 52-54.

10. Cf. God images from the animal world, for example Yahweh as a lion, Hos. 5.14; and from the elementary world, Yahweh as fire, Exod. 3.2-6; as

It is vital in using images to insist that the image is constructed upon both the similarity and the dissimilarity principles. This is expressed in various ways by philosophers and scholars. Max Black has referred to such a metaphor concept as 'an interaction view of metaphor', and agrees with A. Richards's description of what a metaphor is:

> In the simplest formulation, when we use a metaphor we have two thoughts of different things active together supported by a single word, or phrase, whose meaning is a resultant of their interaction.[11]

Or as Paul Ricoeur expresses it:

> To see *the like* is to see the same in spite of, and through, the different. This tension between sameness and difference characterizes the logical structure of likeness.[12]

Images are thus created when two different statements each with its own contexts interact with one another. Not everything that is said by the one statement, the metaphorical, has direct relevance to what the image speaks of, the referent. There are elements of meaning which actually insist on the difference!

To distinguish between imagery and literal speech is of course crucial. Definition of the two forms of speech relative to one another has nevertheless caused great problems for research. One of the scholars who has tried to define wherein the difference lies is the Norwegian exegete, the late Anders J. Bjørndalen, who distinguishes between conjunctive and disjunctive usage. The main idea is that the meaning of a word consists of different elements of meaning, which need not all be actualized in the specific speech situation. If all elements of meaning are functioning, conjunctive usage is concerned; if only a few of these elements are functioning, disjunctive usage is concerned. And it is this disjunctive usage which then asserts itself in metaphorical speech.[13]

This, however, has nothing to say about how we decide in practice whether one usage or the other is concerned. But more often than not

water, Jer. 2.13; as air (wind) Gen. 1.2 and as earth (rock) Ps. 62.3. Cf. the Satan images from the animal world, for example Behemoth and Leviathan in Job 40–41.

11. Cf. M. Black, 'Metaphor', in *Proceedings of the Aristotelian Society*, NS 55 (1954–55), pp. 273-94.

12. Cf. Nielsen, *There is Hope*, p. 52, and P. Ricoeur, 'The Metaphorical Process', p. 146.

13. Cf. also my review of Bjørndalen's works in Nielsen, *There is Hope*, pp. 30-31.

there will be no doubt that an expression must be metaphorical. When in Psalm 62 the psalmist calls the Lord 'my rock', for example, this is clearly a disjunctive use of the word. Several of the potential meanings contained in the word 'rock' are indeed not realized when Israel's God is referred to. Although it is good to support oneself on the Lord and to build on the Lord, God is neither bound to a certain spot nor threatened by weathering.

An important point in Bjørndalen's definition of metaphorical speech is the indication that the same word and expression can be *used* both metaphorically and non-metaphorically. There do not exist different words, metaphorical and non-metaphorical, but the contexts decide whether it is metaphorical or literal *use* of the language.

That an image is created in the tension between two contexts, both of which involve similarities and differences, implies that the images are inexhaustible. They cannot therefore be translated without losing some of the meaning. Moreover, it must be said that images are indeed created in the tension between two contexts, and not in the tension between two words.

This accords well with the indication of recent linguistics that the meaning of a word cannot be defined as something that exists once and for all. The meaning of a word arises in relation to other words. Every word has a semantic field within which its meaning is created. The context-less word is a useless abstraction. And if nevertheless we take an individual word out of its context we immediately create a new context on whose basis the word's meaning is created.

My strong emphasis that metaphors come into being in usage, and that I therefore prefer to speak of metaphors' potential meaning and not, like Bjørndalen, of elements of meaning, is because the reader has such a vital role in the process. It is ourselves as competent users of language who must decide whether a certain term is to be understood metaphorically or literally, that is, whether the text, in the context in which we encounter it, is most meaningful if we interpret it metaphorically.

If we are to try to summarize what is characteristic of imagery, a number of aspects must be included. We have already on several occasions touched on the basic structure of the metaphor: the tension between similarity and difference, and we have indicated that imagery offers new ways of looking at reality. That the image is created in the field of tension between similarity and difference also means that the listener or reader is given a very active role. He must himself enter into the interpretation of the image, involve himself in it and adopt it as a new and more pertinent way of looking at reality. Only then can it be said that an image is successful.

Finally, we must emphasize the image's openness to new interpretation, and thus its suitability for re-use. The image is open to interpretation but, it must be said, not to any interpretation. The specific context in which it is used indicates a number of definite meanings which the listener, on the basis of his premises, will perceive as obvious, and which whoever uses the image will be able to utilize to promote a certain understanding. But if the situation changes and new listeners or readers come to grips with the image, a shift in understanding may occur which results in a re-interpretation of the original image.[14]

Imagery's openness and breadth does not prevent its being perceived in the new situation as extremely precise and pregnant speech. For example, later generations have been able to reuse many of the prophetic oracles with new meaning, without the words thereby becoming less precise. Indeed, the contrary has often been the case. It is difficult to imagine a more precise interpretation of the Lord's suffering Servant in Isaiah 53 than the Christian interpretation, where Jesus of Nazareth is the sacrificial lamb which atones for the sins of the world.

*Exegetic Consequences*

It is self-evident that this has exegetic consequences. What is most important in the analysis of Satan as God's son is the indication of imagery's strong *context-dependence*. The word 'context' should be understood very broadly here as regards the literary placing in the run of a text, the inter-textuality in a broader sense, and the specific situation in which an image is used. Images therefore have a history. There are no 'standard interpretations' which are valid at any time. Image analyses must therefore always contain an element of the image's history of use.[15]

14. Cf. my detailed description of imagery's function in Nielsen, *There is Hope*, pp. 65-66:

a) Imagery acts in a specific context by an interaction between two different statements.

b) Information can be derived from imagery in the form of new proposals for understanding reality.

c) The object of imagery is to involve the hearers in such a way that by entering into the interpretation they take it over as their own perception of reality (performative function).

d) Imagery can be reused in another context with possibilities of new interpretation and new evaluation of the informative and performative functions respectively.

15. Cf. more specifically in Nielsen, *There is Hope*, pp. 66-67.

The father–son image gives rise to narratives and thus to a long section of text. Whereas earlier research has stressed the analysis of the individual word, individual statement, or biblical verse, recent research is characterized by its strong emphasis that language manifests itself in texts whose meaning depends upon the context.

A metaphor should not therefore be analysed in isolation;[16] only on the basis of its context—in a wide sense—is meaning created. Also, an individual text in the Old Testament, a narrative, or a parable, should not be understood or in practice come to be understood in isolation. It must be read in both its syntagmatic and paradigmatic contexts.

Each individual text thus forms part of different networks, each of which influences the reader's interpretation of it. Reading without assumptions does not exist; but the assumptions vary and create different possibilities of meaning. This is also to say that texts can be read, and are read, differently.

Many exegetes have viewed this openness to new meanings, or ambiguity, as a difficulty that should be overcome. One should rather consider it as a richness, and like Northrop Frye maintain that it is indeed a characteristic of good literature that it is ambiguous: '... polysemous meaning is a feature of all deeply serious writing, and the Bible is the model for serious writing.'[17]

What we have now said about metaphors, and generally about the use of imagery, about openness to meaning, and dependence on context and intertextuality, is well in line with the main views asserted in the section on textual understanding in this postmodern period, in which 'intertextuality' is the keyword. It is also on these premises that we shall analyse a part of the intertextuality in which God and Satan are described by means of a 'root metaphor' which is able to create a whole cluster of metaphors: the father–son image with the other images derived therefrom.

As is indirectly apparent, one of these premises is that images are not only meaningful in their intertextuality but can be applied to reality, whereby their significance emerges. The God and Satan images receive their meaning through the mutual relationships in the texts, but point beyond the texts in an attempt to interpret reality.[18]

When in practical exegesis we have to contend with restricting the text

16. Cf. Nielsen, *There is Hope*, pp. 62-67.
17. N. Frye, *The Great Code: The Bible and Literature* (London: Ark Edition, 1983), p. 221.
18. Cf. the referential aspect in Nielsen, *There is Hope*, pp. 53-60.

material which is to be included in an analysis, we also concern ourselves—whether we are aware of this or not—with the images' referent.
Not every metaphorical statement in the Old Testament can be applied
meaningfully to God, and likewise not every metaphorical statement can
be applied to Satan. We are operating in practice with two different
referents to which we normally apply different statements.

How we each individually visualize these referents depends upon the
favourite concepts and favourite metaphors we have for them. For some,
a pair of concepts such as 'good' and 'evil' will be the most natural
description of the two referents. For others, the personal form, 'the Good
One' and 'the Evil One', are more pertinent metaphors, since they belong
to the personal sphere and not to the conceptual sphere.

This clear contrast alone shows something of our prejudices, that is,
that we imagine two opposing principles or two opponents. We are used
to perceiving God and Satan as poles apart, indeed to think in terms of
contrasts, and this despite the fact that the Christian tradition to which we
are indebted is not dualistic in the strict sense.

What I shall try to demonstrate in the text analyses is, then, that the
relationship is far more complicated. It is not opposing principles of life
that are concerned but relationships, which are described, for example, in
the form of a family drama.

### Imagery and Conflict Analysis?

I have now stressed the complexity of imagery, but in this connection I
must return to a subject I have only touched upon. A characteristic of the
images used about fundamental experiences in life is that they are ambiguous. A very widespread image is that of water, which can connote
both life and death. Water is necessary if a person is to live. But conversely
the person dies if immersed in water and prevented from getting oxygen.

There is much human experience to indicate the ambiguity or polysemy
of life, and much thought activity has therefore been devoted to bringing
these charged experiences into linguistic form so that they can be analysed.
But what language is able to do this except imagery itself, with its special
ability to compare complex relationships? It is through imagery itself that
the basic conflicts of life can be subjected to analysis without neglecting
the complexity and without having to supplant part of the experience.

It is part of proper usage to say things as precisely as is possible and
as unambiguously as is now possible. To define means to demarcate, to
catalogue, to separate and grade. But this form of analysis is not sufficient

where experience of which ambivalence is a basic feature is concerned. This applies to basic religious experience, the encounter with the divine. The divine both fascinates and alarms at one and the same time.

If this religious experience is to be given a language, the language used must be able to maintain both these aspects. The Bible with its imagery can preserve the connection between these apparently conflicting features. It is in the light of this that we must understand the necessity for a language in which both good and evil can be maintained without merging and without separation.

Chapter 4

## THE CURRENT VIEW OF RESEARCH INTO THE
## SATAN FIGURE IN THE OLD TESTAMENT

My wish to analyse the Satan figure in the light of one or more 'root metaphors' is not a novel approach. Also, up to the present, research has concerned itself in practice with the Satan image, and tried to define its nature. It is true that investigations have not been described as image analyses, but the difference is slight, since the object has been to disclose the activity in the society of the time upon which the Satan role was modelled.

### *Theories on the Satan Figure's Origin and Function*

The latest monograph on Satan in the Old Testament was written by Peggy L. Day. She calls her book *An Adversary in Heaven: śāṭān in the Hebrew Bible*,[1] and thus refers to *śāṭān* as a celestial opponent. Nevertheless, this work is concerned only ostensibly with Satan. Day's main thesis is that the Old Testament has no concept of Satan in the sense of one specific celestial figure who is opposed to Yahweh. Closer analysis of the use of the word *śāṭān* reveals, however, representations of various satans, each of whom in his way functions as adversary or accuser. There is not one Satan in the Old Testament but the potential for many, believes Day.[2]

---

1. P.L. Day, *An Adversary in Heaven: śāṭān in the Hebrew Bible* (Atlanta: Scholars Press, 1988).
2. 'The present study makes no attempt to identify the origins of Satan; if anything, we must divest ourselves of the notion of Satan if we are to accurately perceive how the noun *śāṭān* functions in each of the passages under examination. As we shall see, the noun *śāṭān* could mean both "adversary" in general and "legal accuser" in particular, and it was used to refer to various beings both terrestrial and divine when they played either of these adversarial roles. Proceeding from this observation, it becomes clear that there is not one celestial *śāṭān* in the Hebrew Bible, but rather the potential for many.' Day, *An Adversary in Heaven*, p. 15. Cf. also p. 63.

The four main texts in her analyses are Num. 22.22-35, Zech. 3.1-7, Job 1-2 and 1 Chron. 21.1–22.1. According to her assessment, they all relate to celestial satans who have their function in the celestial council, whose primary duty was to administer justice.[3]

Peggy L. Day's work criticizes in many ways Rivkah Schärf Kluger's 1948 book, *Die Gestalt des Satans im Alten Testament* (The Figure of Satan in the Old Testament).[4] Schärf Kluger took as her basis her own period's experience of the darkness of evil. Under the impact of this, the visions of Satan's actions on earth in the Revelation to St John become an adequate image of reality. 'The nature and origin of this force has become a terrible actual problem in our time. So it may not be meaningless to trace the image of the devil back to its origins.'[5] But before Schärf Kluger begins her analyses she defines her subject as follows: 'My subject will not be God and devil, not their essence as such—that would be metaphysical speculation—but the psychological contents and the experiences of the superhuman in a religiously creative time, whose expression they are.'[6]

Schärf Kluger then tries to disclose a development in the Satan figure from Numbers 22 via Job 1–2 and Zechariah 3 to an independent demoniac personality with the proper name of Satan in 1 Chron. 21.1. And it is precisely such an interpretation that Peggy Day rejects by her assertion in regard to the various satans.

Day and Schärf Kluger share a wish to analyse the texts available as expressing concepts in the human psyche, but employ different methods of scholarship. Whereas Schärf Kluger relies on C.G. Jung's theories, and thus considers the concepts regarding a devil as archetypes in the human psyche, Day's work is marked by an interest in placing *śāṭān* in the

---

3. Day already declares in the introduction, pp. 1-15, her indebtedness to scholars such as H. Wheeler Robinson, G. Ernest Wright and Frank Moore Cross, and their demonstration that Yahweh, like the Canaanitic gods, presided over a council of divine beings.

4. R. Schärf Kluger, *Die Gestalt des Satans im Alten Testament* (Part 3 of series ed. by C.G. Jung; *Symbolik des Geistes*; Zürich: Rascher & Cie. A.-G. Verlag, 1948) published in an English translation in 1967 in Evanston as *Satan in the Old Testament* (Evanston: Northwestern University Press, 1967). By that time, Rivkah Schärf had become Rivkah Schärf Kluger. My references to the book apply to the English version.

5. Schärf Kluger, *Satan in the Old Testament*, p. 3.

6. Schärf Kluger, *Satan in the Old Testament*, p. 3.

contemporary concepts of a celestial council similar to the council of an earthly king. To characterize their approach to the texts, it might be said that whereas Schärf Kluger utilizes, apart from the traditional exegetic methods, psychology and psychoanalysis, Day employs exclusively the well-known methods in which text criticism and source criticism are very prominent.

With the help of recent investigations into the biblical texts' genesis, Day stresses the importance of arriving at correct datings for the four texts, but she cannot agree that a clear line of development is to be established on this basis. Kluger does not expend nearly as much energy on datings, but she is convinced that there is one definite idea which is developed throughout the various texts. Having demonstrated this development, she believes that she can place the texts in the chronological order which the development reflects.

It will also be seen from Day's study that it was usual in the research which preceded Day and Kluger to see Satan in relation to Yahweh, and thus as part of a greater entity. A. Brock-Utne has suggested, for example, that the background to the Satan figure lies in the political situation in the Near East. The Palestinian princelings were dependent upon the Great King's favour, and feared anyone who was in a position to speak ill of them or accuse them before the Great King.[7] It was likewise imagined that at the court of Yahweh there was a slanderer who acted as described in Job 1–2 and Zechariah 3.

According to H. Torczyner, this was in fact a functionary at the celestial court. Like the Great Kings of the Near East who caused their subjects to be watched, Yahweh employed Satan as 'the king's eye', roaming the world on Yahweh's behalf and testing people's loyalty.[8] A. Lods also sees Satan as a functionary at the celestial court; but he sees him as an agent of the celestial police who also occasionally takes on the office of accuser,

7. Cf. A. Brock-Utne, '"Der Feind": Die alttestamentliche Satansgestalt im Lichte der sozialen Verhältnisse des nahen Orients' ('"The Enemy": The Old Testament Satan Figure in the Light of Social Conditions in the Near East') *Klio, Beiträge zur Alten Geschichte* (Contributions to Ancient History) 28 (1935), pp. 1-9. Brock-Utne refers, *inter alia*, to various Amarna letters: cf., for example, J.A. Knudtzon, *Die El-Amarna-Tafeln I-II* (The El-Amarna Tablets I-II) (Leipzig: J.C. Hinrichs, 1915), No. 254 and No. 286.

8. H. Torczyner, 'How Satan came into the World', *ExpTim* (1936–37), pp. 563-65. This viewpoint is continued by Elaine Pagel, *The Origin of Satan* (Harmondsworth: Penguin Books, 1996), p. 41.

Zechariah 3.[9] In this connection, further reference may be made to Gerhard von Rad's definition of Satan as celestial accuser.[10]

These suggestions exemplify the great importance that this very concept of Yahweh as a king surrounded by a celestial court has meant to Satan research.

Finally, yet another interpretation should be considered, that is, that a number of earlier scholars considered Satan as belonging among the demons, a point of view which has in general been abandoned in recent discussion.[11] In her treatment of this view of Satan, Rivkah Schärf Kluger maintains that scholars such as Hans Duhm and Anton Jirku have not succeeded in reaching an understanding of evil's position in the Old Testament, since they have associated evil with demons and not recognized evil's proximity to Yahweh himself.

Schärf Kluger therefore sees herself as far more in agreement with P. Volz's classic work on the demoniac aspect of Yahweh.[12] Yahweh is seen here as an original demoniac deity, and this makes much clearer why demonology plays such a modest part in the Old Testament. The demoniac is largely incorporated in the image of God. Schärf Kluger is clear and precise as regards what is vital to her, that is, that '... monotheism in its essence is not unity against multiplicity as its absolute opposite; it is rather the *unity of multiplicity*.'[13]

Research in the field has not been comprehensive up to the present time.

9. A. Lods, 'Les Origines de la figure de Satan, ses fonctions à la cour céleste', *Mélanges Syriens offerts à M.R. Dussaud* (Bibliothèque archeologique et historique, 30, Paris. 1939), II, pp. 649-60.

10. Cf. Gerhard von Rad, 'Die at.liche Satansvorstellung', *TWNT* 2 (1935), pp. 71-74, where von Rad argues that Satan is exclusively the accuser at the divine court and in no way a demoniac being.

11. Cf., for example, H. Duhm, *Die bösen Geister im Alten Testament* (Evil Spirits in the Old Testament) (Tübingen: J.C.B. Mohr, 1904), pp. 16-25; pp. 58-63; A. Jirku, *Die Dämonen und ihre Abwehr im Alten Testament* (Demons and their Defence in the Old Testament) (Leipzig: A. Diechert, 1912), and H. Kaupel, *Die Dämonen im Alten Testament* (Demons in the Old Testament) (Augsburg: Dr B. Filser, 1930). When mentioning the earlier research, reference should also be made to Gustav Roskoff's two-volume work on the devil, *Geschichte des Teufels* (The History of the Devil), which dates from 1869 and which contains a large section on Satan in the Old Testament. Cf. also as regards research history the surveys in Day, *An Adversary in Heaven* and Schärf Kluger, *Satan in the Old Testament*.

12. P. Volz, *Das dämonische in Jahwe* (The Demoniac in Yahweh) (Tübingen: J.C.B. Mohr, 1924).

13. Schärf Kluger, *Satan in the Old Testament*, p. 10.

It can be classified relatively easily into the following groups: (a) older research, which wished by using the history of religion to classify the demoniac figures referred to in the Old Testament and to locate Satan there, (b) research following on this which, based on ideas about the celestial court, tried to find a role or an established office for Satan at the court, (c) psychology-orientated research as stressed by Volz and Schärf Kluger, who—without leaving all differences aside—both consider that the Satan figure developed from being part of Yahweh himself into acquiring a more independent function.

In the light of this, I wish briefly to define my own approach to the subject. Like Kluger, I must assert that I am concerned with human ideas. But I must emphasize that these ideas have taken the form of texts which must be read in their intertextuality. I must therefore first adopt an attitude of reserve relative to an all too dogmatic belief that the Old Testament's texts reflect a single line of development. Here, Day's thesis concerning potentially different Satan concepts seems at first more fruitful. But this will not prevent me from raising the question of possible connections between the images of the various texts.

Furthermore, I find Kluger's feeling for the ambivalent in the images of God important, although I cannot follow her Jungian model according to which Satan is Yahweh's split-off dark side.

What I miss in earlier research, however, is a greater awareness that the texts employ images when they describe the relationship between Satan and Yahweh. As will be seen from the previous chapters, I wish to utilize the perceptions of recent literary criticism, including the assumption that all talk of God and Satan must be seen as metaphoric, and must therefore be analysed in the same way as any other metaphoric statement.

This also means that my analyses do *not* pretend—no more than does this section on the history of research—to give a complete overview of the ideas about Satan in biblical and inter-testamentary times. What I wish to examine is one specific way of formulating these ideas, that is, in the image of a personal relationship between a father and his son. I perceive this image as one of those wholly vital to an understanding of the views on God and Satan—but certainly not the only one.

In employing this approach to the text analysis I have not kept firmly to the preconceived view that this specific image must be the original basis of the Satan figure, but I wish to argue in favour of the image's significance in discussing the role of the Satan figure.

But before the text analysis it will be useful to consider briefly the significance of the word *śāṭān*, including the word's etymology.

## *Etymology and Significance of Satan (śāṭān)*

The root *śṭn* is to be found in several Semitic languages besides Hebrew, for example Syrian, Mandaean, Ethiopian and Arabic. It is disputed whether the root *śṭn* exists in Accadian.[14] Some scholars have tried to derive *śāṭān* from the root *śūṭ*; for example H. Torczyner[15] who believes he has found a connection between the Arabic form *šaiṭān* and *śūṭ*. In this regard, however, it should be pointed out that this is not a connection in the history of language but rather in popular etymology. This is to be seen from Job 1.7; 2.2 where Satan speaks of his going to and fro on the earth.[16]

Like the noun *śāṭān*, the noun *śiṭnāh* is probably derived from the verb. A variant is the root *śṭm*, to which the noun *maśṭemāh* belongs. In all, the root *śṭn*, including the variants, occurs 43 times in the Old Testament.

The root *śṭn/śṭm*, refers to various forms of dispute and hostility. Within the family brothers fight, so that hatred and hostility arise (Gen. 27.41; 50.15), and in the extended family shepherds quarrel about wells (Gen. 26.21).

In the political world adversaries appear (1 Sam. 29.4; 2 Sam. 19.23; 1 Kgs 5.18; 11.14, 23, 25, and similarly men fight against one another in war (Gen. 49.23). In the Psalms also, hostility can be referred to using a form of this root (Ps. 38.21; 71.13; 55.4, cf. also Hos. 9.7, 8).

A somewhat narrower meaning is given to the root in Ps. 109.4, 20, 29, where the hostility manifests itself in accusations, as in Zech. 3.1; cf. also Ezra 4.6 where the noun *śiṭnāh* occurs, but the meaning is disputed.[17]

Three areas are therefore present in which *śṭn/śṭm* is used about human adversaries and hostilities: (1) personal discord in the family; (2) political and military hostilities; and (3) the judicial world's accusations.

14. According to K.L. Tallqvist, *Akkadische Götterepitheta* (Accadian God-epithets) (Helsinki: Firsted, 1938/New York: George Olms, 1974), p. 240, the root *śṭn* is used as an epithet for Nergal and *Ištar*, whereas AHw 260b sees *mu-uš-ta-ti-nu* and *mu-uš-te-ti-na-at* as a participle of the root *etēm/nu(m)*. *THAT* II (Wanke) considers the latter convincing, and Day, *An Adversary in Heaven*, p. 23 agrees with this.

15. H. Torczyner, 'Wie Satan in die Welt kam' (How Satan Came into the World), *Mitteilungsblätter der hebräischen Universität Jerusalem* (Information Sheets; Jerusalem: Hebrew University, 1938), IV, pp. 15-21.

16. Cf. Day, *An Adversary in Heaven*, pp. 21-22, and Schärf Kluger, *Satan in the Old Testament*, p. 31.

17. Cf. F. Horst, *Hiob Kapitel 1–19* (Job, Chapters 1–19) (BKAT, XVI.1; Neukirchen-Vluyn: Neukirchener Verlag, 1974), p. 14.

The root is most frequently used in the Book of Job: 14 times in the prologue and twice in the dialogues. In the dialogues, the verb *śāṭām* refers to Yahweh's hostility towards Job. In the prologue the noun *haśśāṭan*, that is with the definite article, is used.[18] According to Job 1.6, *haśśāṭan* belongs to *bᵉnē hāᵉlohîm*. Some scholars see this as a function reference, but which function is concerned is still under debate; this is also to be seen from the research survey.

Rivkah Schärf Kluger defines the root's original meaning as follows, giving Num. 22.22 as the passage where this original meaning is expressed most clearly: 'Consequently, by means of the basic meaning of the secondary form *śāṭām* and the Arabic *šāṭana* as parallel form to *śāṭān*, it can be concluded that the primal meaning of the verb *śāṭān* is *persecution by hindering free forward movement*; i.e., it means to "hinder, to oppose, an existing intention." ... The translation of the noun *śāṭān* by *Widersacher* ("adversary") in most passages by both the Zürich Bible and Luther therefore comes closest to the original meaning.'[19]

Peggy L. Day also holds to the meaning 'adversary' for the noun *śāṭān*. An important element in Day's investigation is the establishment of *śāṭān* as a triliteral word with *nun* as the third radical, and not as derived from some weak verb with the suffix *–ān* added. Day points out that this latter possibility lies behind the placing of *śāṭān* in the Mandaean dictionary under the root *sṭa*.[20] Day carefully examines earlier attempts to see *–ān* as a suffix (thus both Tur-Sinai and Bauer & Leander), but must conclude that there is no reason to consider *śāṭān* as anything other than a triliteral word with *nun* as third radical.

Etymological investigations are often useful, provided one does not allow one's interpretation of the specific passages to be tied down thereby. The danger of enforcing an 'etymologically correct' interpretation on texts where author and listeners have quite forgotten the etymology is scarcely very great in this case. The investigation has shown that the root refers to various forms of adversary and hostility. In analysing texts in which Satan appears, we must therefore accept that different images may be concerned, not only family images but also war images and judicial images.

---

18. Cf. in detail the text analysis to the Book of Job p. 88.

19. Schärf Kluger, *Satan in the Old Testament*, p. 29.

20. Day, *An Adversary in Heaven*, p. 18 n. 7, refers to E.S. Drower and R. Macuch, *A Mandaic Dictionary* (Oxford: Clarendon Press, 1963), p. 324. The meaning of the root *sṭa* is given there as 'turn aside, stray'.

Chapter 5

THE USE OF IMAGES IN THE BOOK OF JOB

The Book of Job is one of the most fascinating texts in the Old Testament. From the very outset we are captured by the narrative of the righteous Job, who not of his own choosing is exposed to Satan's trials and loses everything he owns and loves. We participate in the drama, and chapter by chapter we follow the intense dialogues between Job and his friends, well aware that Job's partners in discussion are scarcely these friends. The friends' rejoinders are rather catchwords for Job's repeated accusations against the hidden God, who in his injustice has smitten the innocent one. The climax of the book is reached when Job summons God before the court and God appears. In two terrific speeches God accounts for himself. Job bows down in the dust, and the book ends with a brief description of how Job gets back double of all he has lost.

It will be seen from the analysis that this is a deliberate composition in which various images are connected to one another in order to carry the action forward. This indicates that an author's volition lies behind the finished text. But this author has not created his text out of nothing. He makes use of the traditional material available in an original way, and creates an entity out of it.

Research has concerned itself in particular with the pre-history of the framework narrative. Some have argued that in general terms the framework goes back to an old legend about a pious man who is rewarded for enduring suffering. The author has then added, as his own independent contribution, the celestial scenes in which Satan appears before Yahweh and is permitted to test Job.[1] If this is correct, it emphasizes the significance

1. Cf., e.g., A. Alt, 'Zur Vorgeschichte des Buches Hiob' (On the Early History of the Book of Job), *ZAW* 55 (1937), pp. 265-68. Cf. also G. Fohrer, 'Zur Vorgeschichte und Komposition des Buches Hiob' (On the Early History and Composition of the Book of Job), *VT* 6 (1956), pp. 249-67, and V. Maag, *Hiob: Wandlung und Verarbeitung des Problems in Novelle, Dialogdichtung und*

of the relationship between Yahweh, Satan and Job to the author's intention in regard to the book, since the element of the divine has not then been taken over from an earlier version but is the author's personal choice of a starting point for recounting the drama of Job.

In our context, however, we shall leave the pre-history behind, since we are reading the Book of Job in its finished version as a literary work of art.[2] Only where it helps to understand the final version of the text shall we include its pre-history. My approach therefore keeps in mind what Norman C. Habel calls his own analysis of the Book of Job, namely 'a composite interpretation of the book of Job as an integrated literary and theological work'.[3]

What we shall investigate are the most important metaphors in the Book of Job. It is especially interesting to discover whether there may be a root metaphor lying not only behind the central metaphors but also helping to bind the book together as an artistic whole. My thesis is, then, that a unifying metaphor of this kind is indeed present: the image of a father and his two sons. This is the root metaphor that controls the drama's development and reflects the relationship between the three persons the author presents to us in the very first chapter of the book: Yahweh, Satan and Job.

An analysis of the Book of Job to reveal a specific root metaphor must begin by considering the metaphors which are to be seen as in any way central to the book's structure and meaning. And here it is natural to take a look at the book's images of God. Which metaphors are used for Yahweh himself? And how do these metaphors formulate Yahweh's relationships with Satan and Job?

The most conspicuous is the image of *Yahweh as creator*. This image is in evidence not only in the great speeches of the Lord at the end of the

*Spätfassungen* (Job: Conversion and Assimilation of the Problem into Short Story, Dialogue Poetry and Late Editions) (Göttingen: Vandenhoeck & Ruprecht, 1982), pp. 48-75 and 41. Cf. also on the early history of the framework, J.A. Baker, *The Book of Job: Unity and Meaning* (Sheffield: JSOT Press, 1978), pp. 17-26, and Y. Hoffmann, 'The Relation Between the Prologue and the Speech Cycles in Job: A Reconsideration', *VT* 31 (1981), pp. 160-70.

2. As regards the history of scholarship in general, I wish merely to refer here to N.C. Habel, *The Book of Job: A Commentary* (OTL; London: SCM Press, 1985), which contains an excellent survey of recent literature, and to H.-P. Müller, *Das Hiobproblem* (The Job Problem) (Erträge der Forschung, 84; Darmstadt: Wissenschaftliche Buchgesellschaft, 1978).

3. Habel, *The Book of Job*, p. 21.

book but also repeatedly as a prerequisite when Job addresses Yahweh in the book's dialogue section. Thereafter appears the very extensive use of *images taken from judicial life*. Job's lament indeed remains a lament but clearly adopts the form of an accusation, and ends in the summoning of Yahweh himself. Almighty God must now appear before the court and present his defence. Yahweh's role in the proceedings between Job and Yahweh thus calls for closer examination.[4]

The creation metaphor and the lawsuit metaphor cannot be evaded in the Book of Job. But we shall take a closer look at this imagery and examine whether it may be of such a nature that it is necessary to include the image of the relationship between *a father and his sons*. The root metaphor is not necessarily of course the metaphor used most frequently but the metaphor which controls the others.

### The Creator Image in the Book of Job

We begin the investigation by considering the creator image, which we already encounter in Job's first long lament about his own life in ch. 3. Job is so tired of life that he curses the day he was born, the night he was conceived. On top of the prologue, this introduction has a shock effect. Satan wished to make Job curse God, and therefore tested him with adversity and suffering. Job's own wife exhorted him with the words: 'Curse God and die!' And in his first speech Job is already so close to cursing God that we must fear the outcome of Satan's test.

But the words do not become a curse on God. They become a curse on his own life and a strong expression of his wish to die, since if he had to be conceived it would have been better had he died in his mother's womb. And if he had to be born it would have been better had he died immediately he left his mother's womb. Then he would have been able to lie in his grave and rest in peace.

Job's lament is formulated as a deliberate transformation of the creation concepts. Light shall become darkness, the boundary between day and night shall disappear, even night will be swallowed up by darkness. The day will never see the dawn because it did not keep the womb closed, preventing Job from coming into the world.

4. In his discussion of the Proverbs' image of God, Lennart Boström emphasizes, e.g., that faith in the creation and faith in God's justice are thematically linked. L. Boström, *The God of the Sages: The Portrayal of God in the Book of Proverbs* (Lund: Almqvist & Wiksell, 1990), p. 242.

What Job desires for his own life is that creation should move in the opposite direction, so that cosmos becomes chaos. Many scholars[5] have pointed out the connection with the creation concepts in Genesis 1, where light is created; light and darkness are given their places, day and night each with its own function; the division of the year is established; light is set in the firmament to light up the world; the great monsters are created; and the seventh day's rest receives its justification as God's own day of rest. Now everything is turned around.

In his thorough analysis of the text, Norman C. Habel expresses the central idea as follows: 'The dominant literary feature of the speech is the intricate pattern of reversals: from birth to prebirth death, from order to primordial chaos, from light to darkness, from gloom in life to pleasure in the underworld, from turmoil and confinement on earth to liberation and peace in Sheol.'[6]

But however much mythological material and however many cosmological concepts are demonstrated, and however strong the precursor the author is fighting against in this chapter, the object is to debate not the cosmic order in general but its collapse as Job personally has experienced it. The starting point is not mistrust of the world order but the existential suffering at whose centre Job finds himself.

*Excursus*

Before we continue, let us consider for a moment one of the images used in ch. 3. Behind the wording of the introductory curse (vv. 3-10) and the subsequent lament (vv. 11-26) is the image of Mother Earth. In the prologue, Mother Earth is the place to which Job will return, naked as when he came from his mother's womb (Job 1.21), that is, the kingdom of the dead. This retort is Job's first speech, and therefore great importance must be attached to it in the context.

Habel considers that in 3.10 there is an inkling of analogous ideas about the mother's womb as more than a womb, since Job's curse in the preceding text is not upon his parents but upon the cosmic beings who permitted

5. Cf., e.g., F. Lindström, *God and the Origin of Evil* (Lund: Almqvist & Wiksell, 1983), pp. 148-49, which interprets this passage as meaning that Job in reality wishes to reverse the process of creation and thus questions the whole of God's creation system. Lindström here builds upon D. Cox, 'The Desire for Oblivion in Job 3', *SBFLA* 23 (1973), pp. 37-49.

6. Cf. Habel, *The Book of Job*, p. 105. In this part of his analysis, Habel builds upon M. Fishbane, 'Jer. 4 and Job 3: A Recovered Use of the Creation Pattern', *VT* 21 (1971), pp. 151-67.

conception and birth. But Habel cautiously says that the term is probably consciously ambiguous, so that at first sight one cannot be certain whether the mother specifically or Mother Earth mythologically is intended, as is the case in 1.21.[7] Moreover, it should be noted that Job's wish consists in finding rest in the grave. From the mother's womb to Mother Earth is the road in Job 1.21; in ch. 3 Job wishes that he has taken the direct road from the outset, so that he would not first have had to experience the afflictions of life.

Here also the road's goal is the grave, that is, the negative side of the Mother Earth concept. Northrop Frye points out that this duality in Mother Earth is a recurrent feature. 'As the womb of all forms of life, she has a cherishing and nourishing aspect; as the tomb of all forms of life, she has a menacing and sinister aspect; as the manifestation of an unending cycle of life and death, she has an inscrutable and elusive aspect.'[8]

The life God gives to the afflicted person is characterized ironically in Job 3 as a secure life (the same word as is used in Satan's description of God's securing of Job and his family and all his property in every way: Job 1.10), but now with the incarceration nuance. Instead of God's way of securing a person—putting a fence around him—Job thus prefers to rest peacefully in his grave.

The womb, the grave as Mother Earth, protection as incarceration, these images appear in the earliest chapters of the Book of Job. Why in fact use the mother image? Might it be that this is an image taken from family life which holds the book together?

By its choice of imagery, the Book of Job convinces the reader that Job's existential problem is of a universal nature. For if God's creation of Job and Job's life can be questioned, then God as creator in general can also be questioned. And if, as Job wishes, God is to answer these profound personal questions of the suffering Job it must be with answers that relate to more than Job's fate alone, as indeed becomes the case in the speeches of the Lord. The personal and the universal aspects are not independent entities but are closely connected.

That Job also sees the creator as Lord of the Universe is clearly apparent

7. Habel, *The Book of Job*, p. 109.
8. Frye, *The Great Code*, p. 68. Cf. also pp. 191-92 of Frye. As regards the concepts of the mother's womb, refer also to Horst, *Hiob Kapitel 1-19*, p. 19, where Horst points out that according to Ps. 139, 13.15, man is created in the mother's womb as well as in the depths of the earth.

from the powerful image of the creator that introduces ch. 9. After Bildad's defence of Yahweh's justice and his clear assertion that God will never reject a blameless person (Job 8.20), Job must fashion his own image of the Almighty. What Job repeatedly stresses is man's nothingness compared with God and his lack of opportunity for securing his rights. For God is indeed wise, and God is strong!

God is he who moves mountains, makes the pillars of the earth shake, orders the sun not to rise, seals up the stars, stretches heaven and does tremendous things. His wrath is so violent that even Rahab's helpers must bow down to it. In other words: God does precisely whatever God himself wishes to do.

In the light of other descriptions of creation, it must be said that here the image of God is a caricature of the creator image. We encounter here the anti-creator side-by-side with the cosmos-creator. And no mortal being can call this creator to account for anything whatsoever. For if it comes to a contest of strength he is the strong one! (Job 9.19). And who indeed can mediate between the Almighty and Job?

But Job has scarcely spoken of the creator of the universe and the impossibility that he will give Job his rights before Job is appealing imploringly to the God who formed him and created him. 'Does it seem good to you to oppress, to despise the work of your hands, and favour the schemes of the wicked?', Job asks his creator (Job 10.3). And Job continues by reminding God that he fashioned him like clay, poured him out like milk and curdled him like cheese, clothed him with skin and flesh and knit him together with bones and sinews. In view of this, shouldn't the creator realize his duty to take care of Job? And Job nevertheless ends his appeal with a complaint that God allowed him to leave his mother's womb at all (Job 10.18).

We can immediately establish that the Book of Job perceives Yahweh as both creator of the universe and creator of the individual. That this is not accidental or particular to the Book of Job is to be seen from Rainer Albertz's analysis of the creation concepts in the Old Testament. According to Rainer Albertz there are two different creation traditions, each with its own *Sitz im Leben* and its own function.[9]

Albertz bases his views on the Deutero-Isaiah creation concepts. Here

9. Cf. R. Albertz, *Weltschöpfung und Menschenschöpfung: Untersucht bei Deuterojesaja, Hiob und in den Psalmen* (Creation of the World and Creation of Mankind: Investigated with Deutero-Isaiah, Job and in the Psalms) (Calwer Theologische Monographien, 3; Stuttgart: Calwer Verlag, 1974).

we encounter, on the one hand, the tradition of the creator of the world who rules over his creations and, on the other hand, the tradition about the creator of man. The purpose of describing God as creator of the world is to praise God's might, whereas the descriptions of the creator of man are employed to call upon God's care and help. The two traditions therefore also have two different *Sitze im Leben*, eulogy and lamentation.[10]

These two traditions are also to be rediscovered in the Psalms. Both can be used to call for Yahweh's intervention, but whereas the creation of man is used as an appeal to the merciful and caring God the motif of the creation of the world appeals to the mighty God. Whereas the first relates to the worshipper's own redemption, the intention of the second is to mobilize God against the worshipper's enemies. In this context, Albertz points out that the image of the creator of the world also contains elements of care and preservation.[11]

As regards the Book of Job, it is particularly applicable that research to date—up to Claus Westermann—has often considered the hymnic elements in the book as foreign bodies, and has not therefore included them to a sufficient degree in the interpretation. But it is precisely from Westermann's demonstration that the Book of Job is more dependent upon the Psalms than upon wisdom that the significance of these creation motifs is renewed. Albertz then shows that the creation images in Job 10.3, 8-12, with their description of the close relationship between the creator and his creation, is intended to induce Yahweh to intervene and save Job. Job appeals not to the creator of the world but to the caring God himself, who has fashioned Job and clothed him in skin and flesh.

The preceding chapter, Job 9.5-9, however, describes the creator of the world. The style has been taken from the eulogy on the ruler of the world; but in Job's mouth the hymn of praise becomes an accusation, strongly emphasizing the distance between God and his creation. The creator is so described in this hymn that whoever knows the Old Testament traditions must perceive Yahweh as an anti-creator who causes chaos instead of cosmos.

According to Rainer Albertz, by including both these creation traditions in the book the author wishes to illustrate the tension which pervades the entire dialogue: on the one hand Job's fear of the mighty God and creator of the world, on the other hand Job's plaintive appeal to the compassionate God, the individual's merciful progenitor.[12]

10. Albertz, *Weltschöpfung*, p. 51.
11. Albertz, *Weltschöpfung*, p. 130-31.
12. Albertz, *Weltschöpfung*, p. 136.

Among the friends, praise of the almighty creator of the world predominates. It is understandable that the lament's appeal to the compassionate creator-God is not to be found here. The close relationship between God and man has no place in the friends' theology.

The creation concepts are voiced most fully, however, in the speeches of the Lord. The many rhetorical questions are intended to bring Job to admit his own impotence and acknowledge God's might. But at the same time these speeches of the Lord clearly emphasize God's care for the work of creation. In genre terms, we are approaching the descriptive eulogy on the majesty of God. Even Albertz must admit that the care motif which he had associated with the lamentation genre is also to be found here.[13]

Evaluated from a form-critical aspect, the speeches of the Lord occupy the place of the redemption oracle. The lament is followed by God's answer. In Deutero-Isaiah, the redemption oracle readopts the motif of man's close relationship with God, which so characterizes the lament. But this is not to be found in the speeches of the Lord in the Book of Job, although Job's plaintive appeal to God as the creator of man in ch. 10 would give good reason for adopting the motif. The speeches of the Lord emphasize rather the distance between God and man. It is made clear to Job that it is not he who has created the world but God, and at the same time it also becomes clear that it is not he who cares for the hungry ravens but God. Albertz rightly points out that the care element is not absent in the speeches of the Lord, but that the care is *not*, as in Deutero-Isaiah, associated with the concepts of man's creation.[14]

This, then, is Albertz's very useful analysis of the two creation traditions in the Old Testament and their different *Sitze im Leben*. In our context the question must be, what consequences does it have for the understanding of the Book of Job's description of the relationship between God, Satan and Job that these different images of Yahweh as creator are used?

On the basis of Albertz's analyses, we must affirm that the care motif is to be found in the Book of Job. In ch. 10, Job appeals to the creator as his personal creator, and in the speeches of the Lord Yahweh presents himself as he who cares for the cosmos. To be creator clearly involves caring for creation.[15]

13. Albertz, *Weltschöpfung*, pp. 144-45.
14. Cf. Albertz, *Weltschöpfung*, p. 145.
15. In his analysis of the image of God in Proverbs, Lennart Boström similarly stresses that God is not only described as the transcendent creator but

Just as the dialogues begin with a lament kept within the framework of man's creation (transformed to Job's lament that the creation, i.e. his own birth, took place at all), so do they end with Yahweh's answer, which rolls out the creation of the whole universe as the first answer to Job's lament. It is the very fact of having been born into a world created by God, but which has in reality proved to be an anti-world, that sets in motion the dialogue section and the speeches of the Lord. Why does a father procreate, why does a mother give birth, why does Yahweh create when he does not ensure that the world is a cosmos, a just world? Why not, then, allow chaos finally to take over power, so that Job can die and lie down to rest in Mother Earth's womb?

The motifs revolve around the relationship between the creator and the created. And both creation traditions include responsibility on the part of the creator towards the created. Therefore, it seems to me not to be crucial whether one can clearly demonstrate different *Sitze im Leben* in regard to the two creation traditions. What is crucial is that two different images of God are at work, and that the two genres are so well known that the reader has his special expectations as regards the use of the hymn and the lament respectively. We know from form criticism that the redemption oracle follows the lament. One may therefore also anticipate that by his repeated use of the lament genre the author makes the reader expect a redemption oracle.

The reader's expectations are indeed met. A redemption oracle appears in answer to Job's accusations. But the redemption oracle does not have the same form as in the Book of Isaiah, for example where Deutero-Isaiah readopts in his redemption oracles the motif of the individual's close relationship with God—the motif so characteristic of the lament. Where one would expect to hear of God's care for Job one hears instead of God's care for the hungry ravens. And this occurs with a strong emphasis that it is God himself who is the creator and sustainer of everything and not Job, who, as is well known, was in no way present when the world was created (Job 38.4).

In this context, I wish to stress that the eulogistic element itself in the speeches of the Lord implies that the purpose of the speeches is not primarily to put Job in his place but to answer the Job who laments over God's lack of care for his world; *in casu*: Job. The praise must be understood according to its function, even when it is in the form of God's

as closely related to man and the world, both exalted God and personal God. L. Boström, *The God of the Sages*, pp. 239-43.

self-praise! The speeches of the Lord create both an insight into God's creative power and comfort for the sufferer. They create understanding and contact, not merely distance and fear. And thus they are an answer to the anxiety which radiates from Job's lamentations.

There has been a tendency to stress the speeches as the frightening encounter with the godhead, the encounter with the holy as *numen tremendum et fascinosum*, the main emphasis being on *tremendum*. But if all the emphasis is on *tremendum* the comforting aspect of the speeches is overlooked. The speeches in fact contain several images which indicate proximity rather than distance. And these images demand much greater attention than has been devoted to them by research to date. They are significant, and not only—as there has been a tendency to believe—linguistic decorations.

One of the images used in the first speech of the Lord is the image of Yahweh, who nurses the sea like a midwife and dresses it in the clouds as a swaddling band (Job 38.8-9). According to Norman Habel, v. 10 should also be comprehended within this image. Yahweh puts the sea, which may be seen as a large chaos monster, into a playpen, according to Habel a deliberately absurd image.[16] But this should not lead one to believe that the image has no meaning in the context. If the author chooses to describe Yahweh's power over the sea as the care a midwife or one of the parents displays towards the child, this is not merely one image among others but must be seen in the context we have already indicated on several occasions: that in the Book of Job Yahweh, apart from being described as creator, is also described as father.

Care also appears in the distribution of the individual creations. The sea receives its specific place, as does the dawn also. Thus the rhythm of day and night is not only regulated but the perpetrators of the night, the evil ones, are shaken off. Yahweh's control over evil is part of being creator of the cosmos (Job 38.12-13).

Yahweh likewise withholds the light from the ungodly and breaks their arm (Job 38.15). In the following passages also an image is drawn of a creator who looks after his creation. Even the most barren desert receives rain, the ibis wisdom, the lion his prey and the raven what it needs for its young.

16. Habel, *The Book of Job*, p. 538: 'Here the control of Sea is reduced to the tending of a baby. The image is deliberately absurd: this violent chaos monster is but an infant, born from a womb, wrapped in baby clothes, placed in a playpen, and told to stay in its place.'

Yahweh's insight into the conduct of animals (Job 39), has also been described as not merely expressing admiration for God's greatness but equally as showing the care lying behind a well-functioning animal world, where the foolish ostrich is ensured the possibility of flight in the hour of danger, and the vulture is so created that it can hide its nest high in the air so that it can spy food for its young far away. Indeed, even the vulture is under God's care, 'its young ones suck up blood; and where the slain are, there it is' (Job 39.30).

If one wishes to appreciate what is special in the description of animals, Othmar Keel's analyses of the connection between the speeches of the Lord and Near Eastern iconography offer good assistance.[17] In this connection, Keel has demonstrated that although one of the images behind the first speech of the Lord is the image of 'the animals' master', that is, the god as the fighter of wild animals, it is combined in this version with the ideas about Yahweh as creator of the cosmos. God's supremacy thus takes the form of control over the chaotic powers; but God does not destroy them. In the description of the supremacy we also notice the care. Where, on the basis of Near Eastern traditions about the god as master of the animals, one might expect a description of Yahweh hunting wild animals and killing them we are instead given a description of Yahweh providing prey for the lions (Job 38.39-41).

The second speech of the Lord must be seen as further proof that Yahweh's care involves restriction of the powers of evil. We shall return later to this speech of the Lord and its association with the father–son image, but just one point will be mentioned here. As Keel shows, the two large animals are not random creations but representations of chaos. Nevertheless, Yahweh speaks of no ordinary chaos-battle when describing these animals, his most outstanding creation. Yahweh is not extolling his adversaries but his own creation, to which only he can set limits.

The speeches of the Lord are addressed to Job, and must be read as contributions to Yahweh's defence against Job's accusations. From the speeches' description of Yahweh as the caring creator of the hungry ravens, and the strong creator compared with the formidable chaos monsters, Job is able to conclude that despite his own experiences up to the present the mighty creator can provide food and procure justice. By referring to the

17. O. Keel, *Jahwes Entgegnung an Ijob: Eine Deutung von Ijob 38–41 vor dem Hintergrund der zeitgenössischen Bildkunst* (Yahweh's Reply to Job: An Interpretation of Job 38–41 against the Background of Contemporary Imagery) (Göttingen: Vandenhoeck & Ruprecht, 1978), pp. 81-125.

greater aspect, the world creator's power and care for the cosmos, Yahweh gives an indirect answer to the question about the lesser aspect, the power of the creator of man and his care for Job. The whole reasoning is based on the assumption that Job, and thus the reader of the Book of Job, can draw the conclusion that whatever applies to the firmament and the animal world applies also to Job.

Many people have rightly remarked on the distance expressed by the speeches of the Lord when Yahweh asks Job where he was on the morning of creation, when the whole universe came into being. But I believe that this should not be overestimated. If we imagine that the first creation narrative is a premise for the author, this is probably not only the case in ch. 3 but also in the connection with the speeches of the Lord. And if Genesis 1 is the strong precursor with which the author struggles, and of which he now gives his transformation, then the question Yahweh raises is not surprisingly new or difficult but merely a reminder of the order in which creation occurred.

Man is not the first creation; the firmament and the animal world were created before man arrived on the scene. This Job should not forget. Job was not, as was wisdom, brought forth at the beginning before the depths of the world were created, cf. Prov. 8.22-36. What Job can be reproached for is not that he was absent at the time but that he has forgotten about it, and reacts as if he had been standing at the side of God, indeed had perhaps even been co-creator with a full insight into the creator role. Job should remember that he is not God's first creation.

Indeed, Job was not even present when the morning stars rejoiced and all the sons of God shouted for joy at the foundation of the earth. Those before Job included these happy sons of God who are mentioned in parallel with the morning stars and who joyfully praise the creator for the creation, Job 38.7. A small detail that can perhaps be ignored as a poetic transcription of the morning theme? Or again a significant element? We shall return to this below, and see how the traditions about the sons of God and the morning stars form part of the book's reasoning.

Instead of urging theophany's frightening strength and Job's submissiveness, it should in my opinion be noted that what the entire structure in the dialogue section is preparing, namely the redemption oracle after the lamentation, appears in fact in the form of these speeches of the Lord. The speeches should therefore be read as the redemption oracles they are, and must be taken at face value when they describe Yahweh's care for the very smallest work of creation and Yahweh's power and will to keep the largest under control.

Two aspects interact here: Albertz rightly points out that the dialogue section takes the form of a lament with a subsequent redemption oracle, and that it is within this that the creation concepts have their natural position. But parallel to this and within this structure we encounter another complex of concepts which interact with the 'lamentations structure', for example, the lawsuit images and the appeal to Yahweh to appear before the court. Thus we cannot understand the course of events in the Book of Job merely by seeing the relationship between Yahweh and Job as a relationship between the creator and the created. The lawsuit image must also be included.

### *The Lawsuit Image in the Book of Job*

When one reads the Book of Job, one perceives repeatedly that complaint and accusation merge into one another. The Book of Job cannot therefore be analysed without applying oneself to the creation concepts and the lawsuit concepts. And a common feature of these concepts is that they herald a meeting between Yahweh and Job. Within the creator image and in combination with the complaint, the reader must expect an oracle from God as a reply to the sufferer's complaint. Within this lawsuit image the reader must await a trial scene in which the accuser meets the accused and the judge pronounces sentence.

An important connecting link between the prologue and the book's other part is thus Satan's formulation of the testing of Job. The vital criterion is then what Job says, whether or not he curses God. The scene is thus set for the speeches-cycles and not for a series of actions to reveal whether Satan is correct in his assertion.[18] By use of the lawsuit image, the various pleadings become a link in a process in which there is room for both accusation speeches and defence speeches, and in which the logical consequence is the confrontation between the contending parties.

It is not surprising, therefore, that in his commentary on the Book of Job Habel is able to show that one of the key concepts in the dialogues is the word for 'face'.[19] Distance must be overcome so that a meeting can take place between Job and Yahweh.

Instead of cursing God to his face, which Satan expected, Job, without hiding before God's face, is to present his summons before God's face,

18. Cf. Hoffmann, 'The Relation between the Prologue and the Speech-Cycles in Job', p. 166.
19. Cf. Habel, *The Book of Job*, p. 64.

the very God who had hidden his face from him (Job 13.13-28). Or, in Job's words in a later speech: 'Oh, that I knew where I might find him, that I might come even to his dwelling! I would lay my case before him [his face], and fill my mouth with arguments' (Job 23.3-4). Job's struggle to meet God is a recurrent theme, which in the passage on the Redeemer is expressed with the confidence that he is finally to see God himself (Job 19.26-27).

That complaint and accusation merge repeatedly is nothing new in Old Testament tradition. Westermann has with good reason indicated the psalm traditions as a basis for understanding the dialogues in the Book of Job. Before we turn to the lawsuit images in the Book of Job, we shall therefore set out briefly the way in which the law-court metaphors function in the Psalms, more specifically in that part of the Psalms sometimes referred to as 'prayers of the accused'.

*Lawsuit Concepts in the Prayers of the Accused*
The 'prayers of the accused' concept is used by Hans Schmidt in regard to quite a large number of individual psalms of lamentation, for example Psalm 7; 17; 26; 27; 35; 109; 139.[20] The prayers of the accused are used when the worshipper arrives at the sanctuary, persecuted by his enemies who pursue him with false accusations and desire his conviction. The judgment must be pronounced by God himself, but before God replies the persecuted one has an opportunity to pour out his troubles, profess his innocence and appeal to God for acquittal.

As in Ps. 7.4-6, the declaration of innocence can take the form of a hypothetical self-condemnation, and thus an oath of innocence (cf. a similar oath of innocence in Job 31). Hans Schmidt based his views on 1 Kgs 8.31-32, Solomon's prayer in the temple, where Solomon asks Yahweh to pronounce a just verdict when one of the people demands an oath before God's altar as a sign of his innocence. Certain established forms of speech which the accused may employ must be expected to have been associated with such a situation, and indeed Schmidt's thesis is that a number of Old Testament psalms of lamentation have had their *Sitz im Leben* in such a judgment of God in the temple.

20. Hans Schmidt, *Das Gebet der Angeklagten im Alten Testament* (The Prayer of the Accused in the Old Testament) (BZAW, 49; Giessen: Töpelmann, 1928). Hans Schmidt's interpretation is followed by, *inter alia*, H.-J. Kraus, *Psalmen* (BKAT, XV.1; Neukirchen–Vluyn: Neukirchener Verlag, 4th edn, 1972). Cf., e.g., the treatment of Ps. 7, pp. 55-64.

H. Schmidt's investigations give rise to the confirmation—in itself banal—that a surprisingly large number of psalms are concerned with what we would refer to as judicial situations. Whether this is because an established institution such as that referred to above existed, where a priest or some other temple official undertook to convey the accused's prayer on the basis of a repertory of prepared texts while another undertook to convey the necessary Yahweh oracle so that the accused's innocence or guilt could be proved, is difficult to determine.

It can be said, however, that although such a procedure existed, for example in the temple in Jerusalem at the time of the kings, the use of judicial terminology was not restricted to this situation alone. This is to be seen from the use of judicial terms in psalms, whose *Sitz im Leben* can scarcely have been the judgment of God in the temple. This applies, for example, to the use of judicial terminology in a national lament such as Psalm 74, where Yahweh is requested to conduct his case against the enemies, Ps. 74.22, but this is clearly imagined as within the framework of warlike events. (Cf. also Ps. 149 and Ps. 75.)

It should also be stressed that use of the accused's prayers was not restricted to the original *Sitz im Leben*. As with the royal psalms, which were 'democratized' in the period after the fall of the monarchy and thus rendered usable by the individual Israelite, so was it with the reuse of the prayers of the accused. The psalms have preserved their usefulness and meaningfulness even beyond the original *Sitz im Leben*. It is not possible therefore to reason simply from 'Gattung' back to *Sitz im Leben*; the use of a text is not always function-typical.[21]

*Reuse of the Concepts in Psalm 139*
In analysing the Book of Job, Psalm 139 is of particular interest. This psalm is also considered by Hans Schmidt, although only one verse is discussed in detail. This is v. 18b, which had hitherto caused great problems for research. For what does it mean that when the worshipper stands up he is still with God? Schmidt interprets the statement on the basis of the situation in which the prayers of the accused originally functioned and which seems to entail a one night's sojourn in the temple before God's judgment is pronounced. In that event the verse indicates confidence that

---

21. Cf. as to this terminology: K. Nielsen, *Yahweh as Prosecutor and Judge: An Investigation of the Prophetic Lawsuit (Rîb-Pattern)* (JSOTSup, 9; Sheffield: JSOT Press, 1978), pp. 3-4.

the judgment will be an acquittal; God will be beside the worshipper with his help.

Although Psalm 139 expresses much greater calm and patience than normally characterizes the prayers of the accused, v. 19 reveals such an earnest cry for help that Schmidt believes the psalm must be perceived as 'ein echtes Angeklagtengebet' (a real prayer of the accused).[22]

This is not the place for a detailed analysis of the psalm, but for our purposes it is important to note that this psalm in fact holds to the close relationship with God. God's knowledge of the psalmist is all-embracing; therefore he can flee nowhere from God's wrath, whether it be heaven or the kingdom of the dead. Not even in the dark can he hide from the God who has knit him together in his mother's womb. This, therefore, is the very God to whom the psalmist can appeal, since he is able to search the worshipper's heart and pronounce a just verdict, now when the enemies propound their lies.

The Book of Job is also concerned with arriving at a just verdict, and here also the appeal is directed to God himself. But the motifs are transformed. Job also speaks of the darkness in his first lament, but whereas the psalmist rejects that darkness can hide anything from God it seems that Job assumes that there is an area where man is beyond the range of God, a land of chaos, a womb with the peace of death. Job also speaks of being created by God's hands, clothed in skin and flesh; but whereas man's creation in Psalm 139 engenders confidence that God also wishes to kill the entreating enemy we encounter the opposite consequence in Job 10. That God has created Job in his mother's womb does not give rise to the eulogy on God's wonderful acts from his lips, but on the contrary makes the accusation even more bitter: for God's intention in the miraculous creation was not to protect his creation but continually to persecute it with his punishment. God's intention in creating man causes man to complain that he was ever brought forth from his mother's womb (Job 10.18).

In the previous chapter Job described the world creator as an anti-creator, and the world judge as an anti-judge who judges without regard for guilt or innocence (Job 9.22). And later we encounter the concept that although Job tried to reach as far as God himself, indeed looked for him east and west, north and south, he did not find God. Here the motif from Psalm 139 is radically reversed. The psalmist considers the possibility of flight, but must abandon hiding himself from the wrath of the omnipresent God.

22. Schmidt, *Das Gebet*, p. 26 n. 2.

Job considers looking for God, but must give this up, since God hides himself. Were they to meet, God would have to allow his testing of Job to redound to Job's advantage and allow Job to appear as gold in the test (Job 23.10).

From the lawsuit aspect, it is not the enemies who in the Book of Job submit false accusations against the worshipper but God himself. Indeed, God does not let it rest at accusations, but has already pronounced judgment without any lawsuit whatsoever by his constant persecution of Job. Job must therefore request that the court is instituted and that the action takes its course.

Both Psalm 139 and the Book of Job utilize the image of man's creator, and revolve around the consequences this will have for a lawsuit. Both texts assume that the creator of man himself should be able to pronounce a just verdict, since of course the creator has the closest possible knowledge of man. But whereas the psalmist expresses his confidence that the creator also wishes what is best for him, Job holds to his mistrust. This mistrust is supported by his despair that it is the creator himself who desires the destruction of his creation. The close relationship between the creator and the created, which in the lawsuit situation should be the creation's guarantee of a just decision, is no guarantee in the case of Job.

If one were to single out from the Old Testament psalms one psalm which has especially functioned as a powerful precursor for the author of the Book of Job, I would indicate Psalm 139.

Job's image of God, perceived as Job's expectations in regard to Yahweh, is close to that of Psalm 139; but Job's experience makes it necessary for him to express himself in continual transformations of this psalm and his own ideal images. And yet Job appeals repeatedly to this terrifying creator-God. How is this in any way possible?

*Lawsuit Image, Creation Image, Father–Son Image*
After Job's repeated laments about the impossibility of bringing a lawsuit against God himself (cf. the list of obstacles in Job 9–10[23]), he might be expected to abandon his action and merely ask for the peace of the grave he dreamt of in ch. 3. But this does not happen. On the contrary, Job holds to his demand for a meeting with God himself; a demand that is in the highest degree a revolt against traditional Israelite thought processes, according to which no person can see God and live.

---

23. A very good survey concerning these obstacles is to be found in Habel, *The Book of Job*, pp. 186-87.

But if Job's experience of his creator directly provokes a negative reaction from Job, in contrast to what was the case in Psalm 139, how then can it be that Job nevertheless expects it to be possible and meaningful to come face to face with God in the court?

Job says on various occasions that there is one who will enter the action on his side, a witness in heaven, an arbitrator or redeemer (cf. 16.19-22; 19.25-27); but here also there seems to be insufficient certainty that in such an event God will be able to guarantee a just hearing for Job. The epilogue makes it clear that it is Job himself who adopts this role in order to save the friends!

How then can the reader of the Book of Job be convinced of the psychological possibility of Job's holding out so stubbornly? Job sees himself as sinless, but of course he knows nothing of the discussion in heaven, and therefore does not realize that God and Satan are of the same opinion! What elements are there in Job's image of God that make possible the endurance and the trust which lie in some form or another behind the stubbornness?

As we have seen, the lawsuit image exists side by side with the creator image. The examination of the creator image clearly showed that this is equivocal. In the Book of Job the creator is the awe-inspiring one, whom Job must accuse of doing what he pleases with his own creations, as well as the caring one. The speeches of the Lord indicate that the latter aspect is the stronger, not forgetting the epilogue which tells of God's care for Job.

In the light of this, however, it must be asked what it is that holds these images of God together and in the final instance makes it understandable that Job demands a face-to-face meeting with God himself, and that enables the book to come to a happy ending. Might it indeed be, as we indicated in the introduction, that the image of God has its root in the perception that the relationship between God and Job is a father–son relationship?

That the lawsuit image may have some connection with the father–son image cannot surprise. We briefly mentioned earlier that in the Near East the father concept includes not only the father's begetting of his children and responsibility for their basic daily needs, but also that he acts as a judicial authority both externally and internally.[24]

In the Book of Job we encounter in Job's presentation of himself in ch. 29 the ideal image of a patriarch surrounded by his extended family.

---

24. Cf. p. 43, where I refer to Thorkild Jacobsen's analysis of the parent image in Mesopotamia.

At that time Job was still under God's care and protection, with his own boys around him, and he was treated with respect wherever he went. He was a regular visitor to the city gate, and he was the champion of the weak, who secured their rights. What this implies is set out clearly in Job 29.16: 'I was a father to the needy, and I championed the cause of the stranger.' Indeed, even when Job's own people turned against him he secured their legal rights for them (Job 31.13). How much more then would Yahweh be a father to his own creations and secure their rights for them?

To be a father to those in a weaker position means not merely securing for them permission to submit their case but also ensuring that they receive the rights due to them. By means of Job's self-portrait, the author of the Book of Job draws a very unequivocal image of the ideal patriarch who acts as a father towards his people and his family. In the narrative generally he draws an image of God's care for Job, which must likewise be designated as fatherly care for his life and property. It is true that Satan is permitted to test Job—and the reason for this we shall return to—but Yahweh draws the line at Job's life. Although Satan is permitted to deprive Job of his children, domestic servants, cattle and property, the book ends with Yahweh returning to Job double his loss.

When in ch. 9 Job listed all the obstacles to a lawsuit against God, he pointed out that God would never respond to a mortal; scarcely listen, indeed. Mortals must ask God for mercy, not demand a judicial hearing, and likewise a person surely cannot endure God's presence. Nevertheless Job acts in complete contrast to what he sets out as possible, and continues with his plan by preparing his action against God (Job 13.6-12), telling his friends that they will be false witnesses in the action in which Job himself intends to meet God face to face (Job 13.13-16). Job is ready, and now challenges God by submitting his complaint (Job 13.18-22). Job is not willing to give in, and indeed ends the dialogue by holding fast to his plan (Job 27.2-6). But Job has one condition: that God no longer lays his hand on him and terrifies him (Job 13.20-21).

Job will not be able to meet God face to face if God terrifies him. If he is to meet Yahweh, Job must set his boundary precisely where the father becomes perverted into a tyrant. If Yahweh chooses violence the relationship between them has been made impossible, and the meeting between Yahweh and Job has become meaningless. If Yahweh chooses violence the boundary of togetherness for father and son is overstepped.

Many readers of Job's plaintive accusations against God have thought similarly: that Job thereby overstepped the boundaries set between the

creator and the created. Yet in the context of the prologue and epilogue
we understand that what would in terms of other images be improper is
possible in the father–son relationship. For it is precisely the son, who
complains with such pain and anger, who feels let down by the father.
The closer is the relationship between the two, the deeper is the sorrow
and anger at being deserted, and the more violently must the reproaches
be formulated.

And so they finally meet, where God speaks to Job in the storm. As
referred to earlier, many scholars interpret this meeting as if Job is suddenly
terror-struck before the holy majesty, and therefore bows down in dust
and ashes. But if one reads this more carefully, what is important is that
Job survives to see God face to face. Job does not need to hide from
God's face, as was anticipated in Job 13.20. On the contrary, Job can react
in Job 42.5 with the words: 'I had heard of you by the hearing of the ear,
but now my eye sees you'; precisely as the patriarch Jacob survives seeing
God's face (Gen. 32.30).

The creator whom Job is able to meet face to face certainly infuses him
with respect and awe, but Job had no need to avert his eyes from his face.
This image of God reminds one of the father image which characterizes
the Near East's perception of the relationship between father and son. And
it corresponds to the image of God we saw in Psalm 139, and found to
be a prerequisite for Job's formulation of his own conflicting experiences.

In our context, it is important to note in the Book of Job the transformation of traditions from the psalms. This is not a direct take-over; the
distribution of roles is strikingly different. Using Bloom's terminology
again, and taking Psalm 139 as the stronger precursor, it must be said that
this is certainly a Job's struggle or a Jacob's struggle between the two
authors. The author of the Book of Job's takes over nothing directly from
the psalm, but transforms it to accord with the intention of his text.

I have now analysed the two most conspicuous images of God in the Book
of Job: the image of Yahweh as the creator and the image of Yahweh as
party to a lawsuit. And in both cases I noted that there were features in
the images which pointed in the direction of father–son concepts. My
observations support the thesis, which was my starting point, that the
father–son image is the book's root metaphor. But these observations are
not in themselves sufficient to sustain the thesis.

Although the family was the backbone of society in ancient Israel, and
although family relationships were often used to indicate relationships
between people other than family members (cf., e.g., the father–son image

behind tribal structures, or the description of the relationship between Israel and Edom as a fraternal relationship), we cannot expect that the reader of the time would immediately have seen the association with a father–son relationship by reason of the use of creator and judicial images. In a completely different and unmistakable way, the reader must be introduced to the thought process that in the case of God and Job the relationship is the same as that between a father and his son. And one must expect to find this introduction in the prologue to the book, where the drama is unfurled and the plot of the book formulated.

If it is to be shown that the father–son metaphor is indeed a root metaphor, we must be able to demonstrate not only the way in which the reader's attention was drawn to this; we must also be able to substantiate that this metaphor is capable of saying something decisive about another important relationship in the book: the relationship between Yahweh and the chaos-powers which we encounter in the speeches of the Lord in the form of the two large animals and which appear in the prologue under the name of Satan. Finally, the analysis must show that the images used can together express the fundamental relationship between Yahweh, Satan and Job.

In the following, therefore, we must look closely at the framework surrounding the dialogues and examine the relationship to one another of the central images in the book's two parts. Whereas most scholars concentrate their interest on the dialogues and often prefer to ignore the framework, I on the contrary believe that the framework contains the key to the interpretation of the drama. If the author did not want this framework, which surrounds Job's struggle with God, he could quite easily have omitted it. We know from the Book of Ezekiel that the Job figure was well known in the first half of the sixth century BCE (Ezek. 14.14, 20). Job therefore did not need to be presented, unless the author wished by doing so to demonstrate his special interpretation of the reason for the blameless Job's exposure to suffering.

But if this is as I suggest, I must expect the book's root metaphor to be introduced immediately in the prologue to Job at the beginning of the work.

### The Father–Son Image as a Root Metaphor in the Book of Job

#### The Prologue
'There was once a man in the land of Uz whose name was Job.' Thus begins the book about the blameless Job's sufferings. The first vital

information presented to us is of a geographical nature: the land of Uz. Scholars have tried to locate this place on the map, and lean mainly towards the opinion that the author has Edom in mind; or perhaps Aram. However, in his commentary on Job, Norman C. Habel argues that the hero does not come from a specific country but from a wonderland out towards the east.[25] Habel emphasizes in his interpretation that Job is described as one of the great figures from the heroic past, a pattern of righteousness (cf. Ezek. 14.14, 20), and for this reason both the time and the place must be far from the Israel they knew.

Habel is correct in saying that the information about the land of Uz is not intended as geographical information in the general sense. But he is scarcely correct when he says that Uz merely connotes a far-away and mysterious country. The reader must use Uz as a point of orientation, but the name is meant to lead us into literary geography, into the geography of tradition.

Edom, the country to the south of Judah, is Esau's territory. Esau became the ancestor of the Edomites, in the same way that his twin brother Jacob became the ancestor of the Israelites' 12 tribes. Aram is the territory to which Jacob fled from Esau, where he procured a family and cattle and became rich in property. The entire introduction to the Book of Job keeps to the popular narrative form. If we compare the narrative method with other texts in the Old Testament we are led naturally to the stories of the patriarchs. In the same way as in Genesis we can read of the lives of Abraham, Isaac and Jacob under the guidance of Yahweh, so in the Book of Job can we read about another patriarch who lived close to God in prosperity and in adversity. Like Jacob, Job procured a family, cattle and

25. Cf. Habel, *The Book of Job*, p. 86, which explains this interpretation by reference to the genealogies in Gen. 36.28, where Uz is linked to Seir and thus to Edom, and Gen. 10.23; 22.21, where Uz is linked to Aram. But he is himself inclined to perceive the indication of locality differently: 'The tone of the narrative suggests that the narrator is using an obscure designation to conjure up an image of antiquity and mystery. A vague land in the distant East is more intriguing as the abode of an ancient hero than a familiar town just across the river Jordan in Edom.'

As regards the traditional designation of Uz as the name of either Edom or Aram, cf. also M.H. Pope, *Job: Introduction, Translation, and Notes* (AB; Garden City, NY: Doubleday, 1973), pp. 3-5, which carefully lists the arguments for the two localities but must abstain from a decision on the matter. R. Gordis, *The Book of Job: Commentary. New Translation, and Special Studies* (New York: Jewish Theological Seminary of America, 1978), p. 10, prefers Edom.

property; but then he lost everything before being re-established in his old dignified position.

A young scholar, Frank H. Polak,[26] has investigated the popular narrative traditions of the Old Testament in order to discover the number of fixed forms of words that are used. One of the results he arrived at was that the framework narrative surrounding the dialogues in the Book of Job is so strongly marked by such fixed forms of words that a late imitation of the popular art of narration must be involved. In other words, it is an artificial product.

As earlier indicated, this does not prevent the author from making use of available material about a blameless man assailed by misfortune, and fashioning this to suit his own specific intention, for example by adding the scenes in heaven. The purpose of the prologues is, then, to make us perceive Job as a patriarch and the story of Job as a patriarch narrative.

If we pursue the idea that the Book of Job consciously imitates the patriarch narratives, we can say more precisely that the author of Job wished not only to take the reader back to the time of the patriarchs but to a specific part of these traditions. We must have in mind the Esau and Jacob traditions when we read the Book of Job and hear tell of the land of Uz.

Using the terminology we are accustomed to employing in such contexts, we would say that the author wanted to make a Midrash on some of the central themes of the Esau-Jacob narrative. Using Harold Bloom's language, we would say that the strong precursor the author is struggling against is the narrator of the Jacob-Esau stories. The narrative style, the location of events in the land of Uz and—as we shall now see—the entire theme and course of events in the book point to such a connection.

The Esau-Jacob narrative is primarily concerned with a fight between two brothers about the right of primogeniture, and thus the blessing the old father can give his elder son. In the Israelite-Jewish mind, the names Esau and Jacob connote jealousy between brothers. There was a man who

26. Frank H. Polak presented his results in a short communication at The XIII Congress of the International Organization for the Study of the Old Testament at Leuven, 30 August 1989, under the heading: 'Epic Formulae and the Evolution of Biblical Prose'. In the published summary in the Congress's programme, he comments briefly as regards the Book of Job: 'In the post-exilic tales of Job, Jonah and Ruth the epic formulae are quite frequent, but we note some departures from the proper use of the convention, as illustrated by patriarchal narrative and the Samuel-Saul-David cycle. These tales then do not represent the ancient tradition but a late revival (cp. Ez., Zach.).'

had two sons. So begins many a story, and the questions which arise for the listener or reader are such questions as: Who, then, of the two is the father's favourite? And how do the brothers react towards each other when they see that they are rivals?

Many family dramas are concerned with the importance of being the elder and of being the favoured younger. According to the well-known literary scholar Northrop Frye, almost all Shakespeare's historical dramas concern the passing over of the elder child. Frye expresses this as follows:

> The theme of the passed-over firstborn seems to have something to do with the insufficiency of the human desire for continuity which underlies the custom of passing the inheritance on to the elder son. All human societies are anxious for a clear and settled line of succession: the intensity of this anxiety is written all over Shakespeare's history plays, and if Shakespeare's particular form of it is no longer with us, the anxiety itself is ... Hence the deliberate choice of a younger son represents a divine intervention in human affairs, a vertical descent into the continuity that breaks its pattern, but gives human life a new dimension by doing so.[27]

What Frye does not mention is that the Book of Job is also the story of a father who had several sons, among whom he preferred the youngest rather than the eldest, so that destructive jealousy arose between the two.

What may also be surprising is that the person who has above all concerned himself with rivalry as a basic element in any culture, René Girard, does not include this jealousy aspect in his great interpretation of Job, *La Route antique des hommes pervers*.[28] But René Girard makes the same mistake as many others;[29] he hastens to do away with the framework narrative—the speeches of the Lord go the same way—in order to read the dialogues alone. Here he indeed finds a description of the scapegoat guiltlessly persecuted by those around him.

Since it is important to Girard that the persecution is real, that it is the scapegoat's kinsmen and neighbours, the society to which he in fact

27. Frye, *The Great Code*, p. 182.

28. R. Girard, *La Route antique des hommes pervers* (Paris: Grasset & Fascelle, 1985).

29. Cf., e.g., E. Würthwein, 'Gott und Mensch in Dialog und Gottesreden des Buches Hiob', in *Wort und Existenz: Studien zum Alten Testament* (God and Man in Dialogue and Speeches of the Lord in the Book of Job in *Word and Existence: Studies on the Old Testament*) (Göttingen: Vandenhoeck & Ruprecht, 1970), pp. 217-92, who while not disregarding the speeches of the Lord believes that he can deal with his subject without taking into consideration the framework narrative.

belongs, who lead the persecution, Girard considers the scene in heaven, and in general everything beyond the experience of everyday life, as facile explanations to conceal the truth, that is that the scapegoat is guiltless. Girard, therefore, has nothing more positive to say about the framework narrative than that these sections 'protect the Dialogues ... they are a kind of woolly bodybelt which posterity has never ceased to wind around the wonderful text ...'[30] and which has been used to safeguard the dialogues against being censored out of existence.

But by eliminating the prologue Girard eliminates one of the important elements of his own theory: the jealousy between equals, the mimetic desire which causes two people to court the same object because they imitate each other's desires. Girard must therefore go outside the Book of Job to find a good example of this envy, that is, to Psalm 73. But the theme is in fact to be found in the first two chapters, provided one understands that what is concerned here is jealousy between brothers, where the elder desires what the younger has received. Whoever wishes to read Job *à la* Girard needs therefore to read the prologue.

The scene in heaven concerns jealousy between brothers and its consequences. The father in the Book of Job is not an earthly father but Yahweh himself. We are told that one day his sons came and stood before this patriarch in heaven, and among them came Satan also. In Job 1.6 the sons are called sons of God. But this is often not interpreted as a figurative expression representing a father–son relationship between Yahweh and sons of God; the use of the word *ben* is understood in the same way as that in which *ben* may refer to a single individual within a species in the context of other nouns.[31] In that event, some indeterminate beings of a divine nature must be concerned who are referred to only as the sons of (the) God(s), that is, the image has rigidified and become a cliché.[32]

30. Girard, *La Route antique*, p. 164.
31. Cf. *ThWAT*'s article on *ben*, in which H. Haag writes: 'Als einzelner wird der Mensch aus der kollektiven Gemeinschaft herausgenommen in den Ausdrücken – ben adam ... Das gleiche wie beim Menschen gilt bei den Tieren: ben baqar ...)' (As an individual, man is removed from the collective community in the terms – ben adam ... The same that applies to man applies to the animals: ben baqar ...), *ThWAT* 2, col. 674.
32. Habel, *The Book of Job*, p. 89. Cf. also Pope, *Job*, p. 9, who writes that these 'sons of the gods' are 'lesser members of the ancient pagan pantheon' who are preserved as angels in later monotheistic theology. Pope therefore translates the term merely as 'the gods'.
Gordis, *The Book of Job*, p. 13 refers to the heavenly beings as 'lit. members

In his analysis of Old Testament concepts of the sons of (the) God(s), Gerald Cooke[33] arrives at the result that the designation 'Sons of (the) God(s)' is only one among many, and occurs in parallel with, for example, the concepts of the heavenly council. But Cooke does not believe that this is a metaphorical usage but a designation of a species, so that the sons of God are divine beings of a lower degree.[34] He nevertheless employs the following usage when he has to summarize the analysis of the Job prologue and emphasize that the sons are lesser gods gathering in the council around Yahweh: 'the divine council is in attendance upon "their father and ruler".'[35] Perhaps, therefore, Cooke would be open to the idea that metaphorics were concerned if his metaphorical concept were different.

It should, however, be added, as regards the emphasis by Cooke and others that the son concept merely indicates the species, that one often returns to the father–son formula to indicate a close relationship between two persons or two things. 'Son' thus refers not only to species but to a relationship.

A thorough survey of the sons of (the) God(s) concept is also to be found in Werner Schlisske's book, *Gottessöhne und Gottessohn im Alten Testament* (Sons of God and Son of God in the Old Testament),[36] where Schlisske demonstrates an increasing demythologization of the mythical concepts which Israel had taken over from the Canaanites, including the concepts of a divine pantheon with El as the father-god. In the Book of Job Satan is such a demythologized son of (the) God(s), which according to Schlisske is included in order to formulate the problem of God's mysterious will in a figurative and thus more poetic way.[37]

Schlisske's analyses open up a greater understanding of the necessity of imagery in formulating difficult theological questions. He thus ends his book with the following demonstration of the theological relevance of the father–son image. Schlisske points out that although the Old Testament's way of referring to the sons of God may be called demythologization compared with the old Canaanitic concepts, it is more than merely a poetic

of the genus 'elohim, "divine beings" ...'

33. G. Cooke, 'The Sons of (the) God(s)', *ZAW* 76 (1961), pp. 22-47.

34. Cf. Cooke, 'The Sons', p. 24.

35. Cooke, 'The Sons', p. 37.

36. W. Schlisske, *Gottessöhne und Gottessohn im Alten Testament: Phasen der Entmythisierung im Alten Testament* (Sons of God and Son of God in the Old Testament: Phases of Demythologization in the Old Testament) (Stuttgart: Kohlhammer, 1973).

37. Cf. Schlisske, *Gottessöhne*, p. 58.

mode of expression. The message of Yahweh as the loving father who repeatedly shows care for his son Israel inherently goes beyond a mere reformulation of the selection concept.[38]

What Schlisske merely indicates here fits in well with the view of recent research that the metaphor is different from and more than a linguistic decoration for poetic purposes. And although in certain contexts the word son may be considered a cliché which merely indicates a species affiliation, a cliché can in a specific context become a living image again, and as we shall see this is what happens in this scene in which the author wishes to describe Yahweh surrounded by his sons, one of whom immediately distinguishes himself and is called by the name of Satan, the adversary.[39]

Rivkah Schärf Kluger also indicates this aspect of the use of the sons of God concept when she writes:

> ... this verbal usage remains an interesting problem in itself. It is as if behind it were a primal image of the relation of the species to the individual, and that is the relation of father to son. The species begets the individual, so to speak ... The son of man is then the idea 'man' realized in the individual, and the son of God is the realized manifestation of God.[40]

In reply to Yahweh's enquiry, Satan tells how he has gone to and fro on the earth, and walked up and down on it. Then comes the question: 'Have you considered my servant Job? There is no one like him on the earth, a blameless and upright man who fears God and turns away from evil.'

Job is not referred to here as Yahweh's son but as 'my servant'. But the servant concept need not clash with the son concept.[41] This is to be seen from, for example the reference to Israel in Deutero-Isaiah: 'But now hear, O Jacob my servant, Israel, whom I have chosen! Thus says the Lord who made you, who found you in the womb and will help you' (Isa. 44.1-2). In Isa. 45.9-12, Yahweh asks whether the people—referred to in v. 4 as 'my servant Jacob'—will demand that he accounts for his sons, in this case especially Cyrus. And the Israelites are referred to directly as

38. Schlisske, *Gottessöhne*, p. 190.

39. Like most other people, I perceive the definite form of the noun as a proper name. Cf. as to this use of the definite article, Gesenius-Kautzsch-Bergsträsser, *Hebräische Grammatik* (Hebrew Grammar) (Hildesheim: Georg Olms, 1963; 1st edn, 1813), p. 423, para. 126 d.

40. R. Schärf Kluger, *Satan in the Old Testament* (Evanston: Northwestern University Press, 1967), p. 99.

41. Cf. Schlisske, *Gottessöhne*, pp. 151-56.

Yahweh's sons in Exod. 4.22-23, and in several places in Deuteronomy such as 32.5, 19, 20. The reference to Job as the servant therefore does not prevent the root metaphor still being father–son.

'Have you considered my servant Job?' Yahweh asked his son Satan. Perhaps there is a reason for this additional description of Job as 'servant'. The servant is he who obeys his master. It is the obedient son and the son who bears the name 'the adversary' whom we confront in this scene. 'Have you considered him?'

We know well this kind of question, the purpose of which is to give the proud father an opportunity to speak about his favourite among his children. And we know the reaction from whoever feels himself neglected by this eternal reference to the excellencies of his favourite son. 'Does Job fear God for nothing? Have you not put a fence around him and his house and all that he has, on every side? You have blessed the work of his hands, and his possessions have increased in the land.' Just try to take away the blessing ('spoiling' is implied) from him and you will see. Then the blessed will curse you to your face. So much for his piety and good deeds! And Yahweh delivers his favourite into the hands of Satan. 'Only do not stretch out your hand against him!'

Satan now smites all Job's property, indeed even his sons and daughters perish in the great wind. No greater pain can befall a man than to lose his own children! But Job does not turn away from his piety; not for a moment does he doubt that it is Yahweh who gave and Yahweh who took away, and that the name of Yahweh must be blessed.

Exegetes have often interpreted this scene in heaven as an example of Yahweh's gathering his council around him in the same way as an earthly king gathers his advisers at court.[42] As we saw earlier,[43] an attempt has also been made to see Satan in the role of a heavenly official, a functionary at court whose task is to spy on God's subjects on earth and submit a report on them to heaven.

On the basis of such an interpretation the root metaphor must be the king, and the actual coining of this metaphor must come from the council where the king assembles his officials for consultation. There is no doubt

42. Cf., e.g., Habel, *The Book of Job*, who reviews the section of Job 1.6-12, under the heading, 'The First Assembly—in Heaven' and interprets the sons of God as members of the divine assembly. Cf. also the research-historical survey in Schärf Kluger, *Satan*, pp. 98-136 and her very special interpretation of the divine assembly in the light of modern depth-psychological research.

43. Cf. the research-historical survey, pp. 52-58.

that Yahweh is frequently described by means of the king image. Tryggve Mettinger[44] has produced several examples of this image's central position in the Old Testament. Indeed, according to Mettinger the king metaphor is quite simply the pervasive metaphor not only in the Book of Job but in the entire Old Testament tradition. Mettinger relies largely on Othmar Keel's demonstration of the possible connection between, on the one hand, the Egyptian concepts of Horos, who can include among his royal achievements the destruction of the hippopotamus and the crocodile, and, on the other hand, the description of Yahweh in the second speech of the Lord in the Book of Job.[45]

I must nevertheless refute that the prologue's root metaphor is the king, for if Yahweh were to be described in the image of a king a number of questions arise. First, how can a king come to agree that one of his subjects, who has hitherto been entirely loyal, should be tested so fiercely in terms of property and health simply because another official expresses suspicion of the motives behind this loyalty? Shouldn't a king be satisfied as long as his subjects obey him? Indeed, Job has shown himself to be an exemplary subject in everything he does.

Secondly, what does Satan hope to achieve? It is seldom profitable to throw suspicion on the king's favourite unless one has strong evidence to support one's case and the certainty of taking over as the person preferred. And here what is involved is not even to find existing evidence but to create a situation in which the person concerned is inveigled into renouncing his allegiance to the king by cursing him to his face.

Thirdly, if Satan is described as the Great King's official, why do we hear nothing of the just punishment of this functionary, who had nearly taken the life of one of the king's most loyal servants?

The answers to these questions may relate to the choice of scene. In contrast to earlier research, I believe that the author does not wish to depict an image of the heavenly council but the image of a father and his sons. But if the scene is not an official meeting between the king and his functionaries but a meeting within the family; it is indeed not unreasonable that one of the sons should yield to his jealousy towards this absent—but in spirit always present—favourite son and attempt to discredit him, so as to be able later to supersede him in his position.

44. T.N.D. Mettinger, *In Search of God: The Meaning and Message of the Everlasting Names* (Philadelphia: Fortress Press, 1988).

45. Cf. Mettinger, *In Search of God*, pp. 195-200, and Keel, *Jahwes Entgegnung an Ijob*, pp. 126-56; 156-59.

In his commentary on the dialogue between Yahweh and Satan, a lone scholar, Francis I. Andersen,[46] has drawn attention to the very free-and-easy tone that Satan uses towards Yahweh. There are no formalities, no court etiquette using 'my Lord!' and 'your servant', but a straightforward, intimate, relationship. Andersen concludes from this observation that we again have evidence that Satan does not belong to the circle of Yahweh's respectful servants. But he is wrong here, because if it is not the heavenly council that meets in the prologue to the Book of Job but a father and his sons, then the familiar form of speech is not offensive but a natural part of the relationship between a father and his eldest son.

If we now compare this with the thesis that the author is struggling with or dialogizing with the Jacob-Esau narratives and read this part of the prologue on the basis of the traditions about Esau who has designs on Jacob's life, since Jacob has cheated him of the blessing, then it is utterly plausible that the author of the Book of Job now causes Satan to try to stretch out his hand towards Jacob.

During his visit to earth, Satan has been able to confirm with his own eyes that this favourite son is blessed by his father. Who else lives in such plenty as this Job? Hasn't this Job, quite unjustifiably, only because of the father's preference for him, received the blessing of a first-born, just as against all right and reason Jacob received the blessing of the first-born?

'Now Esau hated Jacob because of the blessing with which his father had blessed him, and Esau said to himself, "The days of mourning for my father are approaching; then I will kill my brother Jacob"' (Gen. 27.41). Not surprisingly, Satan the son of God also feels jealousy, since no one can possibly doubt that he ranks above Job and should therefore preferably be close to God? It is well known that Job was not even created when the heavenly beings shared in the rejoicing at the creation of the world.

Also, the father's indulgence towards the jealous Satan is more understandable if Satan is one of his sons, and suspicion is sown that the favourite son is a time-server whose loyalty and love are founded solely on calculation. A king can very easily tolerate that his subjects see the advantages of loyalty, and for this very reason show obedience towards their Lord. A father cannot tolerate that his son does not love him, but is obedient only for the sake of gain. A father must know what resides in his son's heart. So it was when Yahweh tested Israel in the desert as a father tests his son (Deut. 8.2-5), and so it is when the son is called Job.

---

46. F.I. Andersen, *Job: An Introduction and Commentary* (TOTC; Leicester: Inter-Varsity Press, 1976), p. 85.

And what about the punishment which did not take place? I shall return to this.

But the parallel between the Jacob-Esau narratives and the Job narrative can be carried further. One of the features which shows that in Jewish tradition the two narrative complexes have been associated with one another is the fact that later Jewish sources link Jacob's family and Job's family. As early as the first century CE, Pseudo-Philo tells that Jacob's daughter Dinah, who was raped by Shechem, became Job's second wife.[47] The mediaeval Jewish legends also concern themselves with the connection between these families, and allow Jacob to be a grandson of Esau as well as son-in-law to Jacob (through Dinah).[48]

I am thus not the only person to have seen a connection between the two narrative complexes, but I have met with no other attempt to see an inherent connection between the Book of Job and the Jacob-Esau narratives. There is in fact more to indicate that the two narratives should be read in the context of one another.

One of the motifs in the Esau-Jacob tradition is the struggle between the two brothers in their mother's womb (Gen. 25.22-26). When Rebecca complains about the struggle between the twins, and would rather be relieved of giving birth to them,[49] Yahweh replies by prophesying the coming distribution of power, where one shall suppress the other and the elder become the slave of the younger. Another motif in the Book of Job is the mother's womb, in part in 1.21, where Job reacts to all the misfortunes with the words that he came naked from his mother's womb and would naked return to it, that is, to the earth's womb/tomb, and in part in ch. 3, where he wishes that he had himself died in, or immediately on leaving, his mother's womb.[50]

47. Cf. Pseudo-Philo in *Antiquitates Biblicae* VIII, 8 (Liber Antiquitatum Biblicarum), II, p. 120.

48. Cf. L. Ginzberg, *The Legends of the Jews II* (Philadelphia: Jewish Publication Society of America, 5730—1969), pp. 225 and 241, and L. Ginzberg, *The Legends of the Jews I* (Philadelphia: Jewish Publication Society of America, 5728—1968), p. 396.

49. It is not quite clear from the text whether Rebecca wishes herself dead or wishes that the sons were never to be born.

50. It might also be considered whether there was a connection between the meals theme and blessing/curse in Gen. 25–26 and the meals and sacrifices referred to in the prologue, where Job's sons and daughters eat and drink together and Job makes a sacrifice to avoid the consequences of any curses. For crucial events to be associated with eating is not unusual. Cf., e.g., also

As we have seen, the father's preference for the younger son is a well-known motif both within the Old Testament and outside it. But in the context of Esau and Jacob some striking transformations have occurred. Their earthly father, Isaac, is not one of the group of fathers who prefer the younger rather than the elder. On the contrary, he wishes to follow the established order in which the elder receives the blessing of the first-born. Isaac loves his elder son, and he has no thought of treating him unfairly.

'Isaac loved Esau, because he was fond of game, but Rebekah loved Jacob', reads Gen. 25.28. The reason seems strange, although several commentators believe they know that fathers prefer sons who like an open-air life, while mothers like to see the boys staying at home! Even if this were so, the object is rather to give the reader a first inkling that a preference for game will play a part later in the story.

Rebecca's love will also play a part at a later date, that is, when she discovers that Isaac wishes to bless Esau, and thus sets the stage for the imposture. It is her idea, not Jacob's, and she gets her way. For clearly there is another who is fond of Jacob: Yahweh himself.

The narratives of Abraham and Sarah tell that Yahweh not only approves but directly supports Sarah in sending away the elder son Ishmael so that Isaac can become 'sole heir'. Although Abraham was hurt, it had to be so (Gen. 21.8-13). Now history in some respects repeats itself. The mother loves the son who is also Yahweh's choice. Rebecca's plan to make Jacob the first heir despite his being the younger thus also becomes reality.

On an earthly level, the motif of the father preferring the younger has been transformed into a narrative about the mother's preference for the younger; but relative to the heavenly father the narrative follows the traditional pattern. Yahweh is well aware that Jacob is to be the ancestor of Israel, although he is the younger of the twins. Thus Rebecca, even before the birth, began to receive the oracle that the elder of the sons shall be the slave of the younger.

It should also be mentioned in this context that in later Jewish legend we find the variation of the Jacob-Esau narrative, that Satan—here referred to as Samael—took part in the dispute between the twin brothers from the very outset. The struggle in the mother's womb was not only their struggle; each had his allies. Samael, who supported Esau, wished to kill Jacob

*Biblia Pauperum* (Copenhagen: Gads Forlag, 1984), pp. 34-35, where Mt. 4.1-11, Jesus' temptation in the wilderness, is associated with the meal by which Jacob bought Esau's birthright and with the Fall's tempting fruit, Gen. 3.

even before they were born, while the Archangel Michael rushed to help Jacob. Michael tried to burn Samael, so the merciful God had to summon a heavenly council hastily to decide the matter. Esau and Jacob—Satan and Job—Satan and Michael.[51]

That God was able to make use of Satan to the advantage of Jacob is also to be seen from the same legends. It is thus told that, in the context of Esau's hunting, the Lord sent out Satan to delay him so that Jacob could meanwhile prepare his meal and receive the blessing of the first-born.[52]

But let us now leave this. It is of course more important that the stories of Esau and Jacob and of Satan and Job concern both a blessing and a curse, and that both tell of the blessing being ensured by a struggle with God himself.

The Esau-Jacob traditions are concerned with obtaining the father's blessing and preserving it. In the Book of Job 'the son' has already received the blessing, but is tested by losing it. The criterion for deciding whether he passes the test is in fact whether he blesses or curses[53] his 'father' Yahweh.

During his struggle with God, Jacob cries: 'I will not let you go, unless you bless me!' And when God finally blesses Jacob he cries out: 'I have seen God face to face, and yet my life is preserved.' And Jacob named the place Peniel, God's face (Gen. 32.30).

As we know, the entire dialogue section of the Book of Job is one long struggle with God, a struggle to come so close to God that Job and Yahweh can meet in a lawsuit. A detailed reading of the Book of Job also shows that the word for face is one of the key concepts. As we have seen, this plays a significant part in Habel's interpretation of the Book of Job. According to Habel, Job challenges the old tradition that man cannot see the holy God. In my reading, the Book of Job keeps to the theme in the

51. Ginzberg, *The Legends of the Jews I*, p. 313.
52. Ginzberg, *The Legends of the Jews I*, p. 330.
53. Yair Hoffmann rightly points out that this criterion is a necessary precondition for the dialogue section. 'By putting in the mouth of Satan the promise "he will curse you to your face" the author shifts the centre of gravity from deeds to words, which from now on will be the sole criterion for Job's personality. Henceforth Job will be examined not in deeds but in words, and so a perfect bridge is built to the poetry, which lacks any element of action but consists only of talk.' Hoffmann, 'The Relation between the Prologue and the Speech Cycles in Job', pp. 166-67.

story of Jacob's struggle with God, where the meeting is a success and becomes a blessing.

Habel is of course correct in saying that this theme should also be seen as a challenge to the opposite and, in the Old Testament, very predominant idea—and thus an intervention against the tradition—that Moses was allowed to see God only from the rear (Exod. 33.20-23). The Book of Job tells us that Satan walks away from Yahweh's face (Job 1.12; 2.7) to tempt Job to curse Yahweh to his face (Job 1.11; 2.5). But precisely by demanding a judicial hearing Job is able to force a meeting with God himself, where he can present his case before God's face (Job 13.15-16; cf. also 13.8, 10, 20, 24; 19.26-27; 23.4, 15-17; 42.5, 9). Both Satan's and Job's strategy thus centres on standing face to face with God.

Then they meet; God speaks to Job out of the storm, and Job submits with the words: 'I had heard of you by the hearing of the ear, but now my eye sees you; therefore I despise myself, and repent in dust and ashes' (Job 42.5-6).

### The Speeches of the Lord

The observation that in his great speeches in chs. 38–41 Yahweh also appears as a father, further supports the argument that the Book of Job should be read as a family drama in which the mutual jealousy between two sons is the basic theme. Let us therefore return for a moment to Othmar Keel's treatment of these chapters.

Othmar Keel,[54] who has studied the speeches of the Lord and their background in Near-Eastern iconography, argues that the author of the Book of Job uses various images of God. In the first speech, God is described on the one hand as the creator of the cosmos, and thus he who is responsible for the ordered world, and on the other hand as 'lord of the animals', a well-known Mesopotamian motif. This has consequences for the description of Yahweh's relationship with the wild animals which represent chaos. Whereas the concepts of 'lord of the animals' normally implies that the lord overcomes the wild animals, the motif in the Book of Job is transformed so that Yahweh becomes he who keeps chaos in check but does not eradicate it, a lord who does not destroy the animals but controls them.

In the second speech, God is described on the same lines as the Egyptian god Horos. From traditional aspects, Keel believes he can find the background to this formulation of the chaos-battle motif in the Egyptian

---

54. Keel, *Jahwes Entgegnung*, pp. 51-156.

concepts of Horos' battle with the evil Seth. In the same way, Yahweh now appears as a king who destroys the hippopotamus and the crocodile, Behemoth and Leviathan.

Othmar Keel has thus given important information on the background to the material the author employs in his formulation of Yahweh's reply to Job. But I should perhaps emphasize more strongly than Keel does that the Mesopotamian and Egyptian material is not used unaltered; it has clearly been the subject of re-interpretation,[55] for the second speech of the Lord (Job 40.6–41.26), outlines no ordinary chaos-battle in which Yahweh proudly presents Behemoth and Leviathan and boasts of their strength. Yahweh asks, who can take Behemoth prisoner? and who can lay hands on Leviathan? And he speaks enthusiastically of their tremendous strength, which Job can under no circumstances match.

We learn that Behemoth is one of God's creations; 'which I made just as I made you'. The accent is on the creator's pride. Behemoth is mighty to behold, unshakeable and inviolable (Job 40.15-25). 'It is God's very first creation, created to rule over the others'.

Yahweh says of Leviathan that 'On earth it has no equal, a creature without fear. It surveys everything that is lofty, it is king over all that are proud' (Job 41.25-26). They are magnificent animals, both Behemoth and Leviathan, created by Yahweh, and Yahweh alone can hold them in check.

The speeches of the Lord thus do not describe the ancient battle when Yahweh killed Leviathan and gave him as food to the creatures of the wilderness (cf. Ps. 74.14). The author's glorification of these creations shows that the traditional concepts have been transformed. Yahweh's delight and pride in his work of creation discloses a proximity to the created which is not characteristic of the myths concerning the overcoming of chaos. What the speeches of the Lord lead us to conclude is that Yahweh has power to restrict the evil that certainly exists as part of the created world.[56]

In this interpretation also I turn against Tryggve Mettinger's reading of

55. Cf. also concerning the mythological background to the use of Behemoth and Leviathan in the speeches of the Lord, Habel, *The Book of Job*, pp. 564-74. A detailed description of the mythological background is also to be found in J.C.L. Gibson, 'On Evil in the Book of Job', in L. Eslinger and G. Taylor (eds.), *Ascribe to the Lord: Biblical and Other Studies in Memory of Peter C. Craigie* (JSOTSup, 67; Sheffield: JSOT Press, 1988), pp. 399-419. Gibson particularly emphasizes the Old Testament mythical traditions about the chaos monster defeated by Yahweh.

56. Cf. also Habel, *The Book of Job*, pp. 568 and 574.

the speeches of the Lord. According to Tryggve Mettinger,[57] this second speech of the Lord is in answer to Job's second, crucial accusation, that is, that Yahweh is a criminal (Job 9.24). Against this assertion Yahweh sets the image of himself as the victor of the chaos-battle. God fights chaos by defeating Behemoth and Leviathan. From a traditio-historical aspect, Mettinger, like Keel, believes he can find the background to this formulation of the chaos-battle motif in the Egyptian concepts of Horos' battle against the evil Seth.

Mettinger's point is that the second speech of the Lord shows Yahweh as he who defeats the powers of evil. Job is not therefore correct when he accuses God of being himself on the side of chaos, indeed of himself creating chaos. To summarize, Mettinger must therefore establish that the image of God which pervades the Book of Job is Yahweh as the fighting king.

Mettinger is on the wrong track as regards the Book of Job in this definition of the fighting king as a root metaphor. The description of Yahweh's relationship to Behemoth and Leviathan is thus not a description of the king fighting and overcoming two chaos monsters but a father's proud description of his strong sons. On two occasions we encounter the emphasis on God's 'first-born' among Creation,[58] but note that the two representatives of the chaos-powers are given this position! Is it possible that the author of the Book of Job also includes these chaos-powers among God's sons, in the same way as he clearly includes Satan? This is indeed quite possible, for if these animals are used as images of the chaos-powers then they represent the same powers of which the son Satan is an image. And it is true of them both that their father must set limits to their development.

What we can conclude, therefore, is that the images of the creator and the father merge—quite naturally—into one another. As creator of the great animals, Yahweh may also be described as their father, but the father aspect means that the care aspect becomes predominant. The chaos-battle motif is subordinated to the father image and is transformed in relation to it.

57. Cf. Mettinger, *In Search of God*, pp. 181-200.
58. Cf. also *2 Bar.* 29.4 according to which Behemoth and Leviathan were created on the fifth day of creation, and *4 Ezra* 6.49-54 where similar concepts are to be found.

### *The Problem of Suffering and the Father–Son Image*

What the narrative of Job thematizes is inexplicable suffering. Where does the suffering come from, and why does it smite the just and not merely the ungodly? The Israelites have tried to talk their way through this great and existential question. They have not erected theses and antitheses or worked out logical deductions, but have used well-known images by which they have been able to verbalize their experience. And one fundamental experience has been that a person can suddenly be struck by misfortune, although there is nothing in that person's life to justify and explain what occurred. Evil is not self-inflicted; it comes from outside. But where does it come from?

The author of the Book of Job has clearly not chosen the model we find in one of the adjacent cultures, the Persian, where good alone leads back to the good god Ahura Mazda, and evil to its opposite Ahriman. The author of the Book of Job was convinced that it is Yahweh who gives and takes, that it is Yahweh who is the creator of both fortune and misfortune. He must nevertheless find a language which makes it possible to some extent to distance misfortune from God himself. And one of the ways is to use the image of a father and his sons.

As regards good and evil this is the situation that everyone recognizes, when the elder son of the family suffers the humiliation that his father prefers the younger. And this is of course what occurs, as the authors of the Old Testament were well aware. We have already spoken of the Jacob-Esau story, where the younger in fact, although fraudulently, barters his way to the right of primogeniture and the blessing. But as we have seen we can also remind ourselves of old Jacob's preference for his son Joseph and after him Benjamin, the two youngest sons. Or think of Joseph's own twins Ephraim and Manasseh who, when old Jacob was to bless them, had to suffer that the elder was treated unfairly compared with the younger. Or Cain in relation to Abel, and Isaac in relation to his big brother Ishmael.

While the Old Testament does not tell of the antagonism between Isaac and Ishmael, but allows jealousy to develop between the two mothers Sarah and Hagar, we find the theme in the New Testament. In the Letter to the Galatians (4.29), Paul is thus able to say quite naturally that as Ishmael persecuted Isaac at that time so is it now.

The father treats one of them unfairly, and jealousy erupts. The two who should have been brothers and companions suddenly become enemies, and the father's love has evil consequences.

He who as a father loves his sons cannot refrain from testing whether his love is reciprocated as soon as any doubt arises. But if the doubt is confounded the elder son is still his son, however much he may favour the younger. Old Isaac by no means abandons his paternal relationship with Esau, but when he realizes the truth he must ask in despair: 'I have already made him your lord, and I have given him all his brothers as servants, and with grain and wine I have sustained him. What then can I do for you, my son?' (Gen. 27.37). And all Isaac can do is to give Esau a dwelling in the infertile land with the sword by which he shall live and the hope of breaking the yoke from his neck (v. 40).

As far as I can see, something similar occurs as regards Satan in the Book of Job. There is good reason to ask, what happens to Satan after ch. 2? Almost all commentators are struck by the remarkable fact that Satan does not appear at all outside the prologue. Has the author, who indeed took the trouble to make Satan one of the main characters at the beginning of the book, forgotten him entirely?[59]

If we read this on the basis of the family drama and the imagery it uses, we are bound to say that Satan is not forgotten. In his copious speeches at the end of the book, Yahweh has in fact something to say about who has power in the world. This is said through the image of the great chaos monsters who stand in a son-relationship to their creator. For although they are the most formidable on earth they can be tamed at will by their father. This also implies that the creator has set limits to these sons' development. Evil has no free rein; it is still restricted by God's will.

And this, we must conclude, is also true of Satan. God sets limits to Satan's activities, in the same way as Rebecca, the mother of Esau and Jacob, ensured that Jacob did not become a victim to Esau's thirst for revenge. We saw this in the prologue, where Satan is not permitted to touch Job's body. And if we look at the speeches of the Lord and perceive them as descriptions of God's relationship to evil we see that what is concerned here is the same as in the prologue. The chaos animals are an image of the same thing as the Satan image. And we must also say that

---

59. Cf. Yair Hoffmann who, in his article on the relationship between the prologue and the dialogues, lists the traditional arguments against the book's unity, including the lack of a reference to Satan in the dialogues. But Hoffmann makes the matter too easy by simply pointing out that Job and his friends know nothing of 'the wager' between Yahweh and Satan, and that by ignoring Satan in the dialogues the author can bring the actual problem into better focus. Hoffmann, 'The Relation between the Prologue and the Speech Cycles in Job', pp. 162-63.

God indeed sets limits to evil; but God no more destroys the chaos animals than he destroys Satan.

The Book of Job therefore does not end with the lawsuit scene, where Yahweh puts on the judge's gown and pronounces judgment on the son who sowed doubt in his soul and tempted him to test his favourite son's love. A father does not destroy his own sons. Neither does God destroy Satan, who plays his tricks in the Book of Job. I thus agree with Northrop Frye when, without going deeper into the problem, he denies that Satan's 'disappearance' after ch. 2 presents any real problem. Frye indeed substantiates his assertion by saying that 'Behemoth and Leviathan are metaphorically identical with Satan'.[60]

But not only in the prologue and the speeches of the Lord do we encounter the father–son image. In Job 15.7-8, Eliphaz says ironically to Job: 'Are you the firstborn of the human race? Were you brought forth before the hills? Have you listened to the council of God? And do you limit wisdom to yourself?' Eliphaz here alludes to the well-known idea about the first Adam, who was the height of wisdom and perfection. These ideas are known from Ezekiel's special version of the Paradise myth, Ezek. 28.12-19, and are probably also behind the narrative in Genesis 2–3.[61]

According to Marvin Pope, it is said of this first Adam that he achieved divine wisdom by eavesdropping on the divine council.[62] Habel, in his commentary, gives weight to the similarity between the first Adam and wisdom. Like wisdom Adam existed from the beginning (Job 15.7; Prov. 8.25), and both have had access to God and thus an opportunity to advise God—an aspect also employed in the speech of the Lord in Job 38.4, 21. The myth even indicates that this first man attempted to usurp wisdom from God. Something similar is to be seen in the Paradise narrative in Genesis 2–3, where the people opposed to God's will tried to become like God in knowledge of good and evil.

On the basis of the father–son metaphor, the ironic address to Job can be read as rejecting that he was said to be God's first-born. This Job is not. According to Job 38.7, it was other heavenly beings who shouted for

---

60. Frye, *The Great Code*, p. 194. Cf. also pp. 195-96 and Frye's 'Table of Demonic Imagery', p. 167. Cf. also Gibson, 'On Evil in the Book of Job', p. 417, who concludes his article on evil by defining Satan as 'a figure of evil', and thus a parallel to Behemoth and Leviathan. Gibson also points out that he has Northrop Frye to thank for this recognition.

61. Cf. Gordis, *The Book of Job*, p. 160, who points out that these concepts are far more developed in apocryphal and rabbinical literature (adam kadmon).

62. Cf. Pope, *Job*, p. 115.

joy when the morning stars sang together. And by the use of feminine-gender forms the description of wisdom shows that a daughter was included among the first-born sons (Prov. 8.22-36). God's family is much more abundant than Job appears to imagine.

We hear nothing of Satan, who initiated the drama, in the epilogue. Here, the role of the negative's representative has been passed on to a group of role-players in the drama: the learned theological friends who believe they know what there is to say about God's administration of the world.

They also know nothing of the meeting in heaven between God and Satan the son of God. But through the dialogues with Job they have in various ways played the role of Satan. They have not, like Job's wife,[63] encouraged Job to curse God, so ensuring that Satan was correct in his assertion. But in contrast to Job they have spoken untruthfully about Yahweh.

The truth about Yahweh is thus Job's image of God. But it should be noted that it is the ambiguous image of God which causes Job to complain and to accuse, and causes Job to appeal to God to meet him in a lawsuit in court, face to face. The true image of God includes the characteristics which have in part been transferred to Satan in the prologue but which we can recognize as acts of God, partly by comparing with other texts in the Old Testament and partly from the specific formulations: attacks by alien peoples or bands of robbers, God's fire from heaven, God's tempest from the desert and destructive disease. As we know, Job also attributed these characteristics to his God (Job 1.21). And there is nothing throughout the book to deny that God is behind such events, although Satan the son of God is the agent in the specific instance.

The friends' image of God included the opportunity for such intervention but gave no place to the child's stubborn will, which despite its experience clings to the father as the one from whom justice and thus redress had to come. The friends know only the simple but severe law of retribution, where all get their just deserts.

And these very friends, who according to their own system should have been convicted for speaking falsely, are spared because Job intercedes for them at God's own request. Here we again encounter aspects of the father–son image when Yahweh shows compassion as a father, although

63. Cf. the classical interpretation of Job's wife as Satan's assistant, *diaboli adjutrix*, as expressed by Augustine. Habel, *The Book of Job*, p. 96.

the friends spoke just as falsely of God himself as Satan spoke of his favourite son Job.

So the drama of Yahweh, Satan and Job takes elegant leave of the friends, and thus indirectly of Satan the son of God who suspected his brother without reason. The stage is left to Yahweh and Job. Yahweh turns Job's fate around, doubles his property and makes him greater once again than the other sons of the East, a patriarch surrounded by his siblings, blessed with wealth and cattle, father of sons and daughters, children and grand-children. He is to see four generations before he dies, old and full of days.

The book gives no ready solution to what we call the problem of suffering, but by telling Job's story it provides the language and images for further work. By choosing the image of a father and his sons the author is able to speak of the proximity of, *and* the distance between, God and the evil one; both are included, not set into a logical formula which 'comes out right' but told as a sequence of events in which one can follow developments, and understand and accept the father's love for *both* his sons and his responsibility for *both* his sons.

I began the review of the Book of Job by pointing out that the name Uz leads us into the traditions of Esau and Jacob. But the book's first verse includes yet another name which may help us to understand the author's intentions. 'There was once a man in the Land of Uz whose name was Job.' What does the name Job really mean? Is it a name chosen at random? Although the author meant to use existing traditions about a just man's sufferings, one should nevertheless, before seeing the name as immaterial to an understanding of the author's intention, examine whether in this instance a conscious choice on the part of the author is also concerned.

The American W.F. Albright has shown in several articles that Job was a very common name in the Near East.[64] We find it in the *a-ya-ab* form in a list of Egyptian slave-names from the eighteenth century BCE, and in one of the Amarna Letters dating from about 1300 BCE. And the name means: Where is father?[65]

64. W.F. Albright, 'Two Little Understood Amarna Letters from the Middle Jordan Valley', *BASOR* 89 (1943), pp. 7-17, and 'North-west Semitic Names in a List of Egyptian Slaves from the Eighteenth Century BC', *JAOS* 74 (1954), pp. 222-33.

65. Cf. also as to this type of name the formulation of the question in Jer. 2.8: 'Where is the Lord?'

Job's problem can scarcely be expressed more simply. So must the son complain who feels let down by his own father.

*Excursus: Satan in the First Book of Chronicles 21.1—An Example of the Book of Job's Historical Effect?*
Before we leave the Book of Job and turn to the New Testament temptation narrative and the question of which strong precursor Matthew the Evangelist struggles against, we must briefly consider the Book of Job's possible influence within the Old Testament itself. Let us therefore look at the second of the three Old Testament texts which tell of Satan, 1 Chronicles 21, and this text's association with the Book of Job.

In 1 Chronicles 21, we read of David's initiation of a census, thereby incurring Yahweh's anger. The story has often been used as evidence that the Old Testament already used the word *śāṭān* (without an article) as the proper name for God's adversary, the devil. The first verse of the chapter indeed tells that it was *śāṭān* who enticed David into counting his people.

It is of course true that the word *śāṭān* need indicate nothing other than a person challenging a king. Solomon had several such political adversaries by the end of his reign, and in 1 Kings 11 the word *śāṭān* (without an article) is used to refer to adversaries such as the Edomite Hadad. That scholars nevertheless believe that 1 Chron. 21.1 is concerned with something other than a political adversary is because at this point the narrative deliberately corrects the Deuteronomists' version of the same episode in 2 Sam. 24.1. But the Deuteronomists do not speak of a Satan. They say that it was Yahweh's anger which was kindled against Israel, and that Yahweh himself incited David to introduce a census. That the Chronicler writes *śāṭān* has been explained in that he did not wish to make God responsible for David's misfortune, but quite logically passed the responsibility on to God's adversary, Satan.

It can scarcely be doubted that 1 Chron. 21.1 is a deliberate reworking of the passage in 2 Samuel 24. It is also reasonable, as hitherto, to seek for the said Satan in what is heavenly and not in what is earthly; for who among David's subjects was in a position to entice him? Even his closest adviser, the army commander Joab, cannot make David change anything in his decision when he warns him against the census. Greater powers are needed to set the action in motion.

That the Chronicler chooses to lay the responsibility on someone other than Yahweh himself accords well with the image of God in Chronicles generally. It was important for the Chronicler to show that Yahweh's actions are always just. Although Yahweh can become wrathful, a reason for the wrath is scrupulously given, usually the people's or the king's defection (cf., e.g., Yahweh's wrath against the people in 1 Chron. 27.24, 2 Chron. 24.18; 29.8, 10; 30.8, or Yahweh's wrath against the kings Jehosaphat, 2 Chron. 19.2, and Hezekiah, 2 Chron. 32.25-26).

Yahweh does not harm a person or his people without reason, even less his favourite David, the hero of 1 Chronicles, of whom the author had no wish to say anything evil. It is indeed an appropriate consequence of the Chronicler's theology that Yahweh is not made directly responsible for David's seduction, and that David is not made the subject of Yahweh's wrath.

But that Yahweh is not directly responsible does not necessarily mean that an adversary of Yahweh is responsible. We must indeed realize the unlikelihood that at a date when the Books of Chronicles were already edited there were ideas about Satan as God's antipole. We must in fact move right up to the second century BCE to find texts that use the word *śāṭān* as a proper name for such an adversary of God, to a pseudepigraphic text, ch. 23 of the Book of *Jubilees*, where we read of the increasing evil in the world from Abraham's death right up to the author's own time, that is, the final centuries before our own era. Only then, it is told, will a change occur. Even children will begin to study the laws and return to the path of righteousness. Happiness will increase, old age will disappear and all will be like children, and 'there will be no Satan and no evil (one) who will destroy, because all of their days will be days of blessing and healing' (*Jub.* 23.29).

Something on the same lines is to be read in *T. Mos.* 10.1, where the coming of the Kingdom of God means that 'then the devil will have an end. Yea, sorrow will be led away with him'. This manuscript is also quite late compared with the Book of Chronicles, since it may be dated to the first century CE.

Moreover, although this does not in itself exclude that the author of 1 Chronicles 21 may already have had a dualist perception of life, in fact only this single verse in the Book of Chronicles may give grounds for such an assertion. It is therefore all the more natural to look at the text in the context of two other Old Testament texts that refer to a Satan—the Book of Zechariah and the Book of Job.

The Book of Zechariah appears to be less directly relevant here. Zechariah 3 concerns a judicial situation in which Satan appears as plaintiff on behalf of Yahweh. Such a situation scarcely arises in the Book of Chronicles. 1 Chronicles 21 does not use judicial language, and there is nothing to indicate that Satan should be regarded here as a plaintiff. In such a case, what would the accusation be about? And if there was reason for accusation, why doesn't the Chronicler present it so that it would become evident to the reader that God punishes justly? With the Chronicler's image of God, this would indeed follow naturally. Comparison with the passage in Zechariah is therefore unlikely to help us, apart from establishing that here also Satan acts on Yahweh's behalf and not as Yahweh's antipole.

But to what sphere does the language of 1 Chronicles 21 belong if not to the judicial? It says in the introduction that Satan tempted David. The word tempted (*hiphil* from the root *swt*) is used in Old Testament texts in the context of trusted persons, such as a spouse, siblings, or friends, who inveigle a person into doing evil and therefore injure him (cf., e.g., Josh. 15.18; 1 Kgs 21.25; Deut. 13.7 and Jer. 38.22).

We encountered earlier a text in which the word *śāṭān* and the root *swt* are used. In the prologue to the Book of Job, Yahweh himself reproaches Satan for having tempted him to destroy Job for no reason. There are perhaps a number of word-plays in the Hebrew text, since *śāṭān* in Job 1.7 plays on the verb 'going to and fro' from the root *šwt*, while there is a play on the verb 'tempt' from the root *swt* in Job 2.3.

These two situations are in fact somewhat reminiscent of one another. It must be assumed in both passages that close relationships are involved in which it is easy to allow oneself to be persuaded by another. In the Book of Job it is one of God's sons, Satan, who entices his father to test the younger brother's love and loyalty. The father allows himself to be enticed, but regrets it (Job 2.3). In 1 Chronicles it is Satan who tempted David. David also gives way, but regrets it later (1 Chron. 21.8).

If, therefore, we were to look for a text that may have caused the Chronicler to speak of Satan specifically as he who tempted David it is probably to be found in this prologue, where Satan is not God's adversary but one who stands close to God and Job.

If this is correct, we must conclude that 1 Chron. 21.1 is not an instance of Old Testament ideas of a dualistic nature in which God and Satan confront one another in a struggle for the world. On the contrary, the Chronicler has chosen a model reminiscent of the family image in the Book of Job, and we can find the reason for this in the Chronicler's theology. For if he perceives Satan not as an adversary but as one of God's sons, then he can maintain the proximity between God and what is happening in the world as well as a certain distance from the misfortunes which innocent people suffer. And thereby both God's might and God's justice are defended.

Let us for a moment look at these considerations in the context of the Chronicler's view of the relationship between Yahweh and David. In the Chronicler's eyes, David may well remind him of the righteous Job. In any event, the Chronicler is very anxious that his reader should see David as a person whose sins are not so serious that he deserves Satan's temptation, but serious enough to deserve Yahweh's just punishment when he allows himself to be beguiled by Satan! The Chronicler therefore wisely avoids recounting the story of David's relationship with Bathsheba and the murder of her husband Uriah. The Prophet Nathan's accusations can thus also be disregarded in the historical record, and similarly there is no place for the story of Absalom's rebellion against his father.

For the Chronicler, David is the true founder of the Jerusalemite cult. The Chronicler is aware of the psalms literature, and leaves his reader in no doubt that when the ark was taken to Jerusalem it was with rejoicing and hymns of praise (1 Chron. 16). He therefore concluded that it is David who is referred to in Psalm 2, where it reads: 'You are my son; today I have begotten you.' To see the relationship between Yahweh and David as a father–son relationship was therefore scarcely a remote thought for him.

David is the ideal king of the Books of Chronicles. He is the chosen servant, God's favourite. Within this relationship, therefore, Satan can be interpreted as the one who is close to both parties, as is the case in the Book of Job where the family image closely links the three main protagonists. The seduction of David is indeed not an incidental plot against David but an integrated part of the narrative of Yahweh's selection at David's time of Araunah's threshing floor as a holy place. Satan's role as initiator of events must therefore be seen as a stage in Yahweh's plan involving David and Jerusalem. Had the Chronicler not perceived Satan in this way he could simply have omitted this introduction about Satan and David, and allowed the people's iniquity to be the cause of the plague. The Chronicler is not normally afraid of arranging the material to suit his theology.

Because of the scantiness of the text, one should of course be wary of drawing obvious conclusions from the apparent association with themes in the Book of Job. But we can at least say that the relationship between Satan and David is closer to the relationship between family members than to that between, for example, an accuser and the accused.

In addition, it may be added that the relationship between Yahweh and David seems to have been considered on the basis of a father–son relationship. We indeed find again in this narrative the theme of the father who must punish his disobedient son but later takes pity on him. In the description of David's reaction to the choice between punishment by famine, sword, or plague, we recognize the image of the merciful father: 'David said to Gad: "I am in great distress; let me fall into the hand of the Lord, for his mercy is very great; but let me not fall into human hands"' (1 Chron. 21.13).

And in what follows God also appears as the merciful father who sets a limit to the suffering that will assail his favourite son. The plague arrives, but God relents as it approaches Jerusalem and arrests it at Araunah's threshing floor. Here David then builds the altar which later became part of Solomon's temple (1 Chron. 22.1).

From the aspect of the history of tradition, the story of the census and the plague is a holy-place legend. The text's most important point is not who tempted David. This is a lesser aspect we have chosen to concentrate on in this context. The purpose of the story is to establish the location of the great altar for burnt offerings.

The text thereby becomes closely associated with another of the great holy-place legends of the Old Testament, the narrative of Isaac's sacrifice, Genesis 22. The Isaac story is also intended to substantiate that the location of the altar for burnt offerings was selected by God himself. And who indeed other that the Chronicler can recount that Mount Moriah where Isaac was to be sacrificed is the same place as Araunah's threshing floor, where David built his altar and Solomon the temple of the Lord? (Cf. 2 Chron. 3.1.)

And then the themes intersect again, for the story of the sacrifice of Isaac is introduced with the words that Yahweh himself put his chosen one to the test (Gen. 22.1). Before the designation of the holy place there is a test. Abraham passed it; David did not. But David repented, confessed his sins and accepted the punishment. If we now follow the causation of this narrative, we find that it occurs in a new version in the pseudepigraphic work, the Book of *Jubilees*. Here we can read that Satan took charge of the testing of Abraham (cf. *Jub.* 17.15-18 where Satan is called Mastema, which is derived from the root *śāṭān/m*) and that the mountain where Abraham built his altar was Mount Zion.

The question then arises, what has the testing motif to do with the traditions of Jerusalem's holy place? If we bring in the third text in the Old Testament which refers to Satan, Zechariah 3, it transpires that here a test precedes the *re*-consecration of the holy place. In Zechariah's vision, Yahweh is referred to as he who tests his people before they can live together again. 'The Lord rebuke you, O Satan! The Lord who has chosen Jerusalem rebuke you!', it reads, when Yahweh refuses to listen to Satan's accusation against Joshua the high priest and instead initiates the necessary purification of him (cf. on this in detail in Chapter 7).

By using the father–son image, we can perhaps express the concept of a connection between testing and designating the holy place as follows: The designation of the place for Jerusalem's temple denotes the establishment of the place where Yahweh has promised to live. But before Yahweh can choose the place where his dwelling among men is to be he must know what is in the heart of his favourite son, the representative of the people among whom God will live.

The Deuteronomists wish to express it in this way, since they thus see the period in the desert before the conquest of the Promised Land: 'Remember the long way that the Lord your God has led you these forty years in the wilderness, in order to humble you, testing you to know what was in your heart, whether or not you would keep his commandments' (Deut. 8.2). Before the creation of the place where the chosen people can meet their God as the son meets his father, there is the period of trial in the desert. Paternal love and testing belong together. I shall look more closely at this in the next chapter.

Chapter 6

THE TEMPTATION NARRATIVE IN MATTHEW 4.1-11, READ AS
THE STORY OF A FATHER AND HIS TWO SONS

In the Gospel according to Matthew, the temptation in the wilderness
follows immediately after the narrative of Jesus' baptism in the Jordan.
Scarcely have we learnt that the spirit of God descended over Jesus while
a voice proclaimed, 'This is my Son the Beloved, with whom I am well
pleased' (Mt. 3.17), when we are told that Jesus was led up by the spirit
into the wilderness to be tempted by the devil. The meeting is not fortuitous,
but planned by the God who had proclaimed Jesus as his son.

And so begins the dialogue between Jesus and the devil. Without
introductory manoeuvring, the devil tempts Jesus with the words: 'If you
are the Son of God, command these stones to become loaves of bread.'
If we read on, we soon discover that this form of words is also not
fortuitous. Whatever the devil's temptations are directed towards, they
relate to the question: 'Are you *the son of God*'? And Jesus' reply expresses
precisely what it means to be a true son of God.

In all three temptations Jesus refuses to adopt any position other than
that of the son. Jesus has no desire to create bread from stones, as if he
were the creator himself. Neither does he wish to call upon the protection
of the angels and thereby tempt the creator to demonstrate his care for his
creation. To be the son of God thus means neither to act like God nor to
set oneself up as lord over God's actions.[1] And one thing more is rejected
by Jesus: rule over the kingdoms of the world and their splendour. When
the devil offers him dominion over the world there is a condition that

1. Günther Bornkamm emphasizes that the description of Jesus' rejection
also implies rejection that he as son of God must be a magician who justifies
himself by miracles, as the 'Son of God' was imagined as doing given
Hellenistic thought-processes. G. Bornkamm, G. Barth and H.J. Held, *Überlieferung und Auslegung im Matthäusevangelium* (Tradition and Interpretation
in the Gospel according to Matthew) (Neukirchen–Vluyn: Neukirchener Verlag, 7th edn, 1975), p. 34.

Jesus falls down before him and worships him. But Jesus rejects this offer also. The son's service must apply only to the father; he owes him his obedience and loyalty.

It is well known that the father–son relationship played a vital part in Israelite-Jewish society. We also know that Jesus himself referred to God as his father. But how frequently do we encounter the father–son image in the Old Testament as an image of the relationship to God?

*Excursus: The Father–Son Image in Old Testament Tradition and its Use in the Relationship between Yahweh and Israel*
In the Old Testament psalms, we find in some passages a description of God as the merciful father who cares for the individual person. According to Ps. 68.6 Yahweh is the father of the fatherless, and in Ps. 103.13 we can read that his compassion was like that of a father. But in fact the psalms make surprisingly little use of this image of God and the individual worshipper.

Reference to the king and the relationship between God and the king is used somewhat more frequently. According to Ps. 2.7, Yahweh has proclaimed to the king that this is his son, just as Yahweh promises to be a father to the House of David in 2 Sam. 7.14. The same theme is found in Ps. 89.27-28: Yahweh is the father, and the king is like the first-born.

But we find the most frequent use in the context of the people themselves. The Deuteronomists' interpretation of the choosing of Israel includes the father–son image in a characteristic way. It is understandable that under the impact of Jerusalem's destruction and the peoples' exile it was vital to maintain that suffering also may be a stage in God's plan. And here the image of the loving father who must also put his son to the test makes good sense.

In the exile period, the wilderness traditions can be used as a key in interpreting the crisis, and the people can find comfort in Moses' encouraging words to the troubled Israelites: that they should look back to the wilderness period and remember how at that time God carried them as a man carries his son (Deut. 1.31). But to be a son also involves being tested, and during the 40 years in the wilderness Yahweh had to humiliate them and test them in order to discover 'what was in your heart, whether or not you would keep his commandments' (Deut. 8.2). And the passage continues by making it clear that God has disciplined the people as a man disciplines his son so that they can become an obedient people. 'Therefore keep the commandments of the Lord your God ...' (Deut. 8.5-6).

To be a son means to obey one's father. For the very reason that they are Yahweh's children they must avoid all kinds of alien cult and distinguish carefully between what is pure and what is impure (Deut. 14.1-21). Moses must therefore rebuke them sternly when they sin against God, and thus put themselves outside the father–son relationship: 'Do you thus repay the Lord, O foolish and senseless people? Is he not your father who created you, who made you and established you?' (Deut. 32.6).

The relationship between God and the people is described in even stronger terms in Deut. 32.18-20, where Yahweh decides to hide his face from his children, for they are a faithless people, children one cannot rely on, who have even forgotten the 'Rock that bore you, the God who gave you birth.'

A further example from the Pentateuch is Numbers 11, where the people complain about the wretched conditions they live under in the wilderness and long to return to Egypt's flesh-pots. 'If only we had flesh to eat! We remember the fish we used to eat in Egypt for nothing, the cucumbers, the melons, the leeks, the onions and the garlic; but now our strength is dried up, and there is nothing at all but this manna to look at' (Num. 11.4-6). They mope about food like children. Then Moses becomes annoyed, turns to Yahweh and complains that God has burdened him with the task of leading these people. Why do you 'lay the burden of all this people on me? Did I conceive all this people? Did I give birth to them, that you should say to me, "Carry them in your bosom, as a nurse carries a sucking child," to the land that you promised on oath to their ancestors?' (Num. 11.11-12).

The answer is obvious. It is not Moses who has born or begotten the people, and so it is also not Moses who must take care of their necessities as the nurse cares for the infant. This is and remains Yahweh's own responsibility, for who else brought Israel into the world?

The father image as an image of God is also known from the prophetic texts. Yahweh says in Hos. 11.1: 'When Israel was a child, I loved him, and out of Egypt I called my son.' And the same idea is taken up by Jeremiah, who causes Yahweh to present himself as Israel's father and Ephraim as his first-born (Jer. 31.9), although the people have forsaken their father and do not wish to use the paternal name they have previously invoked (Jer. 3.4,19).

It is indeed at the time of Jeremiah and his disciples, that is, during the Babylonian exile, that we often encounter the father–son image in the context of God's relationship with the chosen people. In Isa. 45.9-11 and 64.7, the image is juxtaposed with the potter image and the idea that man is only clay in God's hand, while in Isa. 63.16 we meet it as a step in an earnest prayer to God to show himself as his people's helper.

The Old Testament proverbs clearly show that the father role involves not only the loving care and protection of sons but also disciplining, in the sense of testing what is in the heart, whether or not the son is dutiful. It is not concealed here that the Lord punishes the son he loves (Prov. 3.12); something that earthly fathers should also bear in mind, one senses. Similarly, in the prophet Malachi we find Yahweh's complaint that his sons do not honour and fear him as they should (Mal. 1.6).

If we pursue the Old Testament view of the relationship between father and son to the Apocrypha and pseudepigrapha, we find an increasing number of examples of the use of the father image as God. That Israel is God's first-born and must therefore be disciplined is to be seen from, for example, Sir. 36.14 and several other passages in Wisdom (cf., e.g., Wis. 11.10 and 12.19-22). Or, as it says in the Pss. Sol. 18.4: 'Your discipline for us (is) as (for) a firstborn son, an only child.' Indeed, it is in fact seen as the sons' privilege to be tested and disciplined by God.

The image of a father is thus well known in the Old Testament texts, but it should be asserted that it does not occupy the central position it has in the New Testament. The father image is used only rarely in the Old Testament in regard to God's relationship to the individual Israelite, but somewhat more frequently in regard to the relationship to the people, or to the king as representative of the people.

### *The Temptation Narrative as a Midrash of the Wilderness Traditions in Deuteronomy 6–8*

As we have indicated, the relationship between father and son is a main theme in the temptation narrative. In his book on the temptation of the son of God, Birger Gerhardsson[2] has shown that the narrative in Matthew

2. B. Gerhardsson, *The Testing of God's Son (Mt. 4:1-11 & Par): An Analysis of an Early Christian Midrash* (Lund: C.W.K. Gleerup, 1966). Cf. also B. Gerhardsson, 'Gottes Sohn als diener Gottes: Messias, Agape und Himmelsherrschaft nach dem Matthäusevangelium' (God's Son as the Servant of God: Messiah, Agape and Dominion of Heaven according to Matthew's Gospel), *ST* 27 (1973), pp. 73-106.

As regards the role of Satan in the temptation narrative, reference may also be made to E. Fascher, *Jesus und der Satan: Eine Studie zur Auslegung der Versuchungsgeschichte* (Jesus and Satan: A study of the Interpretation of the Temptation Narrative) (Halle: Niemeyer, 1949).

is built up as a Midrash of parts of Deuteronomy, that is, as a commentary on the traditions about Yahweh's testing of Israel in the wilderness. The Midrash genre was popular in New Testament times, and it is no surprise that it is in fact Matthew the Evangelist, with his deep roots in Judaism, who makes use of this genre.

The starting point of a Midrash is a text taken from the tradition, a sentence, or merely a single word, which is then expanded partly by association and partly by other quotations. A text-mosaic is thus created, which receives convincing strength especially from its association with well-known and popular Scripture or exegeses. The Midrash genre clearly reflects the intertextuality technique which we expounded in the section on the present-day text-concept.

The reader of a Midrash such as the temptation narrative is drawn into a network of texts, of which the narrative of the testing of Israel in the wilderness is quite determinative, according to Gerhardsson. When one reads of Jesus' temptation, one must read in parallel in one's mind the narrative of Israel's trials. Only in the light of this does the Matthew text yield its full significance.

That this was the author's intention is clear from Jesus' reply to Satan. All three replies originate from Deuteronomy 6–8, where we are told that God allowed his son Israel to wander in the wilderness for 40 years in order to discipline him and to test him.[3] Chapters 6–8 are of course themselves a Midrash of the desert-wandering traditions in Exodus, Leviticus and Numbers, expressed as Moses' great speech to the people before the immigration. Israel must now bear in mind its suffering in the wilderness, that this was a stage in God's testing of his people. And they must remember that these tests do not express Yahweh's casual whims but rather a father's disciplining of his son.

Gerhardsson sees it as important that the material in Matthew's narrative of the temptation has been taken primarily from a text in which the people are referred to as *the son of God*. Deut. 7.7 reads that Yahweh has chosen Israel, and justifies the choice: 'It was not because you are more numerous than any other people that the Lord set his heart on you and chose you—for you were the fewest of all peoples. It was because the Lord loved you and kept the oath he swore to your ancestors that the Lord has brought you out with a mighty hand, and redeemed you from the house of slavery, from the hand of Pharaoh, king of Egypt.' (Cf. also the reference to God's love of the people in Deut. 4.37.) We are to understand in the light of this

3. Gerhardsson, *The Testing of God's Son*, p. 11.

fatherly love the words directed to Israel in Deut. 8.5: 'Know then in your heart that as a parent disciplines a child so the Lord your God disciplines you.'

That Israel has not only been chosen but is God's beloved son is also to be seen from Exod. 4.22, where the son-motif is linked to the deliverance from Egypt. Yahweh orders Moses to go to Pharaoh and to tell him: 'Thus says the Lord: Israel is my firstborn son. I said to you, "Let my son go that he may worship me." But you refused to let him go; now I will kill your firstborn son' (Exod. 4.22-23). But whereas here the son-relationship gives rise to Yahweh's great acts of deliverance for Israel by the slaughter of the enemy's first-born and liberation from imprisonment, in Moses' speech in Deuteronomy it is justification for the great tests to which Israel is subjected in the wilderness. To test is part of fatherly love. And whatever may occur between father and son the point of reference is the father's love for his son, both when obedient and when disobedient. What the father wishes from his son is his reciprocal love.

Birger Gerhardsson refers not only to the son-image in the wilderness tradition but rightly points out that the 'God's son' designation was originally a king-epithet.[4] Best known in this context is Ps. 2.7, which says at the induction of the king: 'You are my son; today I have begotten you', and the promise to Nathan in 2 Sam. 7.14. In New Testament times, however, the image was used more frequently of God's people than of the chosen king, Messiah.

The material used by Matthew also indicates that we must be conscious of the term 'God's son' in the temptation narrative, and that we must read it using the Old Testament wilderness traditions as a background text. If we read it in this way, we expect the temptation narrative to deal with how the son is tested so that the father can know what is in his heart, whether or not his love is reciprocated—just as Yahweh had to test his son Job.

The central statement in the baptism narrative are the words that Jesus is the beloved and chosen son of God. The words in Mt. 3.17 reflect Isa. 42.1, where the first servant song reads: 'Here is my servant, whom I uphold, my chosen, in whom my soul delights.' But in the narrative of the flight to Egypt also there is an association with the son-motif, that is, with the Hosea quotation: 'Out of Egypt I have called my son' (Mt. 2.15). Jesus thereby becomes the beginning of the new Israel, which like the old Israel stands in a son-relationship to God.[5]

---

4. Gerhardsson, *The Testing of God's Son*, pp. 22-24.
5. Cf. also Mt. 8.29; 14.33; 16.16; 26.63; 27.43.54.

If we then glance at the Gospel according to Luke and its placing of the temptation narrative, we are given a similar impression of the importance of the 'God's son' concept. Both gospels agree that the Jordan baptism and the pledge of being the beloved and chosen son precede the temptation in the wilderness. The water of baptism and the drought of the wilderness are cosmos and chaos in beautiful contrast. But in Luke, after the pledge, Jesus' earthly genealogical table is added as a commentary on the question that must arise for whoever hears that God has called someone 'My son, the beloved, my chosen one, my trusted one': What is meant by saying that he is a son of God? Has he no earthly parents whatsoever? And to this the genealogical table replies that to be 'true God' (to use the words of the Creed) does not exclude also being 'true man', son of Joseph and son in a direct line of, for example, David, Jacob, Isaac, Abraham, Noah, Seth, Adam and GOD. In the Luke version also, the crux of the matter is the meeting between the son of God and the devil.

But let us return to the temptation narrative in Matthew. The first temptation occurs in the wilderness and is directly linked to the wilderness traditions. In the same way as the people at that time suffered hunger, so must God's son Jesus be tested by the torment of hunger: the people for 40 years; Jesus for 40 days, like Moses who also fasted for 40 days according to Exod. 34.28. A situation so similar and yet so different; for whereas the Israelites grumbled and tempted the Lord Jesus reacts as the obedient son who trusts the creator to take care of the destitute.

Jesus rejects the temptation to decide for himself the food due to the son with a quotation from Deut. 8.3: 'One does not live by bread alone, but by every word that comes from the mouth of God.' (Cf. also Job 5.17-23 on God's nurture and God's help, even in famine.)

The second temptation takes place in Jerusalem on the pinnacle of the temple. The main theme is God's protection, a theme linked to the sojourn in the wilderness and to the holy place as an asylum. In the same way here as in Matthew 4, Ps. 91.11-12 refers to protection by angels, so that the worshipper does not dash his foot against a stone. The wilderness traditions also tell of angels when Yahweh promises to send his angel in front of the people to guard them on the way and bring them to the place he has prepared (Exod. 23.20).

With a quotation from Deut. 6.16, where there is a ban on testing the Lord, Jesus resists the temptation to summon the protection of angels by throwing himself from the high pinnacle. Jesus does not wish to test whether God will keep his word about protecting his chosen one. He does not wish to verify whether God is with him, as did the Israelites at Massah (Exod. 17.7).

The third and most important of the temptations takes place on a high mountain. In extension of Gerhardsson's indication of the link to the wilderness traditions, it should be mentioned that, before Jesus, Moses also had stood on a high mountain and looked out over a promised land. Then it was Yahweh who showed it to him and said: 'I have let you see it with your own eyes, but you shall not cross over there' (Deut. 34.4). God shows Moses the land but will not allow him to partake of it. According to later rabbinical speculation, Moses also met Satan on the mountain; but of course Moses withstood Satan's temptation.

According to Matthew, the temptation itself consists of the worship of Satan as lord of the world. Luke emphasizes that all power has been transferred to the devil, and he can give the power to whoever he pleases. And if we ask who has given the devil this power, there is only one answer: God himself has done this. Only God can distribute this power to whoever he pleases. Matthew 4 reads more tersely: 'All these I will give you, if you will fall down and worship me.' Here also the temptation is linked to the *God's son* theme, since the choice is between being the son of God or of the devil, between the paths of suffering and of power.

The temptation narrative constitutes the high point in the first main section of the Gospel according to Matthew. It has now been made clear that Jesus is the son of God, and that the son-relationship consists in obedience towards the father: Jesus wishes neither to tempt God by acting as if he were himself God, nor to acknowledge any lord other than God himself. The son-relationship here indicates total obedience, and not a special physical or metaphysical relationship to God.[6]

The narrative has sometimes been interpreted as meaning that the devil wishes to make Jesus doubt whether he is in fact the son of God. But this is scarcely the intention. The pledge at the baptism stands firm. Jesus has himself heard the words about being chosen and loved as a son. What the devil wishes is not that Jesus should undervalue his own role but, on the contrary, that he should overplay it, for Satan is well aware that real

6. Cf. F.W. Beare, *The Gospel according to Matthew: A Commentary* (Oxford: Basil Blackwell, 1981), p. 102, in which Beare emphasizes that 'son' indicates a relation. The declaration that Jesus is God's son is therefore 'not an affirmation of the divinity of Jesus, but an appointment to office, perhaps even to sacrifice and to service.' Cf. also G. Cooke, 'The Israelite King as Son of God', *ZAW* 73 (1961), p. 46.

temptation has to do with the use of our strengths, not of our weaknesses. It is in fact our strong points which tempt us towards misuse of them and self-promotion.

In support of his thesis that Mt. 4.1-11 is a Midrash of Deut. 6–8, Gerhardsson points out that there is not only a close link between many details of the two texts; he also points out that as a whole the temptation narrative has its basis in a text from this Old Testament passage.[7] It turns on Israel's fundamental creed: 'Hear, O Israel! The Lord is our God, the Lord alone. You shall love the Lord your God with all your heart, and with all your soul, and with all your might' (Deut. 6.4-5). This is the unconditional love of the father which is required of Israel and now of Jesus.

Jesus is tested not on a series of casual commandments but on the commandment that demands perfect love, for only when Jesus has passed this test does his father know what is in his son's heart. In rabbinical interpretation also, this love in its absoluteness plays the decisive part. And as an example of meeting this commandment, the rabbis in fact frequently refer to Job's unconditional love and obedience, as expressed in Job 2.10 and 1.21.

Gerhardsson[8] refers to the word 'tempt' as the second most important word in the narrative, that is, after the words 'God's son', and emphasizes the link with Deuteronomy and the wilderness tradition. The Hebrew word for to tempt, *nissā*, also refers to testing, for example when the Queen of Sheba tests Solomon's wisdom. But the word is used in a religious context especially as concerns the Covenant people and God's wish to test whether the Covenant community is keeping to its part of the agreement (Gen. 22.1; Exod. 16.4, Deut. 13.2-5).

Part of the Lord of the Covenant's right is to test the loyalty of his Covenant community, as a father must test his son's obedience. When the devil is called 'the tempter' in Mt. 4.3, it is therefore in the sense of 'he who tests'. But the subtlety is that the first temptation consists in causing Jesus to act not as the son of God but as God himself, the second in causing Jesus to tempt God to manifest himself as God, and the third temptation in giving the devil God's place. But no son of God is entitled to act as God himself, and no son of God may tempt his father to prove his divine might, for as it reads in Deut. 6.16: 'Do not put the Lord your God to the test.'

7. Gerhardsson, *The Testing of God's Son*, pp. 71-80.
8. Cf. Gerhardsson, *The Testing of God's Son*, pp. 25-32.

Read in our context, however, it is difficult not to allow our thoughts to return to Job and ask whether he is perhaps the famous exception that proves the rule. For perhaps Job's strategy throughout the dialogue is to entice Yahweh out of the cloud and to manifest himself as God?

Gerhardsson is also aware that in rabbinical literature, where the words of Ps. 11.5, 'The Lord tests the righteous and the wicked', are frequently quoted, a link is created between testing and exaltation via a play on words between the two Hebrew words *nissā* and *nāśā*.[9] The rabbis wish by this means to indicate that before exaltation there must be a test. Gerhardsson sees the same theme in Deuteronomy, where by ch. 8.4 we hear of testing but thereafter look ahead to exaltation.

We must nevertheless establish that it is not God himself who meets his son on the high mountain and tests his obedience, as occurred on Mount Moriah, where it was God who demanded of Abraham his first-born son, 'your only son, he whom you love', to test his obedience. In Matthew Satan is the tool, and thus we see the same trend as we encountered in the Book of Job and the First Book of Chronicles. A certain distance must be created between the testing of the chosen son and the father.

And what in fact is at stake between the pair in the wilderness? Can we consolidate this into one question: What if *you* are the son of God? Perhaps the devilish question has this undertone: Which of us two is the true *Son of God*? Is it you, Jesus, you who have seen the heavens open above you, or is it I, I who have been given dominion over the world, I who am also among the sons of God? Or expressed more directly on the basis of biblical narrative tradition: 'Which of us two is the elder son and thus he who has the birthright?' Isn't the author struggling here with precisely the Old Testament narratives on the passing over of the elder brother? There are indications that Matthew is the scribe here, who like a master of a household brings out of his treasure what is new and what is old.

The very last piece of information in the text perhaps also expresses that it is this 'birthright' which is at stake in the temptation narrative. When Jesus refused to accept world dominion from Satan's hand, we learn that Satan left him and angels came to wait on him. Now even the heavenly powers are put at the service of Jesus, not only so that they can bring him bread and ensure his protection but as a tribute to Jesus who as son of God should be surrounded by the heavenly hosts; a new proclamation that Jesus is the beloved and chosen son of God.

9. Gerhardsson, *The Testing of God's Son*, p. 34.

*Jesus and Satan—Two Brothers?*

The theme of the struggle for the birthright leads us back to the tradition
of Esau and Jacob. But in Matthew one of the sons is called Satan. It is
not enough, therefore, to be mindful of the narrative of Isaac's twin sons;
the Book of Job's description of the relationship between a father and his
sons must also be considered. Gerhardsson's reference to the wilderness
traditions does not explain why it is Satan who tests Jesus. Given the
Deuteronomistic traditions, it should far preferably be God himself who
tests his son. The narrative of the testing of Abraham similarly suggests
that God himself should be the one to test the obedience of his chosen
son. Only by bringing in the scenario of the Book of Job can it be perceived
that the tempter is in fact Satan.

To employ Harold Bloom's terminology, one of the strong precursors
against whom Matthew struggles is the author of the Book of Job. From
the aspect of this struggle, the temptation narrative is created not only as
the story of God's testing of Jesus as a father tests his son; it becomes a
family drama in which the elder brother is given a vital role. Through the
struggle with the Job tradition, the temptation narrative becomes the story
of a father and his two sons, a story of God, Satan and Jesus.

And thus we have presented the missing link in Gerhardsson's demonstration of the Old Testament background to Mt. 4.1-11. One might well
ask of Gerhardsson, where does Satan in fact come from if the temptation
narrative is merely a Midrash of Deut. 6–8?

But what will be the consequences for the analysis of the temptation
narrative? My first thought would be that, given this, we must take far
more seriously than we are accustomed to the content of the dialogue
between Jesus and Satan. For if the dispute concerns what it means to be
the son of God, then it is no casual opponent who tempts Jesus but the
very Satan who, according to the Book of Job, is *also* God's son.

So there are two sons of God in dispute about who is God's true heir,
a dispute which certainly ends with Jesus resisting the temptation but NOT
with God's punishment of Satan for trying to tempt his brother Jesus.
Given our normal perceptions of the devil, it might perhaps be expected
that he would suffer a cruel fate after the temptation in the wilderness.
But this no more happens in Luke's narrative than it does in the version
in the Gospel according to Matthew.

We also notice here the similarity to the Book of Job. The two testing
narratives have in common that the elder brother is not punished for his

active part in the testing, for the elder brother's testing of the younger is a stage in the father's testing of what is in the heart of his favourite son. The fact that it is the elder brother who carries out the testing and not the father himself creates the necessary distance between the father and the—as becomes apparent—unfounded suspicion of the son. Whereas the Deuteronomists had no more problems than did the author of the narrative of Isaac's sacrifice in allowing God himself to test his chosen ones (whether obedient or disobedient), we note in texts such as the Book of Job, 1 Chronicles and Matthew 4 the need for a more subtle way of imagining the relationship between good and evil. It is true that the tests do not take place without the will of God, but nevertheless they are performed by someone who might have his own reasons for putting God's favourite son to the test—the envious elder brother.

It is thus neither God nor an antipole to God who tempts Jesus in the wilderness but another of God's sons. And he also is temporarily under God's protection.

But then there is also reason to ask: Has God any need whatsoever to probe into what is in his son's heart? Doesn't God know his people inside out? Doesn't God know, as Psalm 139 says, when I am sitting down and when I am rising up, whether I am walking or lying down? And to this we must answer that within the image of the father and his sons this is not so. The son is free to love or to hate his father. In his love, the father cannot compel his son. Love has its limits here; limits of which the author of Psalm 139 is also aware. For although the creator knows him and has knitted him together in his mother's womb he can end his prayer with a plea that God will search him and know his heart, ensure that he is on the right path and not, as his accusers assert, on the path of evil.

The temptation of Jesus must therefore be seen as including a real possibility that the son will fail in his obedience toward the father and will put either himself or his elder brother in the father's place. This might have occurred in line with the temptation story's narrative logic. Had this occurred, the redemption story would have been different. And we can only guess at how the story would then have been told, and whether another of the sons, the son who already has dominion over this world, would have been a suitable protagonist in God's plans for the world. In any event, this elder brother much more resembled the Messiah, whom the majority were backing at the time as an authoritative answer to the Roman occupying power, than the younger son who in loving obedience to the father chose the path of powerlessness rather than the path of power.

But the son chose obedience and thus the path of suffering. His story is therefore part of the intertextuality created by both the suffering Job and the suffering Servant of the Lord who, according to Isaiah 53, was appointed to be the scapegoat of the people. 'He was wounded for our transgressions, crushed for our iniquities; upon him was the punishment that made us whole, and by his bruises we are healed ... He was oppressed, and he was afflicted, yet he did not open his mouth; like a lamb that is led to the slaughter ...' (Isa. 53.5-7).

It is also theologically important to look at Jesus' temptation in relation to the Lord's Prayer. Here we ask God not to lead us into temptation but to deliver us from *the evil one*, as it should probably be rendered. It is thus God himself who may be imagined as leading us into the kind of temptation where what is in our heart is tested by Satan. In the light of New Testament imagery, in which the family image includes not only God as father and Jesus and Satan as sons but also the baptized community, the petition thus applies to our father, and the assumption is that we have Jesus as a brother. We know of this brother that his task on earth was that of a substitute. He was crucified for our sake. Might it then be that the temptation in the wilderness was also as a substitute?

If this is so, the Lord's Prayer must also be a prayer that God will refrain from putting us to the test, because he has already tested our brother. The testing of Jesus in the wilderness was the zenith of the temptation story that began with the fall of Eve and Adam. The Christian knows that if the test were to be repeated today none of us would be able to pass it. If Satan were to investigate what is in our hearts, the test might well reveal that what we are striving for is indeed our daily bread, so that we do not hunger; protection from danger, so that we do not dash our foot against anything; and the power and the glory of this world.

If the Lord's Prayer is to make sense, it must indeed be assumed that we ourselves realize that our only escape is for God to spare us from the test, and that all we have to offer as an argument for being spared is that the father has already tested our brother in our place.

But it is not only ourselves, who as readers develop an idea and continue to recount the biblical narratives of a father and his sons. In one of the non-canonical texts from Christian times we encounter this version of the devil's role as the tempter.

*The* Life of Adam and Eve

The collection of pseudepigrapha[10] includes a text called the *Life of Adam and Eve*. The text is of Jewish origin, but has survived in Latin. Comparison of the Latin text with the two other books about Adam and Eve, the *Apocalypse of Moses* and the *Slavonic Book of Adam*, shows that the Latin text contains a special tradition in regard to the devil's reason for seducing mankind, that is chs. 12–17 of the *Life of Adam and Eve*. The problem of the origin of this material is still unresolved. It has similarities to the Fathers of the Church, such as Tertullian, Irenaeus and Augustine, and corresponds even more to certain Slavonic texts. It can be seen that the source of the Latin version was Greek. But when the translation was made is not known, and likewise it is impossible to determine whether the source itself may go back to a Semitic text.

From the genre aspect, the way in which the three Books of Adam treat the Old Testament narratives may be described as a Jewish Midrash. Direct Christian ideas can be detected in some places, but these are plainly later insertions into the Jewish text. The contents of the Books of Adam include speculations about the angels and the last judgment; but the main problem is the origin of sin and suffering.

A single text probably lies behind the three books. That this was Jewish and not Christian is apparent not only from the ideas which characterize the texts but also from the fact that Christ's role at the end of time is nowhere clearly expressed. On the other hand, there are no polemics against the Christians. It must therefore be a relatively early text, and most people indeed consider the second to fourth century CE period as the probable date of the basic manuscript.

The *Life of Adam and Eve* tells that when Adam and Eve were driven out of Paradise they built themselves a hut where for seven days they grieved and lamented over their distress. After seven days Eve became hungry. 'Then Eve said to Adam: 'My lord, I am hungry. Go, and seek for us that we may eat. Perhaps the Lord God will consider us' (ch. 2).

But Adam walked across the entire country for seven days without

10. As regards the pseudepigraphic texts, reference is made to J.H. Charlesworth (ed.), *The Old Testament Pseudepigrapha*. I. *Apocalyptic Literature and Testaments* (London: Darton, Longman & Todd, 1983); *idem, The Old Testament Pseudepigrapha*. II. *Expansions of the 'Old Testament' and Legends, Wisdom and Philosophical Literature, Prayers, Psalms, and Odes, Fragments of Lost Judeo-Hellenistic Works* (London: Darton, Longman & Todd, 1985).

finding food. Eve now offered her life for Adam, for perhaps God will allow Adam to return to Paradise if she sacrifices herself. But Adam refuses and chooses instead to do penance. And Adam said to Eve: 'You are not able to do as much as I, but do as much as you have strength for. I will spend 40 days fasting' (ch. 6). The place Adam chooses for his fast and penance is the River Jordan, whereas Eve is to stand in the River Tigris. Eve is to stand in the water up to her neck for 37 days and Adam for 40 days, and they will utter not a word.

Eighteen days go by, and Satan becomes angry. He transforms himself into the brightness of angels and finds Eve in the River Tigris. Satan now inveigles her into believing that God has sent him to tell her that God has had compassion on them and will give them food. 'Therefore come out of the water and I will lead you to the place where your food has been prepared' (ch. 9).

And Satan takes Eve to Adam who immediately sees through the devil's ruse. Eve is in despair when Adam tells her who it is she has again listened to, and plaintively she now asks Satan: 'Woe to you, O devil. Why do you assault us for nothing? What have you to do with us? What have we done to you that you should pursue us with deceit? Why does your malice fall on us? Have we stolen your glory and made you to be without honour? Why do you treacherously and enviously pursue us, O enemy, all the way to death?' Eve's questions hit the mark, for this is precisely what they have done: deprived Satan of his glory (chs. 10–11).

The devil then replies with a long description of how Adam and Eve were to blame for his being cast out of heaven (chs. 12–17).[11]

What is most important in the devil's narrative is the following: One day when the devil was still part of the heavenly world with its many angels, God created Adam in his own image. The Angel Michael then asked the others to worship this creation of God. But the devil refused: 'I do not worship one inferior and subsequent to me. I am prior to him in Creation; before he was made I was already made. He ought to worship me' (ch. 14).

Then the other angels also refuse to worship Adam, but Michael threatens them with God's wrath. This causes the devil to exclaim: 'If he be wrathful with me, I will set my throne above the stars of heaven and be like the Most High' (ch. 15). And then the inevitable happened. The Lord God

---

11. These chapters constitute a special material in the Latin version. Where the material originates from cannot be determined, but there are similarities with the church fathers and with some Slavonic traditions.

became angry with the devil and cast him and his angels out of heaven and expelled them to earth, where they subsequently harassed Adam and Eve. For as it reads in the introduction to the narrative: 'O Adam, all my enmity and envy and sorrow concern you, since because of you I am expelled and deprived of my glory which I had in the heavens in the midst of angels, and because of you I was cast out onto the earth' (ch. 12).

In this tradition, in which we recognize the motifs from, for example, the baptism narrative and the temptation narrative, Satan receives his just punishment when he refuses to worship the first Adam, man created in God's image.

It is clear that the elder son's envy of the younger, the last created, led to Satan's refusal. Satan is one of the angels. He himself has a host of angels under him, and has no wish to worship what is created after himself. And when Michael presses him he threatens to set his throne above the stars, that is, to seize power not only over the entire earth and its glory, as Satan is said in the New Testament to have power over the whole world, but even over heaven so that he becomes equal to the highest.

That the narrative is a Midrash of the Old Testament Fall narrative is quite clear. But what is of interest in our context is not so much the connection with the serpent's temptation of Eve in Genesis 3 but rather the link to some of the motifs we have encountered in the Book of Job and the New Testament temptation narrative, for where does the author find the elements that are not known from the Fall narrative? Is it purely imagination, or does his Midrash also consist in a continual retelling on the basis of the biblical texts themselves, so that his great precursor is not only the author of the Fall narrative but also the author of the Book of Job and the author of the temptation narrative?

### *Comparison between the Book of Job, Matthew 4 and the* Life of Adam and Eve

Comparison of these three texts from the Old Testament, the New Testament and the Old Testament pseudepigrapha brings to light both similarities and differences. The oldest text is the Book of Job, in which the monistic aspect dominates. Satan is one of the sons of God, and visits the earth only occasionally. His domicile is heaven, where his father speaks to him as a confidant and treats his words so seriously that he agrees to test the younger brother Job.

The father and the elder brother here discuss together the younger brother; and later in the book the father and the younger son meet face to face. The brothers do not meet, indeed the younger is not even aware that the misfortunes which befall him originate from none other than the father himself. In Job's eyes it is taken for granted that it is the Lord who both gives and takes. And given Old Testament thought-processes it is quite natural to consider catastrophes of the kind we hear of in the Book of Job's first chapters as acts of God, for when according to 2 Samuel 24 / 1 Chronicles 21 David was himself required to choose his punishment from God the choice was between famine, devastation by enemies, or plague. The misfortunes which befall Job are indeed the enemies' devastating attack, which slays both cattle and farm-hands, the storm which kills his children and the boils which threaten his own life. These clearly belong in the same category, and must equally be attributed to God himself or, as is the case in 2 Sam. 24.16, to the angel of the Lord.

In the Book of Job it is God's son Satan who carries out the destructive acts, but with God's agreement and within the limits set by God. When Satan asks Yahweh to stretch out his hand towards Job, power over Job is made over to Satan himself. In 2 Samuel 24 it is God's messenger, the angel, who stretches out his hand towards the land of Israel and performs God's will.

In the somewhat later New Testament text, it is the two sons who meet. The father is not on the scene, but no one is in any doubt that the relationship with the father plays the crucial part. In Matthew, the devil is the lord of this world. His dominion is not contested, and the Gospel according to Luke says directly that world power has been made over to him. Nothing is said about who has given this to him, but it can only be God himself. And the fact that God has given Satan power over the world indicates a relationship between the two which accords well with the relationship between a father and his son. As a father can share the inheritance among his sons, so can God distribute his dominion.

In this tradition, therefore, the devil is not depicted as a usurper. Also, his temptation is not described as his own malevolent caprice but as a step in God's plan of redemption. It was the spirit of God which led Jesus into the wilderness to be tempted by the devil. The devil belongs to this world, with the power and the right given to him by his father. The temptation is thus most profoundly serious, and must as we have seen be regarded as an extension of the Old Testament traditions about God's testing of his son.

The reader of the Old Testament temptation traditions is not told directly why God wishes to tempt the chosen one, whether this be Abraham, Job or Israel. On the basis of the father–son image, it should also be unnecessary to question the father's right to test his son. But bearing in mind the suffering of the exile period and of the post-exile period the question cannot be suppressed. God's justice is at stake. The problem of evil must be put into words so that it can be dealt with, and one of the linguistic forms that proved useful was the narrative of a father and his two sons.

Triangular dramas of this kind among closely related and yet different persons make it possible to deal with the significance of the suffering in such a way that those affected may be sure that the suffering is a step in the father's testing of the son, without being the father's direct action. And this is what happens in Mt. 4.1-11, where we encounter both the favourite son and the elder brother, who at the beginning of Jesus' activity asserts his influence and tries to tempt his younger brother into an unacceptable role-change.

The temptation narrative with its imagery is a vital contribution to the theological discussion of the distribution of power in heaven and on earth. When we read the narrative within the paradigm that we have called 'a father and his two sons' we perceive that the proclamation of Jesus as God's chosen son *must* provoke objection from the lord of this world. And by including the pseudepigraphic text from the *Life of Adam and Eve* we can see that this motif is used at a later date as an explanatory model for Satan's role at the Fall.

It is important to bear in mind that the temptation is not merely a matter of routine. The testing is serious, and the parallel with the wilderness traditions does not make it directly probable that the new Israel's representative should act in any way other than did the old Israel when it was tested and fell. The hope of a successful outcome scarcely comes from the wilderness traditions; it comes rather from the tradition which tells of God's servant Job, a man who feared God and turned away from evil.

The devil's most important task in the temptation narrative is perhaps in that case to call to mind the text concerning Job. For we are thereby made aware that we should read in parallel with the wilderness traditions not only Mt. 4.1-11 but also the Book of Job. The narrative of Jesus' activity, his suffering and death receives its full significance in the light of the narrative of the righteous Job, who is tested by Satan but is raised up to his former elevation and glory when against all expectations he comes face to face with God and is giving back all that was lost.

If the devil is to bring to mind the Book of Job and thus remind us of the righteous sufferer, this is perhaps also an aspect of the father image we should reflect on. When we speak of the problem of suffering in a biblical context, we tend to think only of the suffering of 'the sons'. This is what happens to a marked degree in René Girard's interpretation of the Book of Job, where the innocent Job is the scapegoat which is exposed to the violence of the multitude. Quite logically, Girard disregards the framework narrative[12] and the entire scenario in heaven. What interests him is the all-too-earthly events and the sufferings to which Job's laments bear witness.

If we concern ourselves with the father image in the Old Testament, we must remember that the father role also is associated with suffering. We encounter in several passages the sorrowing father who must give up his child. Jacob's sorrow over the loss of Joseph and the fear that Benjamin, the last of his favourite wife's sons, would suffer the same fate is vividly expressed in the story of Joseph in Genesis 37. And although the authors of the two sacrifice narratives—Isaac's sacrifice and Jephthah's daughter— do not permit the sorrow to be directly expressed the deep pain of having to renounce one's only child can nevertheless be sensed in the dialogues between father and son and between father and daughter.

These emotions are expressed most beautifully in David's sorrow that the first-born of himself and Bathsheba must die. It tells in 2 Sam. 12.15 that the Lord 'struck the child that Uriah's wife bore to David, and it became very ill'. David prays for the boy's life, and begins a strict fast. But the boy dies on the seventh day. No one dare to tell the father of his son's death, since David is so stricken by sorrow that a calamity is feared when he hears of it. When David nevertheless realizes that the child is dead, he rises, washes and anoints himself, and goes into the temple to pray; he then goes home and sits down to eat.

When he has eaten, the servants ask him why he has acted so entirely differently from what is customary. The time for mourning rites and fasting should be now that the boy is dead. But David answers: 'While the child was still alive, I fasted and wept; for I said, 'Who knows? The Lord may be gracious to me, and the child may live.' But now he is dead, why should I fast? Can I bring him back again? I shall go to him, but he will not return to me' (2 Sam. 12.22-23). The pain of the irrevocable in parting from the first-born son is clearly apparent in David's simple words.

Perhaps the father–son image used of the relationship between God, Job and Satan includes this aspect? Or the narrative of God, Jesus and Satan? And perhaps also the pseudepigraphic descriptions of Satan's fall? Is it so evident that God is seen as an insensitive lord who, without regret, puts

12. R. Girard, *La Route antique des hommes pervers* (Paris: Grasset & Fascelle, 1985), p. 40.

his favourite sons to the test and painlessly casts out the son who is envious of his younger brother, or who desires his father's position? As we know, in the Book of Job Satan is indeed not punished, and in the temptation narrative Satan is also allowed to go when the task he is performing for the father is completed. Is this perhaps because the father loves both his sons and suffers with them?

The texts are not much help to us in answering the question, unless we in fact read them in the intertextuality in which other father–son narratives can be supplemented by some of the emotions which also agitate a father's heart. And here we might also refer to the text we are to deal with in the next chapter, the parable of the prodigal son, which has also been called the parable of the tender-hearted father.

The author of the temptation narrative thus also imagines that the relationship between God and the devil is close. They are not, as in other New Testament traditions, one another's adversaries. The devil's behaviour on earth is not therefore explained by reference to an earlier fall, but must be seen as a stage in God's plans. In Luke, only at a later date (Lk. 10.18), do we hear the mysterious words that Jesus has seen Satan fall from heaven like lightening.

If, then, we turn to the most recent of the three texts, the Jewish Midrash about the Fall, the *Life of Adam and Eve*, that the devil has been rejected and physically cast out of heaven plays a crucial part. For this reason, the devil's temptation of Adam and Eve has become a personal act of revenge. Originally the devil was in heaven, where he enjoyed his splendour among all the angels. But because he would not submit to God's favourite, Adam, and even threatened to set his throne above the world's stars and make himself an equal to God, he was cast down to earth.

The distance between God and the devil is obvious here, and we can see how the original, monistic perception of Satan as part of God's heavenly world is supplemented by a dualistic view of the relationship between God and Satan. The original proximity between Satan and God is maintained, but like Adam falling to the temptation to become like God himself Satan was seized by hubris and as punishment had to be banished to earth away from the divine world.

That Satan wishes to set his throne above the stars contributes to Satan's fall. We are also aware of a variant of the theme from another pseudepigraphic text, the *Apocalypse of Moses*. When Adam is dead and the angels have brought him back to Paradise, God promises Adam that he will be allowed to take over Satan's throne: '... I will establish you in your dominion on the throne of your seducer. But that one shall be cast into this place, so that you might sit above him. Then he himself and those who listen to him shall be condemned, and they shall greatly mourn and weep when they see you sitting on his glorious throne' (*Apoc. Mos.* 39.2-3).

The text, which belongs to the group of Adam books, is written in Greek, but from a Hebrew source. It is very similar to the two other texts, the *Life of Adam and Eve* and the *Slavonic Book of Adam*, and like them must go back to the common basic text from the second to fourth century CE. There is good reason to incorporate this variant in order to indicate that we also encounter the rivalry between the two brothers in association with the throne motif. Satan originally sat on his glorious throne in heaven, but this is now taken over by God's favourite creation, Adam, while the elder brother, Satan, is degraded to a lower position.

Comparison of the three main texts may give an impression of a clear linear development from a monistic to a more dualistic model, in which the Bible holds to the monistic whereas the later Judaeo-Christian text moves in the direction of the dualistic. We should quickly be able to establish that the matter is not so simple by including other New Testament texts, for example the Gospel according to John and its world of imagery. For the time being, however, we must be content with regarding the Book of Job, the temptation narrative and the narrative in the *Life of Adam and Eve* as varying examples of how the relationship between God and Satan was perceived in the period between the Babylonian exile and about 400 CE and as examples of the continuous adaptation of the same root metaphor: there was a father who had two sons.

### *'Son of God' as a Metaphor in the Temptation Narrative*

If we ask the question: 'How can God, who is not of the world, be apprehended in the world?', the answer must be, as regards the Old Testament, that what is told about God is told in human terms by means of imagery from this world, for otherwise God could not be known to the world. But this is indeed possible only in imagery, since God himself is not of the world and therefore cannot be identified with anything of the world. And this is likewise true when God uses the devil as his tool. This son of God must also be spoken of in imagery.

But from this follows the logical question: Should the temptation narrative in Matthew 4 be read as imagery, and what effect does this have in understanding the other son of God, Jesus of Nazareth? Is Jesus merely an image of God, a metaphor? Might we just as well forget about historic reality—Augustus, Rome, Joseph and Mary, Bethlehem, John the Baptist and the River Jordan—and instead concentrate solely on the imagery the New Testament uses, saying that Jesus is nothing more than these proclaimed words and imagery?

Of course not! Jesus was a living person of flesh and blood who walked about in a specific country at a specific time in history. We must not forget this, and for the same reasons we should not sweep too quickly over the wealth of historic information in the gospels. We must not use this information to conclude that all which is written is to be interpreted literally as historic fact but to assert that God has met man face to face in a way that the Old Testament would not have been able to conceive.

No one can see God and live, it reads there. Therefore even Moses was not allowed to see God's face but had to be content with seeing God from the rear, while with his hand God concealed himself from Moses (Exod. 33.18-23). The Prophet Isaiah was thus able to look at the Lord of Hosts sitting on a lofty throne in the temple at Jerusalem, although with the limitation to his view that the hem of God's robe filled the entire temple (Isa. 6.1). And therefore the prophet Ezekiel, who saw God on a throne carriage arriving on clouds to his exiles, had continuously to resort to comparisons. He had to emphasize that although he saw he did not see God face to face. What he saw was something 'that looked like a human form. And I saw something like gleaming amber, something that looked like fire enclosed all around; and downward from what looked like the loins ...' (Ezek. 1.26-28). He saw and did not see God himself.

The visions speak of seeing and yet not seeing. And Job fights his battle against Jacob for the possibility of meeting the Almighty just once face to face. With the New Testament there comes the assertion: In Jesus of Nazareth man has been able to see God face to face. But how can one tell of this God in human form, and what language is appropriate? What the disciples and evangelists wished to express was that here was more than Solomon; here was the son of God. They could not be content, therefore, with a description of Jesus. They had to interpret his life and his deeds. And to do this they had to resort to the imagery and narrative traditions on which they had themselves been reared.

It can be difficult for us today to decide whether they spoke consciously in imagery when they described the dove hovering over Jesus at his baptism, or whether they intended to give an historically correct rendering of an actual phenomenon. But we can be sure that they were not content with presenting phenomena. Phenomena are in themselves mute. They must be interpreted. And the same applies to the narrative of the temptation in the wilderness. What we must be convinced of as readers of the Gospels is that the Jesus who was born as man is God's appearance in the world. He is God's way of making himself known. As it reads in the Gospel according to John, he was to be God's interpreter. 'No one has ever seen God. It is God the only Son, who is close to the Father's heart, who has made him known' (Jn 1.18).

We as readers must therefore also expect historic facts and interpretations of these facts, explanations of what Jesus means, to be intermixed in the Gospels. The Gospels refer to Jesus both in literal speech and in imagery, for he was true man and true God. Language can behave in no other way in this unique situation, in which God becomes man. We must therefore ask of the narratives: What happened, and what was the meaning of what happened? We sometimes cannot get back to what happened, but we have the interpretation of this. Some occasionally believe that we can get back to historic facts, while others doubt this. We have no method available to decide which statements rest on historic events and which speak in imagery.

What is decisive in this context is not whether we can reach an agreement on what precisely may be considered as history and what must be described as imagery. What is decisive is that given the linguistic form of the Gospel texts we cannot disregard the fundamental tension: in the Gospels we encounter both the assertion that Jesus' life was lived in this world within its temporal and spatial limits, and the assertion that this Jesus was God himself who came into the world in human form, the God whom not even the highest heavens can contain, the God whom no orthodox Jew could see face to face and which no man can comprehend. If we abandon the assertion that it is in this world that God allowed himself to be born the message loses its relevance for us, who are of this world. If we abandon the assertion that here is God himself the message loses its evangelism, that Jesus is the saviour of the world. The naked facts are in themselves mute, and only the imagery and the narratives about Jesus can interpret them.

The narrative of the temptation in the wilderness is also subject to this tension. We can speak of God and the devil only in imagery. We must speak literally and in imagery of the son of God, Jesus. And for all three in the drama the images have reference. They not only draw attention to one another; they also draw attention to the reality which is indeed accessible to us through the imagery.

Chapter 7

## The Parable of a Father and his Two Sons in the Light of the Satan Traditions

The Book of Job begins and ends with Job. In the temptation narrative we first encounter Jesus and then the devil, and when the devil leaves the scene Jesus is left standing alone until the angels come and serve him. But the parable of the two sons begins with the father, and whereas in the two other narratives we realize only gradually that the action is taking place between a father and his two sons we are left in no doubt in the Luke narrative.

It may seem straightforward that the basic motif is the father with the two sons; but nevertheless several interpretations concentrate on one of the three. This may be the younger of the sons, the one who leaves home and squanders his inheritance abroad but is nevertheless received with open arms when he returns. Or the interpreter may be interested in the elder son. The big brother is the one who stays at home. He attends to his day-to-day affairs, but when his younger brother returns and, without a word of reproach from the father, is received as a son of the house he is seized with intense anger and jealousy. But the portrait of the father is also fascinating, for the father's love is overwhelming and has undesirable consequences. The love for the younger son creates jealousy in the elder brother, who now feels he is being passed over. And the parable ends without our knowing whether the elder brother accepts his father's loving request to take part in the feast of welcome for the younger son.

The parable clearly makes use of the image that has concerned us throughout: the father with his two differing sons. We encountered in the earlier analyses the image of God's relationship to Job and Satan on the one hand and to Jesus and Satan on the other hand, and regarded in this intertextuality the question arises whether we should also try to understand Jesus' parable as a parable about God and two sons of God, Jesus and Satan. It might indeed have been that Jesus originally told the parable in order to say something about himself, and not to create an exemplary narrative in which humans can see a reflection of themselves.

But let us first see how the story is rendered in Luke 15, and how the relationship between the father and his sons develops.

### The Father and the Younger Son

'A man had two sons.' This is the beginning of the narrative, simple and clear. Nothing more need be said for everyone to know that this is a story of rivalry. How does the father treat his sons relative to one another, and how do they fare reciprocally? Both are probably trying to win their father's love.

We learn first of all that the younger son asks for his part of the inheritance to be paid out to him; and that the father does as his son asks. Recent investigation[1] into the rules of inheritance in the society of the time has shown that the son's request is fully legal, and that it should not be interpreted as unusual or as an expression of disobedience. This was simply one of the younger son's opportunities to create a future for himself. The greater part of the property was in any event to go to the elder, who therefore remained at home and looked after it.

The apocryphal text, the Book of Sirach, indeed warned fathers against surrendering anything whatsoever of their property to a son, a wife, a brother, or a friend before death approaches and it becomes urgently necessary. This perhaps reflects that younger sons had an opportunity to ask for their inheritance, and that fathers were inclined to indulge them in this. For who would voluntarily make himself dependent upon others? (Sir. 33.20-24).

For many younger sons the future lay in the outside world. Many of them set out in the hope that what they could not achieve at home, where the elder son would eventually get the lion's share, was awaiting them abroad. This younger son also sets off abroad with his fortune to make his own way. But this does not turn out as one might have wished. He fritters away his fortune, and when the money has run out he is left to his

---

1. W. Pöhlmann, 'Die Abschichtung des verlorenen Sohnes (Lk. 15.12f.)' (The Distribution to the Prodigal Son), *ZNW* 70 (1979), pp. 194-213. Cf. also T. Schramm, 'Bibliodrama und Exegese: Anmerkungen zum Gleichnis vom gütigen Vater (Lk. 15, 11-32)' (Bibliodrama and Exegesis: Commentary on the Parable of the Indulgent Father), *Kieler Entwürfe für Schule und Kirche* 11 (Kiel: Pädagogisch-Theologisches Institut Nordelbien, 1990), pp. 21-51.

own devices. No one gives him anything, and in addition severe famine besets the country. He must now be content with a job as swineherd to one of the farmers. Only then does his thought turn to his former existence at home with his father.

He still has enough common sense to realize that he has destroyed the original father–son relationship. He has had his inheritance, has squandered it, and no longer deserves to be called a son of the house. What he can still hope for is a job as a hired servant on the same level as the other hired servants. The son has realized the consequences of his actions. He has condemned himself, and is prepared to meet his father with the words: 'Father, I have sinned against heaven and before you; I am no longer worthy to be called your son.' So it must be if justice is to be seen to be done.

What then happens is entirely against all expectations. While he is still far off his father catches sight of him and feels compassion for him. He runs lovingly towards him, embraces him and kisses him. All paternal dignity is forgotten, and overcome with joy the father takes back his son as if nothing had happened between the two.

Once before in biblical history is there a story of such a reunion, and interestingly enough this occurs in the Esau-Jacob traditions. After the struggle at the River Jabbok, Jacob must now meet the brother who was bent on killing him because he had cheated him of his birthright. He has awaited the reunion with anxiety, and like a good strategist he has prepared for all eventualities, but scarcely this: 'But Esau ran to meet him, and embraced him, and fell on his neck and kissed him, and they wept' (Gen. 33.4). It may be surprising that in this context Esau acts as the loving brother, and later rabbinic interpreters have indeed keenly discussed this passage, advancing the possibility that Esau did not in fact kiss Jacob when he put his arms around his neck but gave him a powerful bite![2]

In Luke 15, no one can be in any doubt that the father is overwhelmed by love towards his long-lost son. But the father's joy is so irrational that the son simply does not react to what he is experiencing. He continues in the role he has rightly assigned to himself: the former son who still uses the 'Father!' form of address but must immediately afterwards confess that he no longer deserves to be called his son.

Again, the father's reaction is different from that expected. There is

---

2. Cf. O. Hofius, 'Alttestamentliche Motive im Gleichnis vom verlorenen Sohn' (Old Testament Motifs in the Parable of the Prodigal Son), *NTS* 24 (1978), p. 245.

indeed good cause for the son's self-accusation, and given normal justice and equity we would expect the words to be acted upon. But this does not happen. Instead of telling us of the father's feelings, Luke tells us of his actions. The servants are told to step lively; they are to fetch festal clothes and a ring for the son, and put shoes on his feet; then will the fatted calf be slaughtered, and the festivities can begin.

Then follows the episode with the elder brother, who is not immediately disposed to welcome the brother who was lost and is found again.

### The Father and the Elder Son

'Now his elder son was in the field.' While the younger son is abroad in a distant land the elder remains where he should be, in the midst of the daily routine with its work and its duties. And there we find him when the brother returns home. The festivities have already begun when the elder brother comes home; apparently no one had thought to fetch him before the end of the day's work. After all, he had always said that work must come first! Now he stops work, calls one of the farm hands, and is told the reason for the dancing and music. When he hears that his father has slaughtered the fatted calf because his brother has come home safely he becomes angry and refuses to go indoors.

Quite unlike the father, who rushes to meet his returning son, he indignantly keeps his distance. The reason for his indignation is clearly his father's unfair treatment of him. If anyone deserved a party, with dancing, music and a fattened calf on the spit, shouldn't it be he, who has served his father more faithfully than anyone and has never had a thing in return?

The father's reaction towards this son is sustained by the same love which we have already seen. He does not begin to discuss whether justice has been done but quite simply tries to persuade his son to take part in the rejoicing. 'Son, you are always with me, and all that is mine is yours.'

The inheritance was indeed divided between the two brothers at the beginning of the parable. And although the property is of course at the full disposal of the father in the last instance everything belongs to the elder son. In this sense he represents the father, and he is therefore asked to act like a father towards his younger brother. And we who read the parable are invited to rejoice, and are given as reason for this the words about the brother who is found again: 'It was fitting to make merry and be glad, for this your brother was dead, and is alive; he was lost, and is found.' And in this way we are given cause for further thought; that is, to think about our own lives and our own reaction to existence.

We do not know whether the elder brother allowed himself to be persuaded to join in the celebrations, or whether he chose to keep out of them. But this is often considered to be the very point of the parable. The question must be left open so that it can be passed on to us, the hearers of the parable.

The Danish theologian Johannes Sløk[3] has pointed out that whoever hears the parable must decide for himself his attitude towards its challenge. Sløk expresses this as follows:

> To illustrate this, I can refer to the parable of the man who had two sons or—as it is usually called—the parable of the prodigal son. What is interesting, of course, is that the story the parable tells is not completed. We hear of the home-coming of the prodigal son, of the feast, of the brother's indignation and sullenness, of the father who goes out and speaks to him lovingly and exhortatively. But then we hear nothing more, and if it is a true story we should be told how it ends: how the brother replied, what he did, whether he went in to welcome his younger brother, or whether he stayed outside wrapped up in his own resentment. The story demands an ending and a resolution of the problem. We are not given this. Why? Because the listeners themselves must compose the ending. In the absence of an ending the story collapses as a story; it becomes a reality; it ceases to be about a father with two sons; it is instead about the listener; and the moment it stops the story is complete reality, the listener's own reality; he is placed in a radical situation, and whatever he now does will be the ending of the story.

What Sløk here presents is the existential encounter with a text, and something different from the interpretation of the parable which can also take place: 'If, however, one interprets the parable, this point of course lapses. One can draw attention to it, explain it, expound that this is the "meaning" of the story, but the explanation can never be transformed into reality; it can only be transformed into a clearer insight into a piece of interesting literature.'

It can scarcely be presented more precisely. And having read Sløk it is easy to come to the conclusion that since 'clearer insight into a piece of interesting literature' is nothing to enthuse about we should keep away from this kind of exercise. It may be, however, that insight and understanding present no obstacle to existential experience, and were necessary preconditions for the *repeated* encounter with the text. Let us not shrink, therefore, from investigating what the text may have meant originally, on

3. J. Sløk, *Det absurde teater og Jesu forkyndelse* (The Absurd Theatre and Jesus' Preaching) (Copenhagen: Gyldendal, 1968), pp. 81-82.

the one hand when it was told for the first time and on the other hand when the evangelist gave it place in his evangelical context. But to throw light on this we must first enquire about the purpose of the narrative.

## *Is the Parable an Exemplary Narrative?*

The basis of the following considerations is the observation that a remarkable number of Jesus' parables are unethical or absurd. We know the parables so well that we become used to swallowing one shocking breach of justice and equity after another. But what preacher has not had difficulty in finding an interpretation relevant to the present day of the parable of the workers in the vineyard, which turns up as the text for the sermon on Septuagesima Sunday at the very time when Denmark, for example, is engaged in collective bargaining on the labour market. The preacher is almost forced to add that any similarity to the present situation is unintentional. For the parable is in no way concerned with how we make our arrangements in this world and resolve topical problems, but with the Kingdom of God.

Or consider the parable of the dishonest manager, who makes use of the threatening bankruptcy to his own advantage and is praised by his master. Here too the preacher falls into dire trouble if he or she tries, like the author of the Gospel according to Luke, to apply the parable to this world (Lk 16.9-13). Moralizing interpretations are hopelessly inadequate.

We should therefore be very cautious in using moralizing interpretations of the parable of the prodigal son. As we know, the parable is situated directly before the parable of the dishonest manager, and before it are two other parables about lost things, the parable of the lost sheep and the parable of the lost coin (Lk. 15.1-7 and 15.8-10). These two little parables also are clearly not intended to cause us to act likewise. It is more economic to take good care of one's 99 sheep than to put them at risk for the sake of a single stray. And a good profit is scarcely to be expected from calling together one's neighbours just because one small lost coin has been found. Here also the framework is the Kingdom of God and its circumstances.

Since Adolf Jülicher's great work on the parables of Jesus, it has been considered a good exegetic method to distinguish between two different forms of imagery: parable and allegory. Jülicher wanted to have done with former times' allegorizing interpretations of Jesus' parables. According to Jülicher, a characteristic of an allegory is that it consists of many metaphors which must be interpreted individually. But a parable is a simple comparison which consists of an image part and a subject part, and only the point of the image part is to be compared with the subject. The *tertium comparationis* is what the interpreter is to identify. For example, it is in the light of this that Luke 15 is often interpreted as a narrative of a father's boundless love for 'the prodigal son *alone*'.[4]

An axiom for Jülicher was that parables, as opposed to allegories, were easy for listeners to understand. Jesus was an ordinary man from Galilee who did not make use of erudite allegories but spoke intelligibly and simply. But I think that Jülicher's preconception has tricked him here. What we consider today to be cryptic speech because we ourselves do not immediately understand what is said need not have been unintelligible at that time. It may well be that they were familiar with the intertextuality on the basis of which utterances were to be understood to a degree quite different from ourselves. Also, the fact that we shall read below the entire parable as a metaphoric narrative does not mean that we therefore turn the parable into a secret dogma reserved for the few and the elect. It rather means that we take the narrative seriously as a story of a father and his *two* sons.

Perhaps we must first establish that the father in the narrative should not be seen as an earthly father but as an image of God himself. The sons are depicted as two different types: one squanders away all his worldly goods in the company of prostitutes, whereas the other clings desperately to his property. When the elder son criticizes his father for having been so miserly that he has never given him a calf so that he can have a party, this is probably a projection of his own attitude towards life. So would a man speak who would not himself consider slaughtering a calf to share it with his friends. The father is aware of this, and points out quietly that all he has in fact belongs to the son.

Neither of the two sons can be said to represent suitable role-models, unless the focus is on the younger son's remorse and repentance. Then, of course, it is unfortunate that the father wholly disregards what would be so useful to us as preachers. But the theme of the parable is not the return of the penitent sinner, no matter how many good sermons may have been written on this subject. The two sons are scarcely suitable role-models if the whole sequence of events is taken into consideration.

4. A. Jülicher, *Die Gleichnisreden Jesu. I. Die Gleichnisreden im Allgemeinen* (Jesus' Parables. I. The Parables in General) (repr. Tübingen: J.C.B. Mohr, 2nd edn, 1910). A brief survey of Jülicher's view on parables and the consequences thereof are to be found in K. Nielsen, *There is Hope for a Tree: The Tree as Metaphor in Isaiah* (JSOTSup, 65, Sheffield: JSOT Press, 1989), pp. 35-42.

The parable might instead be a deterrent from which one should learn. In this perspective, it would follow naturally to interpret the parable as addressed to the Pharisees, Jesus' adversaries. These upright people must see themselves in the image of the elder brother, people who cannot take pleasure in the father's excessive love but instead demand justice and equity, and who prefer the brother who has husbanded his resources and served the father all these years without disobeying any of his commands.

Such an interpretation falls neatly into line with the editorial introduction to Luke 15, in which Jesus' association with publicans and sinners creates such anger among the scribes and Pharisees that they grumble: 'The fellow welcomes sinners and eats with them.' And in replying to this sulkiness Jesus tells about the feast for the resurrected 'prodigal son', to which the elder brother is also invited.

The function of the parable thereby becomes to question the Pharisees' view of what is pure and what is impure. For although they and Jesus could agree that God in his love forgives people their sins they could not accept that a consequence of this must be that Jesus shares the table with publicans and sinners. Jesus' parable then becomes a point of debate in the ongoing dispute about Jesus' attitude towards the Law.

But if we read the text not only in its editorial context but also with the traditions of a father and his sons as strong precursors we become aware of yet another layer of significance. Perhaps Jesus originally wished to say something different—and something more than Luke considers important in his context.

### *Is the Parable an Example of Narrative Theology?*

The parable of the father with the two sons belongs to the intertextuality which includes the Book of Job and the temptation narrative. Read in the light of this, we can expect the following model: God is depicted as the father who has not only a younger son, Jesus the favourite, but also an elder son who envies the younger brother his father's love. Two brothers with the same father, and yet so different. If we interpret this on the basis of Matthew 4, the two brothers are an image of Jesus and Satan. And the point of the narrative is that the father loves *both* his sons. Not only does he wish to celebrate the return of his resurrected younger son, he also wishes to share the rejoicing with the elder brother who has been with him all along.

In his final rejoinders, the father says of the younger son that not only was he lost but that he has been found again. The father speaks of the son as having been dead but coming to life again. And commentators rightly see a Messianic theme in this form of words. Thus it became Jesus' fate to be the Christ. He went abroad, did not keep his inheritance 'as an exchange', but became like those he lived among. The humiliation towards the human continues even unto death. (Cf. Phil. 2.5-11.)

But is this interpretation in fact convincing? Is it really possible that the evangelist would convey an image of Jesus as a son who wastes his fortune in evil company? We scarcely expect this to be so; but in that event the parable would belong among the group of 'unethical' parables which time and again causes difficulties for interpreters because the 'father-figure' behaves in complete contrast to what one might expect. As we have already said, this is the case when a man praises his dishonest manager, or when a shepherd is foolish enough to leave 99 sheep in the wilderness, or a king is wasteful enough to fill his house with all kinds of riff-raff from the highways and byways just because he has conceived the idea that there must be a party. Or an employer who acts subversively to a degree approaching the criminal when he calmly pays the same wage for a whole day's hard work as for a single hour's work in the cool of the evening.

Looked at in this context, we must then point out that it is not only the father who behaves unexpectedly. The image of the younger son is also unexpected, if this is intended to be a 'self-portrait' of Jesus. But can it indeed be that both the father and the father's son behave so surprisingly as to astonish us? The evangelist Luke has indeed an extremely positive image of God's will to redeem.[5] Several of the so-called 'unethical parables' are indeed to be found in this Gospel, where together they give quite a surprising image of who God is and who God's son is. In the light of this, the parable of the prodigal son might be one of the texts which speak of the incarnation of Jesus; a piece of narrative theology, not about the tiny baby in the crib but about the realization of the incarnation in the adult's deeds among sinners.

Working from psychological analyses of the Jesus-figure, some scholars[6] have considered whether there must lie behind the description of the younger son who leaves home and goes abroad the historic memory that Jesus also was a younger son who at a certain time left Joseph and Mary. Certain passages in the Gospels, for example Mt. 12.46-50 and Mk 3.21,

5. Cf. G. Franzoni, *Der Teufel—mein Bruder: Der Abschied von der ewigen Verdamnis* (The Devil—My Brother: Farewell to Eternal Damnation) (Munich: Kösel, 1990; publ. in Italian in 1986).

6. Cf. T. Schramm, 'Bibliodrama und Exegese', pp. 21-51.

give the impression that the family finds this wandering son embarrassing. They therefore go to find him, and try to make him come home again. Timm Schramm thus considers it quite appropriate psychologically that James the Righteous might be the family's elder son, conservative as he is in his whole attitude and with the elder child's tendency to adapt to the parents' standards; the law-abiding James. Younger children are different; they are gregarious and want to be in the company of others; they do not conform. This must suggest that Jesus was not in fact the first-born but one of the younger members of Joseph and Mary's quiverful of children. Schramm therefore thinks it probable that behind the drafting of this parable lie experiences from Jesus' own life.

However this may be, we must insist that in a christological perspective this is not related to any childhood and adolescent experiences but to the interpretation of Jesus as the son of God who left his heavenly home and cast in his lot with fallen mankind.

I find it difficult to believe that the parable's way of depicting Jesus should be only that of the evangelist or the church, since the form of the parable is such that the image is not only provocative but is in fact an image which Jesus' adversaries have drawn of him, this friend of prostitutes and publicans. Perhaps it was Jesus himself who adopted the image, and with gentle irony made it his own. Isn't this how you see me? Aren't you saying this about me? that I was prodigal with myself and with all I own, whereas you of course are good housekeepers of God's gifts. But I say to you that my father loves me and longs for the day when we shall share a meal together at home, he and I and my elder brother, and all those who belong with my father.

In setting their framework the evangelists often emphasized that Jesus was in conflict with the scribes and Pharisees, and that his parables were contributions to a dispute. At the beginning of Luke 15 the scribes and Pharisees are grumbling about him, and it is then perhaps natural to see the parables which follow as a contribution to a dispute, on the same lines as when Jesus was struggling with the Jews in John 8.

This approach is certainly useful in many respects, and covers a number of specific situations. But can we be sure that every dialogue between Jesus and the scribes degenerated into wrangling and dispute? How significant may Jesus' subsequent fate be in understanding his attitude towards the Pharisees? Shouldn't one occasionally consider whether some of the parables were primarily an expression of Jesus' proclamation of his identity and his importance in God's plan for the world? Imagery is of course a well-known teaching tool; remember the frequent use of images in rabbinic tradition!

Some scholars will probably refute that Jesus may have engaged in proclaiming his own role in the drama of redemption. They would rather consider such statements as the community's interpretation of Jesus' identity, viewed in the light of his crucifixion, death and resurrection. But it is not inconceivable that Jesus spoke of his actual identity. At a time when there were several pretender-Messiahs and when the question of the coming of the Kingdom of God was hotly debated, he also may well have spoken about himself. According to the Gospels, not only John the Baptist but also the disciples wished, of course, to learn more about whether Jesus was the Messiah. Might not this parable perhaps be read as Jesus' answer to the question of his true identity, and how it is that God loves not only him and all who belong with him but also the son who sets justice above pleasure? And Luke may well be right when he says that scribes and Pharisees were among Jesus' listeners because they also wanted clear information on the identity of this Jesus.

In consequence of this, the image of the older brother must be one of the New Testament's Satan images: Satan as the one who takes great care of what he has, and prefers to hoard assets rather than to throw them away in festivities. We know from the somewhat later text, the *Life of Adam and Eve*,[7] that Satan has been represented as someone who indeed insists on his rights, and also from Matthew 4 where Satan is clearly in charge and only spends where it is worthwhile. The offer to Jesus of the kingdoms of this world and their splendour does not suggest that Satan is about to renounce any of his own power. It is rather a stage in his upward striving. He wants to take the father's place through the son's worship, an ambition we also encounter in other passages of the pseudepigrapha where the devil is depicted as he who wishes to set his throne high above the stars.[8]

Although some may find the older brother far too respectable to be an image of Satan, I would rather see the older brother's attitude as symptomatic of evil: to keep to himself what has been given to him, desperately, as if it were plunder; not to be able to join in others' pleasure; never to be able to temper justice with mercy. Therein lies damnation; therein lies the demonic.

God, says Jesus, is like a father who has two sons: one who squanders away everything and another who insists on justice and equity. So different,

7. Cf. Chapter 6, pp. 107-14.
8. Cf. The *Life of Adam and Eve*, ch. 15, and *2 En.* 29.

and yet sons of the same father. And the father loves them both! In this narrative, the normal boundaries within which everyone knows what is good and what is evil are overstepped. But then perhaps in this version of the narrative it is primarily the father, God himself, who is the subject of the narrative. We are given no unequivocal image of the father; it does not fit into our definitions and classified boxes; but neither does it reject that there are and must be differences in existence. But the father does not see the differences; he sees his sons.

### *Love that Tempers Justice with Mercy*

The parable of the father is not alone in describing God's love as a love that tempers justice with mercy. We encounter the same message in the Old Testament, although not always proclaimed by means of the father–son image. The lawsuit image, which as we saw earlier is closely associated with the father–son image, can also show that love is stronger than justice. If, therefore, we seek strong precursors for the parable of the father and the two sons we must examine closely a text from the Old Testament. This is the third of the texts that refer to Satan, Zechariah 3. Here in fact we encounter a sequence of events which is in many ways reminiscent of the events between the father and the *younger* son in Luke.

### *Zechariah's Vision*
Chapter 3 of Zechariah contains the prophet's fourth vision, in which Zechariah sees the high priest Joshua standing before the angel of the Lord. Joshua is dressed in filthy clothes, and Satan is standing at his right hand to accuse him. But scarcely has Zechariah noticed Joshua and Satan when he hears Yahweh reprimanding Satan. Then follows a purification scene in which the high priest is clothed in festal apparel and a clean turban. Guilt is taken from him, and he is installed in his office.

And what is the background to this vision? In his commentary on Zechariah 1–8, David Petersen[9] gives an exhaustive account of the political circumstances in Zechariah's time. Zechariah acted as a prophet during the period after the return from Babylon. The temple was now to be rebuilt and the temple services to begin again. But resumption of the cult in Jerusalem clearly caused difficulties, *inter alia* of a theological nature.

The community must have had scruples about how the temple cult could

9. D.L. Petersen, *Haggai and Zechariah 1–8* (OTL; Philadelphia: Westminster Press, 1984), pp. 112-20.

begin on a new, pure foundation. Was not the high priest, who must ritually bear the people's guilt and procure atonement for them, himself unclean? And Zechariah's answer to the disputed question was that the prerequisite for the high priest's correct functioning was inherent in the ritual purification of Joshua which had taken place in the divine council and was witnessed by the prophet.[10]

Having thus clarified the political and theological background to the vision, we must examine the literary preconditions for the vision. In his handling of the Satan figure, David Petersen mentions that a judicial framework is concerned which corresponds to the situation that we know from Ps. 109.6.[11] As in Zechariah 3, the formula employed is of a Satan standing on the right-hand side.

Petersen goes no further as regards the connection between the two texts. But let us for a moment look at this a little more closely. Hans Schmidt also saw Psalm 109 as the prayer of an accuser.[12] In the light of the great problem of whether the high priest can lead a pure temple cult, it would follow that the vision thoroughly reflects the accusation which Satan is caused to present: How can an unclean person lead the cult in the right way?

Although this accusation is not submitted as part of the vision, it must be seen as the inevitable precondition. It covers all that anyone might ask at that time. But Zechariah now proclaims that this question has also been of relevance to the divine council, where Satan had acted as the accuser.

It had been sufficient to begin the description of the divine scene in the middle of the case because the prophet has been able, by introducing a *śāṭān* standing at Joshua's right side, to anticipate a certain preconception. The listeners to whom the temple cult was known must also have been aware of such prayers of an accused. They have therefore understood that a courtroom scene was involved, where a decision had to be pronounced on the accusations submitted: Are the accusations true or false? And they were aware that only Yahweh could pronounce this judgment.

10. Cf. Petersen, *Haggai and Zechariah 1–8*, p. 201: 'Zechariah's concerns here involve meta-ritual. How can the whole temple ritual system be set in motion again if everyone is unclean? The high priest cannot bear anyone's guilt since he, or at least his clothing, is soiled. What happens in this vision of Zechariah makes the restoration of the ritual system possible, and this by means of an ad hoc cleansing ritual in the divine council.'

11. Petersen, *Haggai and Zechariah 1–8*, p. 189.

12. H. Schmidt, *Das Gebet der Angeklagten* (The Prayer of the Accused) (BZAW, 49; Giessen: Töpelmann, 1928), pp. 40-46.

But surprisingly the vision does not continue with a decision. Yahweh certainly makes a statement on the matter, but his words take the form of censuring Satan the accuser.[13] May this perhaps mean that Satan's accusations against Joshua are false? Or is it indeed because the accusations are true that Yahweh has no alternative but to send the accuser away so that the proceedings can instead end with the necessary purification? The specific background to the vision renders it probable that the accusations were considered to be true at the time, and for this very reason they were worried.

The vision further reads that it is 'the Lord who has chosen Jerusalem' who rebukes Satan. The expression can also be translated as 'the Lord who has tested Jerusalem'. In a 1970 article, Robert North[14] pointed out that the verb can mean both choose and test. He himself considers it more correct to read the verb as meaning 'test' and to associate it with Satan, so that the meaning becomes that Satan is he who has tested Jerusalem. This corresponds to the function as Satan in Ps. 109.6, thinks North.

It would perhaps be simpler to maintain that Yahweh is still the subject, and then in return to follow North as regards the meaning of the verb. In that case it is the Yahweh who has already tested Jerusalem through the destruction of the city by the Babylonians who refutes Satan and causes the angel to take over the case in the form of a purification. But if this is a correct interpretation we must also reject the prevalent interpretation of Satan as God's adversary in this text; for Satan, like the angel, is Yahweh's tool.

Everything indicates that the accusations are true, and that Satan is expelled because Yahweh wishes to save his high priest. At the same time it must be asserted that Satan's presence is an expression of Yahweh's will. Since the accusations are true, Yahweh cannot let them pass unnoticed. Arrangements for judicial proceedings *must* be made. But for the sake of Jerusalem, which has already been severely tested, justice will not be done. Here also justice will be tempered by mercy.

13. MT has Yahweh as the subject, whereas Pershitta has Yahweh's angel. I consider Peshitta's rendition of 'Yahweh's angel' as an attempt to make the text flow more easily. I therefore do not agree with Petersen, who follows Peshitta, and I consider it significant that Yahweh should be absent.

14. Cf. R. North, 'Angel-Prophet or Satan-Prophet?', *ZAW* 82 (1970), pp. 31-67. Cf. in particular p. 59. In *ThWAT*, Wildberger mentions a few examples of the meaning of 'to test', but does not include the Zechariah passage. In contrast to North and Wildberger, Seebass (cf. *ThWAT*) found no support for this meaning in the Old Testament, but probably in Accadian texts.

We must ask, what then resulted from this testing of Jerusalem? And the answer can scarcely be: 'Despite all this Jerusalem did not sin and did not reproach God for anything', for Jerusalem is no righteous Job. The answer is rather that when God saw what was in the hearts of the people punishment was the proper outcome; but love was greater than the demand for justice, and so the high priest, the representative of the people, was saved like a brand from the fire. And if this high priest is to be reinstated in his office purification rather than condemnation is necessary.

The judicial procedure is therefore replaced by a purification. Joshua is not the first to undergo purification before his installation. It is said of the prophet Isaiah that to his great horror he saw Yahweh in the Temple at Jerusalem. 'Then one of the seraphs flew to me, holding a live coal that had been taken from the altar with a pair of tongs. The seraph touched my mouth with it and said: "Now that this has touched your lips, your guilt has departed and your sin is blotted out"' (Isa. 6.5-7).

It must follow that this very passage from Isaiah is included in the interpretation of the scene in heaven where the high priest is to be prepared for his office in the temple, and must therefore be clad in clean clothing. It also in fact says of this high priest that he is like a brand plucked from the fire (Zech. 3.2). And why is this very image used in the middle of the refusal to bring proceedings on 'the premises of the law'?

David Petersen[15] rightly draws attention to the ambiguity of the image. Fire can consume and fire can purify. The wood that comes into contact with fire will usually be seriously damaged. Remember the use of the same image in Isa. 7.4 about the two foreign kings who should not inspire more fear in Ahaz than a pair of smouldering stumps of firebrands.[16] But in the case of Joshua he was after all saved from the fire. He has thus already undergone one purification initiated by the Yahweh who tested Jerusalem.[17]

To summarize, therefore, we must say that Satan acts on Yahweh's behalf when he presents the accusation against Joshua, and that what is concerned is a dramatic description of Yahweh's dual function in relation to Joshua.

It is well documented that in the prophetic addresses to the court Yahweh

15. Petersen, *Haggai and Zechariah 1–8*, p. 192.

16. The tree image in Isa. 7.4 has been covered in Nielsen, *There is Hope*, pp. 164, 212, and more generally on pp. 84-85.

17. Cf. Petersen, *Haggai and Zechariah 1–8*, pp. 192-93, where Petersen refers to the parallel in Amos 4.11.

acts as both accuser and judge.[18] As a modification of this, Zechariah 3
shows us how the roles can be distributed, so that someone from Yahweh's
divine environment, Satan, can take it upon himself to be the accuser.
This scene, as is often the case, therefore gives no reason to speak of
Satan as God's adversary,[19] but rather of Satan as God's proxy.

### The Zechariah Vision and Luke 15

But what have 'the prodigal son' and Joshua the high priest to do with
one another? Let us begin by establishing that in both Zechariah 3 and
Luke 15 the sentence which would be the natural consequence of the
judicial process is avoided. Joshua the high priest is one of those who
according to Ezra 2.2 returned home to Jerusalem from the Babylonian
exile. Unlike the younger son in Luke 15 he did not voluntarily seek his
fortune abroad, to end up among the unclean animals there. His father had
been taken to Babylon as a prisoner by Nebuchadnezzar, and had grown
up there. Both Joshua and 'the prodigal son' then decided at some time
to return.

Before Joshua's appointment as high priest there must be a judicial
process. The accuser is on the stage, but the judge will not even listen to
him and rejects him. The returning son also considered it necessary to go
through a trial process. In his case the judge is of course his father, but
he expresses the accusation himself. Then, in the parable, this is thoroughly
consolidated by his elder brother, who can well imagine what the inheritance has been squandered on.

The accusation against the younger brother is true. We are not confronted
here with one of the prayers of the innocently accused. He even appears
twice as his own accuser. In the same way as the high priest's impurity
is an obstacle to his office, so is the sin against the father an obstacle to
the son-relationship. Neither of them has a right to what they want to be:
Yahweh's high priest, the father's son.

But in both cases the accusation is rejected. Not by counter-arguments.
No defender appears on the scene, for no defence will stand. The whole
system of justice is swept from the table in favour of an entirely different

18. In this context I merely refer to K. Nielsen, *Yahweh as Prosecutor and
Judge: An Investigation of the Prophetic Lawsuit (Rîb-Pattern)* (JSOTSup, 9;
Sheffield: JSOT Press, 1978).

19. Cf. as to this the section on Old Testament research's view of Satan and
the section on the word's etymology.

way of living: love which forgives, since Yahweh can forgive his people's high priest as a father can forgive his son.

In both cases there is a restitution of the rights which belong to their positions. And in both cases this is effected by attiring them in new clothes: a clean turban and festal robes for the high priest; festal clothing, shoes and a ring for the son.

The son is clad in festal clothing. We normally interpret this last feature of the parable as purely an expression of the father's loving generosity. But in the light of the tradition of Joshua the high priest being clad in festal robes and thereby cleansed of his sin we are also given this narrative to point out that the seriousness of the accusation is not denied, but that the judge himself supplies the necessary justice by cleansing the guilty of his sin. The younger son is thus one of those who must undergo purification before installation in his office.

In his book on the re-investiture of the prodigal son, Karl Heinrich Rengstorf[20] has pointed out that the clothes the father gives the son are those he earlier used as son of the house. He is now reinstated in his original function, and they are therefore referred to as 'the first', clothes he has previously. The reference is thus not to the quality of the clothes but to their emblematic nature, as Rengstorf terms it.

Similarly, the ring is not referred to because it is a costly jewel and thus a splendid reunion gift but because it is the signet ring which restores his old rights to him. And the shoes are not merely something comfortable rather than bare feet but a symbol that the owner is entitled to have landed property at his disposal. The son who returned home to become a slave is reinstated in his dignity as a son.

And so the father wishes to celebrate his son's return, while in Zechariah 3 Yahweh promises Israel that on the day he effaces Israel's guilt they shall invite each other to come under their vine and fig tree.

By comparing these two stories, we can establish that there is a tendency not to permit the lawsuit language to carry the day. I have analysed elsewhere the prophetic lawsuits in the Old Testament,[21] and I have been able to establish a somewhat similar tendency. The accusations are always rendered very carefully, whether directed against Israel itself or against the alien gods. But there is never any attempt to present a defence, either

20. K.H. Rengstorf, *Die Re-Investitur des verlorenen Sohnes in der Gleichniserzählung Jesu Luke 15, 11-32* (The Re-investiture of the Prodigal Son in Jesus' Parables) (Cologne/Opladen: Westdeutscher Verlag, 1967).

21. Cf. Nielsen, *Yahweh as Prosecutor and Judge*.

from Israel or from the alien side. Nonetheless it usually happens that when Israel is accused judgment is either not given or is replaced by a warning.

There has been a tendency, not least from the Christian side, to draw attention to the Old Testament's nature as a code of law. No one of course wants to refute that the Old Testament contains legal material or that the Law is of crucial importance to Judaism, but it is worth noting how often the lawsuit metaphor puts into words *unimplemented* legal actions.

The Old Testament's Yahweh is well aware that justice must be tempered by mercy. We might also formulate this in a different way: Within the family it is natural for the father to be the highest judicial instance. But it is just as natural for the relationship between a father and his sons to be *based* not on law but on love. The father–son relationship is not outside the law, but the law alone does not determine the relationship. And indeed law is not the dominant aspect of the relationship. What is of supreme importance is love.

It is not surprising therefore that we frequently find the family image used as a root metaphor. Neither is it surprising that a later author, in his struggle with Zechariah 3, causes the parable to concern a father and his two sons. The root metaphor we can most easily glimpse behind the Zechariah vision is clearly played out in the parable of the prodigal son, for the image of a father and his sons allows us to argue convincingly that God's love is stronger than a demand for equity, however justified this may be.

In Zechariah 3 it is Satan who represents justice and equity. His unexpressed accusation necessitates purification of the high priest. Joshua's guilt is not denied, but it is taken from him. Yahweh allows justice to be tempered by mercy because of his love for sorely-tried Jerusalem. In Luke 15, the elder brother perhaps primarily represents justice and equity. As readers, this is our own perception of him, but we should not overlook that it is in fact the younger brother himself who formulates the accusation, whereas the older brother merely repeats and amplifies it. Here the younger plays Satan's role of his own accuser, and the older continues where he leaves off.

In the light of the Satan traditions, we must say that the distribution of roles is far less clear in this parable. Both sons can appear as accusers; where one accuses himself the other accuses his brother. But as Satan is rebuked in Zechariah 3 so are both sons' accusations swept aside by the father, for love is stronger than both sin and jealousy. However different the two brothers may be, the older comes to imitate the younger in his relationship to his father. Both believe that equity is the fundamental consideration, and both are taught the contrary by the father's action.

The parable's proclamation of the father's love when the so-called prodigal son returns home, as well as when his brother loses control of himself under his own feeling of having been passed over, is what turns the narrative into a complete story. We cannot be content with one of the sons and his relationship to the father. In the light of the traditions we have hitherto discussed, we must therefore say that whereas previously in this parable we heard mostly about the sons it is now the father who is at the centre. Both sons are delivered up to his mercy and compassion, and both are themselves lost.

And so we must again ask whether this parable can really be interpreted as the story of the relationship between God and his two sons, Jesus and Satan. For what has the sinless son of God, of whom the Gospels tell, to do with this younger son? Is it conceivable that Jesus wished to draw a self-portrait which included such words as 'I am no longer worthy to be called your son', words which the parable in no way disclaims but which are vanquished by love?

By their very nature interpretations must be drafts for discussion. But we can support our interpretation by other texts in which analogous ideas manifest themselves. If therefore we are to render the interpretation more probable we must bring in the New Testament texts which emphasize Jesus' human side. I have in mind here the depictions of the Jesus who is afraid of entering into God's plan of redemption and asks that the cup may pass from him, and the accounts that Jesus feels himself forsaken by God on the Cross. But a narrative such as Jn 8.1-11 in which Jesus refuses to cast the first stone, although the sinner is rightly accused of adultery, and the temptation in the wilderness, when God must test Jesus to learn what is in his son's heart, belong in this context.

The New Testament not only says that Jesus was true God but that he was also true man. And it can often be immensely difficult to decide whether certain actions are to be understood as expressing Jesus' humanity or Jesus' divinity. This is true, for example, of the many times when Jesus revolts against contemporary laws and regulations. The reason seems to be that there are occasions when adherence to the law leads to inhumanity and absence of love.

In this perspective, the life of Jesus, with its surprising breaches of the Law, can indeed be told by using the image of the son who, although guilty of squandering his inheritance, never loses his father's love. The son's self-accusation thus contains that element of the father which we may call 'the father in the judge's robe'. We meet it again in the older brother's recriminations against the father, and we should not believe—in misplaced sentimentality about paternal love's all-effacing nature—that the father and the son are therefore indifferent to justice and equity. The accusations, with all their weight, prevent us from allowing matters to take their course.

But the order to be found in the Kingdom of God cannot be brought under one formula automatically. It can only be narrated. Similarly, Jesus' life also cannot be organized into one formula. It can be recounted, and sometimes these stories may take the form of surprising parables, so that we can sense that there is more here than Solomon. Here the law is breached and upheld in the love between a father and his sons.

### *Jesus and Satan, Sinners and Pharisees?*

We have now shown that Jesus may originally have employed the parable to say something of God's love both for himself and for his elder brother, Satan. But this does not mean that we have completed the interpretation of the parable. A parable such as this contains several potential meanings, and some of these emerge in earnest only when we read the parable in the context given it by the evangelist.

As already mentioned, Luke wished to link the parable to Jesus' association with sinners and the Pharisees' outrage at this. What Luke will have us to understand is therefore primarily concerned with God's love for mankind, sinners as well as righteous. But it is not in fact a big leap from the interpretation of the three persons in the parable as images of God, Jesus and Satan to the interpretation of the parable as a rejoinder in the disputes between Jesus and the Pharisees.

Jesus' solidarity with publicans and sinners is a recurrent theme in the New Testament, and it is not surprising therefore that the image Jesus presents of God's love for him is also well adapted to saying something about God's love for those who associated closely with Jesus. To this may be added that the parable is not the only passage in the New Testament in which the Jews are associated with God's sons. We shall therefore study in depth this aspect of the parable's use in order see how the Gospel according to John describes the connection between Satan and the Jews.

This concerns the disputatious dialogue between Jesus and the Jews in Jn 8.31-59. The chapter is introduced by the story of the woman caught in adultery, where Jesus does not wish to cast the first stone. One must ask, was he also not sinless? Then follows the speech about Jesus as the light of the world, in which one of the points is the Pharisees' failure to recognize who Jesus is, where he comes from and where he is going. Jesus links their lack of comprehension to the fact that they also do not know the Father. The next part of the discussion also centres on the question: Who are you? But they did not understand what he was saying to them about the Father. And thus they also did not understand Jesus' son-relationship.

Then follows a discussion between Jesus and the Jews who had come to believe in him (Jn 8.31-59). Here also identity is concerned. Who is Jesus, who is his father, and whose sons are the Jews? On the face of it the discussion is difficult to step into, since both parties have a preconception which is not automatically that of the modern reader. One of the scholars who has interested himself in this is Nils Alstrup Dahl.[22] In his 1964 article, Alstrup Dahl presented three texts which have acted as the texts behind the disputatious exchange in the Gospel according to John, and so made it possible to follow the discussion between Jesus and the Jews.

This commences with Jesus' words that truth will make the Jews free, and their reaction: 'We are descendants of Abraham and have never been slaves to anyone.' Jesus does not at first deny that they are descendants of Abraham, but points out that they seek to kill him because his words have not sunk in. 'I declare what I have seen in the Father's presence; as for you, you should do what you have heard from the Father.'

When the Jews stubbornly repeat the assertion that they have Abraham as their father, Jesus replies by showing that if they were really Abraham's children they would be doing what Abraham did. 'But now you are trying to kill me, a man who has told you the truth that I heard from God. This is not what Abraham did. You are indeed doing what your father does.'

What Jesus says here provokes a—to our ears—quite unexpected and inexplicable reaction. The Jews reply with the words: 'We are not illegitimate children; we have one father, God himself.' This gives the immediate impression that they are talking at cross purposes, for what connection is there between the accusation of wishing to attack Jesus and the rejection that they are illegitimate children?

22. N.A. Dahl, 'Der erstgeborene Satans und der Vater des Teufels (Polyk. 7.1 und Joh 8.44)', in Walther Eltester (ed.), *Apophoreta, Festschrift für Ernst Haenchen zu seinem siebzigsten Geburtstag am 10. Dezember 1964* ('Satan's First-born and the Devil's Father [Polyk. 7.1 and John 8.44]', in Walther Eltester (ed.), *Apophereta, Festschrift for Ernst Haenchen on his seventieth birthday on 10 December 1964*) (Berlin: Töpelmann, 1964), pp. 70-84.

Like Alstrup Dahl, one must bring in here the two parties' common preconception. The Jews' assertion that they are Abraham's children is contradicted, according to Jesus, by the fact that they do not act as Abraham did. Their actions bear witness against them, and therefore their father must be a murderer. As we know, Abraham was no murderer; but someone else was, that is, the first murderer referred to in the Bible, the fratricide Cain.

Not a word is said about Cain in the text. But that Jesus has Cain in mind and that the Jews understand his taunt is apparent from their answer. They are well aware that Jesus accuses them indirectly of having not only Cain as a forefather but also Satan himself. And why is this so?

Nils Alstrup Dahl in his article shows that part of the Jewish tradition is that Cain and Abel have different fathers: Satan and God respectively. Cain is not only Eve's first-born but also Satan's. Gen. 4.1 tells of the birth of Cain. The wording itself creates difficulties. Most people try to translate the passage as meaning, 'With God's help I have begotten a son'. But in fact it reads that Eve has begotten a man by God or through God, or that she has had Yahweh himself as a husband. According to Alstrup Dahl, the rabbinic scholars interpreted Eve's words to mean that Eve believes it is the angel of God who has on God's behalf made her pregnant. But on this occasion also, says tradition, Eve has been deceived, for this angel was of course none other than the devil himself, who shortly before had seduced her in the form of a serpent.

In regard to this reconstruction, Alstrup Dahl refers to the Palestinian Targum and Pirqe Rabbi Eliezer. The Talmud, however, does not mention this tradition. Similar ideas are to be found among the gnostics, since the following is to be read in the apocryphal Gospel according to Philip: 'First adultery came into being, afterwards murder. And he was begotten in adultery, for he was the child of the serpent. So he became a murderer, just like his father.'[23]

A parallel to this tradition is also to be found in another apocryphal gospel, the Protevangelium of James, according to which Joseph feared that history had repeated itself, so that it fared for him as it did for Adam when Mary became pregnant; the Protevangelium of Jas 13.1. And if we

---

23. H.W. Bartsch (ed.), *Koptisch-gnostische Schriften übersetzt von (Lei-poldt-)Schenke* (Coptic-gnostic texts translated by ...) (*TF*, 20; Hamburg: Herbert Reich Evangelischer Verlag, 1960). Cf. in particular p. 109.5 = Spr. 42 concerning the quotation from the Gospel according to Philip. Cf. the English rendering of the passage, *The Nag Hammadi Library in English* (ed. J.M. Robinson; Leiden: E.J. Brill, 3rd edn, 1988), p. 146 (NH CII 61, 5-10).

wish to follow the tradition in the Jewish context, Ginzberg can also contribute here with Jewish legendary material.[24]

In the light of this the dialogue between Jesus and the Jews is far easier to understand. Jesus thus accuses them not only of being descended from the first murderer, Cain, but also of being begotten in adultery by Satan himself. They must therefore retort with the words that they are not illegitimate children but in fact have God as their father. It is evident that the discussion continues along these lines. It says directly: 'You are from your father the devil, and you choose to do your father's desires. He was a murderer from the beginning and does not stand in the truth, because there is no truth in him' (Jn 8.44).

As regards these Cain traditions, the First Letter of Jn 3.12 may also be referred to, where the reader is warned against being like Cain, 'who was from the evil one and murdered his brother.' One senses in this letter from 'the apostle of love' the clear contrast between the Gospel's demand that one should love one's brother and Cain's murderous example.

But this idea also does not stand alone. For example, there was a group of gnostics which referred to themselves as Cainites. According to their teaching, they originate from a power stronger than Abel. This, Alstrup Dahl asserts, must be based upon a special rendition of the rabbinic interpretation of the story of Cain. Perhaps the background is that a group of marginal Jews were at some time accused of being of Cain's lineage, adopted the accusation as a title of honour, and tried to rehabilitate Cain.

Alstrup Dahl can also add that Markion in particular valued Cain. Markion thus teaches that when the Lord descended to the kingdom of the dead he rescued Cain and his like, whereas Abel, Abraham and all the favourites of the Jewish God of Creation had no part in the redemption. Perhaps Markion's sympathy for Cain is in fact because he himself had been marked as a heretic by Polykarp, and designated 'Satan's firstborn'.

These Cain and Abel traditions must therefore be included when dealing with texts whose leading principle is the father-son motif; but here in the form in which the motif is two fathers with two sons, one of whom is envious of the other and kills him. The envy arises because 'the father of the younger', Yahweh, prefers the offering of the younger and rejects the offering of the son of Satan, the older.

In interpreting the story of Cain, the Jewish tradition thus wished for a more dualistic model than the Old Testament narrative of one father with

24. L. Ginzberg, *The Legends of the Jews I* (Philadelphia: The Jewish Publication Society of America, 5728-1968). Cf. in particular pp. 105-107.

two sons. If the fathers are different, the sons also can differ profoundly. This is the model upon which the Gospel according to John continues to rely— not the Genesis version. It is perhaps not surprising, therefore, that in fact the author of the Gospel according to John chooses a family image of a more dualistic form.

If we are to try to gain an impression of who in Jesus' words are the devil's children, or—to express it directly—represent Satan himself, there are indeed in this text according to John some Jews who despite having come to believe in Jesus had designs on his life, and did not want the servant relationship he offered. When we read in the Gospel according to Matthew of those who may be considered as belonging to Satan we see that Jesus' own disciple Peter was called Satan when he wished to prevent Jesus from subjecting himself to humiliation, suffering and death in obedience to the father (the obedience Satan tested in the wilderness). For Peter, the way was much preferably that of the Old Testament, the triumphal procession after the defeat of the enemy, the way Satan in fact offered (Mt. 16.21-23). The traditions that Satan entered into Judas, when in his treachery he was about to help in carrying out God's plan of redemption (Lk. 22.3 and Jn 13.2, 27), perhaps also belong here.

It is therefore in the New Testament that, side by side with the traditions of Satan as the demonic adversary against whom Jesus struggles when he heals the sick and the possessed, there are passages in which Satan represents generally accepted values such as observance of the law and of the way to victory then expected for the kingdom of God: the way of power and not of suffering. The Satan image is thus not as unambiguous as we normally make it out to be. Satan is not necessarily depicted in the image of an adversary; Satan may also be compared to a jealous older brother who insists on justice and equity, or to a well-meaning disciple who pays no regard to what is God's will.

The survey has thus demonstrated that the New Testament can speak of the Jews as the children of Satan himself. It has also shown that the redactional interpretation of the parable as an intervention against the Pharisees, who behave like the older brother Satan and do not understand the father's love of the younger son and thus of the sinners with whom he surrounds himself, is a proper extension of this. And finally we have amplified the Satan image to be found in the New Testament. Satan is not necessarily depicted clearly as an adversary, so that it cannot be said out-of-hand that it is he we must renounce. It is rather that the Satan image has several features which make it natural to identify him particularly with the older brother in the drama.

## The Parable as the Story of the Heavenly Father's Boundless Love?

In analysing the parable, we have seen that the image of the two sons astonishes time after time. Characteristics which do not correspond to the traditional image of Jesus are here indeed associated with the younger son, and characteristics which we would not expect in Satan are those of the elder brother. But nevertheless what is most astonishing is the father's love for *both* his sons.

Love's boundlessness is and remains the true message of the parable. But this very elasticity of the father has always been a stumbling-block, both for those who are outraged by the unconditional love of the 'prodigal' younger son and for those who are outraged by the 'righteous' elder brother's failure to rejoice. As we know, elasticity is a poor starting point for creating a strong community. The clear boundaries which mark a 'within' and an 'outside' are far more alluring.

It is therefore difficult for us to render the parable in a way that takes both sons seriously. It is usually easier to give an accentuated account of the father's love for the younger brother, or to concentrate on the effort to induce the elder son to join in the festivities. But this distorts the narrative's original meaning: There was a father who had two sons, and whatever may have then occurred he could be a father only if both his sons were with him and rejoiced with him.

So is it with the heavenly father when, as the Gospel according to Luke recounts, he causes one of his sons to be born in a humble stable in Bethlehem, whereas the other son is entrusted with all the power and the glory of the kingdoms of the world. Luke also causes the two sons to meet in the wilderness after Jesus' baptism. Luke also causes the devil to leave Jesus without interference from the father. But then he adds: 'When the Devil had finished every test, he departed from him until an opportune time' (Lk. 4.13).

If we continue to read the chapter, we note that the question of Jesus' identity remains the central subject, and that those present in the synagogue at Nazareth, who must ask in wonder: 'Is not this Joseph's son?', had not understood Jesus' son-relationship (Lk. 4.22). The unclean spirit whom Jesus expels shortly afterwards knew his true identity far better: 'Let us alone, Jesus of Nazareth! Have you come to destroy us? I know who you are, the Holy One of God' (Lk. 4.34). And the demons express themselves even more precisely when they come out of the possessed shouting: 'You are the Son of God!' (Lk. 4.41).

But where in the temptation narrative we meet the devil juxtaposed with Jesus as the Lord of this world and thus also one of God's sons, we observe in the context of the traditions relating to the driving out of demons an imagery in which the contrast between Jesus and the powers the demons represent becomes clear. These are the very powers which know intuitively who Jesus is, because they are in league with the brother who tested Jesus and saw what was in his heart: the obedient son's full love for the father.

In the context of the studies of the family image, it is important to assert that this is not the only image that covers the relationship between the good and evil powers of existence. If we only had the image of the father with his two sons we might be led to believe that the father's love obliterated any difference between the two. But this is clearly not the case. They have the same father, but the two brothers are utterly different. This is indeed why they are two and not one. Compared with the Gospel narratives concerning, for example, God's actions to heal and relieve the sick and the possessed, which play a very crucial role among the synoptists, it becomes clear that the New Testament does not obliterate the differences. It is and remains the difference between a blessed life and an accursed life.

The Gospel according to John's statement about light and darkness also maintains the difference, and in 1 John 3 the boundary is drawn with particular clarity. On the one side are the children of God, who are of God and therefore do not sin. On the other side are the devil's children, those who sin. But for this very reason the son of God was revealed 'to destroy the works of the devil' (1 Jn 3.8). And in Revelation's visions also we encounter this insistence on the contrast between good and evil, the lamb and the great dragon.

But as opposed to these thought-models with their clear division into positive and negative, God's world and Satan's world, the narratives of the father with the sons present themselves as a fundamental part of biblical tradition. In this universe of tales, the world drama is played out between three persons, all bound to one another in a love that hurts. For envy emanates from love and leads to rivalry and malice, and love generates the suffering that the father must experience when he sees the evil consequences of love.

Therefore, not only the image of the loving father belongs to the narrative complex of the father and his two sons but also the image of the suffering father. It is so natural in Christian theology to speak of the son's suffering that in our Western tradition we seldom speak of the father's suffering. But the image in itself also includes this aspect: the deep suffering over the evil consequences of love.

What can we read from our image analyses is mainly the following: when a father has sons, painful situations arise which normally require judgment and punishment. But when the father is God himself the sons feel that, time after time, the proceedings become a mock trial. The case is stayed before it reaches a final decision or, as is recounted in the New Testament, the case is decided to the advantage of the accused in a different way by another person taking the place of the accused.

That such thoughts are also to be found in modern Christian theology may be illustrated by the following poem by Kurt Marti,[25] where the images have been taken from the 'Big Brother' society we imagine in our worst nightmares, and where the lawsuit never in fact gets off the ground because the accusations anticipated turn out never to have been recorded.

### When The Books Are Opened Up

When
the books are opened up

when it transpires
that they were never kept:

neither registers of ideas nor catalogues of sins
neither microfilms nor computer files

when
the books are opened up

then see: on page one
    'Did you take me for a copper?'
then see: on page two
    'Big Brother—it was your invention'
then see: on page three
    'your sins were not too great—
    your joy was too small'

when
the books are opened up.

'Your joy was too small' reads the poem. 'Son, you are always with me, and all that is mine is yours. But we had to celebrate and rejoice, because this brother of yours was dead but has come to life; he was lost and has been found', says the father in the parable of the two sons.

25. G. Heinz-Mohr, *Plädoyer für den Hymnus* (Speech in Defence of the Hymn) (Kassel: Johannes Stauda, 1981), p. 234.

Chapter 8

VARIATIONS ON THE THEME: THE SON OF GOD

*The Fall among the Sons of God, Genesis 6.1-4, and its Reuse*
*in the Old Testament Pseudepigrapha*

How can one speak of evil in relation to good, of Satan in relation to God? This is the question which lies behind this book's investigation of the image of a father and his sons. I have so far observed in particular the emphasis on the nearness between the father and the sons. But the distance is also part of the image. The two generations are not inseparable. I shall therefore examine below a few examples of how the distance can be brought into line. A well-known means of achieving this is the travel motif.

At the beginning father and son are together, but at a certain time their paths separate. This may occur by mutual agreement and amicably, but the son's departure may also be in the nature of a rupture with the father. The biblical traditions have many stories about sons who leave home, but very few are concerned with sons of God who leave their father and thus leave the heavenly in favour of the earthly.

We encountered Satan in the Book of Job as the son of God who for some time roamed the earth. Here he observed Job's progress and happiness, and then he returned to his father. He lived among the other sons of God, close to his father. There is nothing to indicate that he was denied this position after he had tested Job, neither was there a revolt against his father or any fall from the heavenly to the earthly.

Only in the later Jewish legends concerning Job do we encounter the idea that Satan is banished from heaven. Ginzberg[1] thus refers to a legend which tells of Satan's trying in many different ways to pester Job out of his wits. But Satan does not succeed in causing him to defect. Rather, in

1. L. Ginzberg, *The Legends of the Jews II* (Philadelphia: The Jewish Publication Society of America, 5730–1969). Cf. in particular pp. 239-42.

his suffering and pain, Job holds fast to his piety and thanks God for all he has done for him. And the narrative ends with the Lord deciding to cast Satan out of heaven.

The temptation narrative in the Gospel according to Matthew does not tell us directly that Satan has left heaven, but his presence on earth is apparently fully in accordance with the father's will. For quite simply all power on earth has been given to him, and he is now where his father wishes him to be. The narrative does not give the impression that after this assignment Satan returns home to the father; rather, he is in a wait-ing-mode on earth, leaving it to the angels to serve Jesus. Whereas Matthew is silent on this point, Luke indicates the waiting aspect of Satan's role: 'When the Devil had finished every test, he departed from him for an opportune time' (Lk. 4.13). This is not the last time the two sons of God meet.

Finally we must mention the Gospel according to Luke's parable of the father and the two sons, in which one of the sons goes abroad. Recent research stresses the normality of the younger son's journey. The father has himself distributed the inheritance, as one did when the youngest wished to make his own way abroad. The departure is not an expression of rebellion but rather of practical necessity. But what distinguishes the narrative is not the journey abroad but the return home to the father. This son makes a twofold move, and the parable is in no doubt that where the father is there should the son be also.

Whereas the Bible texts referred to present a harmonious relationship in the context of the son's journey, other traditions say that the departure results from a revolt in heaven, and that it is more of a banishment or a fall. We have referred briefly to the legend of the banishment of Satan following the testing of Job, and we might likewise have referred to the traditions in the *Life of Adam and Eve*, which also tells of Satan's fall from heaven (cf. pp. 107-109).

We shall examine below the various traditions about the sons of God who descend to the earth and marry the daughters of men. We shall begin with the Old Testament tradition, and examine how this regards the presence on earth of the sons of God. Do they leave home of their own free will and following agreement with the father, or does it result from a breach with the father? And in extension of this: Is it a positive or negative outcome that sons of God and daughters of men become so close that a conjugal relationship arises in which a son leaves his father and keeps to his wife so that the two become one flesh?

*Genesis 6.1-4*

The narrative is very short. It follows immediately after the genealogical table in ch. 5, which lists Adam's descendants through his son Seth up to the time when Noah becomes father to Shem, Ham and Japheth. After this information, ch. 6 begins its story.

We are told that people have begun to multiply on earth. Daughters are born to them, and the sons of God see that they are fair. The sons of God now take the women they desire, enter into them and have children by them. Then follows a saying of Yahweh (v. 3). Yahweh reacts to the event by announcing that from now on his spirit would not abide in mortals for ever; for they are flesh; their days shall be 120 years.

Verse 4 also reads that at the time when the sons of God went into the women there were giants on earth. This information must be understood as a specific definition of the common progeny. No ordinary people or ordinary sons of God stem from sons of God and daughters of men, but intermediate beings of special size and strength. That there were also giants later on is added as a matter of fact. And a final item of information tells us that these are the great heroes of old.

Despite its limited extent, the story is very complex. The first two verses, which recount briefly and concisely the marriages of the sons of God, reflect a popular narrative accounting for a strange phenomenon of existence, namely the giants and heroes we are told about in v. 4. The Bible's early chapters are filled with such aetiologies basing subsequent phenomena on events at the beginning of time. A great many things have caused surprise: Why does the snake have no legs? Why does it eat dust? Why does the woman desire her husband? And why is it he who rules over her? And the answer is given in the form of a narrative about events at the beginning of time. The mixed marriages are thus intended to explain that there were once giants and heroes of great repute on the earth.

In popular tradition the explanation has been brief and concise. It was because they had not only a mother who was a woman but also a father who was a son of God. This is how it was, for everything has a natural explanation!

But such straightforward explanations do not stand up in the long run. Theological speculation begins, and the marriage between heaven and earth becomes open to question. The mixture of the heavenly and the human conflicts with belief in Yahweh and must therefore invoke God's punishment on mankind, as it did when Adam and Eve dwelt in the Garden of Eden and tried to become like God. And what else is mankind trying to achieve by cohabitation with the sons of God? The God-given distance was not to their liking; they had to try again to overstep the boundary between the heavenly and the human in order to become like God. But again this will not succeed. Their days must be numbered.

For this reason the editor must supplement the narrative by v. 3, which expresses God's punishment of mankind and at the same time explains that mortals' days are numbered. For this also has been a question which calls for explanation. Why do we live for such a short time compared with the great ones of the past?

But in its biblical context the narrative is not presented merely to answer such questions. It is placed just before the story of the Flood, and is thus given a further function. The editorial process concerned with the location of Gen. 6.1-4 is complicated.[2] We must assume that there was an earlier version of the protohistory which included neither the genealogical table nor the marriage story. At that time the Flood followed directly after the Cain and Abel story, probably so that Lemech's song of revenge, which ends at 4.24, was a fitting prelude to establishing in 6.5-6 that the increasing evil of mankind on earth caused God to regret his creation.

But at some time the connection between the song of revenge and the Flood narrative was broken. An editor added the genealogical table (ch. 5), to give the—in his eyes important and necessary—information about Adam's lineage through the pious Seth, Noah's progenitor. But a problem arises here. The people of the genealogical table are indeed devout persons who live a life pleasing to God, and who are accordingly given long life and progeny. Indeed one of them, Enoch, is even gathered up directly to God without having died. How then is the increasing evil, which is the reason for the Flood, to be explained? It is not enough that we have already heard of Cain and Abel; another narrative must be included which retains the theology of the Fall story and the fratricide.

Some believe that the editor has at this point chosen to add the story of the marriage of the sons of God to the daughters of men because he has interpreted the sons of God as Seth's descendants and the daughters of men as Cain's kin. Perceiving the connection between the three chapters (Gen. 4–6) in this way makes it possible to uphold God's justice when he wipes out most of mankind (Cain's kin) as well as when he saves Noah's family (Seth's kin).

We do not know whether this is in fact the reason. It is more important

2. Cf. as regards the text's genesis, J. Scharbert, 'Traditions- und Redaktionsgeschichte von Gen 6.1-4' (Traditional and Editorial History of Gen. 6.1-4), *BZ* 11 (1967), pp. 66-78.

to note the editor's wording of the story of the mixed marriages. He was not in fact content with the popular aetiology; he has created a story which gives a theological interpretation of the connection between heaven and earth. He has transformed the old aetiology into a Fall narrative, telling of man's attempt to become like God. These mixed marriages evoke God's wrath and punishment; not in relation to the sons of God, who took the initiative, but in relation to the human race as a whole.

In the light of the paradigm of the father and his sons, we can say that in both the theologically-worded narrative and the popular aetiology the sons' departure is treated as presenting no problem. It is the sons' own independent decision; they have not been thrown out of their home, and we are not told that the father protested at their leaving home. But the journey of the sons of God to the earth has evil consequences for mankind.

The editor wishes us to read his version of the marriages of the sons of God as a story concerned with the fall of mankind; not the fall of the sons of God. The meaning is quite clear, although one cannot accuse him of producing an elegant text; rather the contrary. On the other hand, the form of the text makes it clear that we are concerned with re-edited traditions of various origins. And if, glancing at other narratives of a similar nature, we were to ponder on how some of the material the editor has worked up may have looked it might be appropriate to comment as follows.

At the editor's time there were various versions of the theme of a god who chooses his wife from among mankind. By choosing a woman and not a goddess the god identifies himself with mankind and gives them a share in the heavenly. We shall consider a little later whether ideas about such a distribution of heavenly gifts to mankind is within the editor's horizon when we look at the similar narrative in the Book of *Enoch*. For the time being we wish merely to establish that the editor of the Old Testament version had no desire to expand on that part of the narrative which concerns the sons of God and any good intentions they may have had to share their lives with the daughters of mankind. The editor has not created an Old Testament Promethean myth. He does not even say that Yahweh became angry at the descent to earth of these sons of God, for which he had to punish them. To put it no higher, the editor is very sparing of words where heavenly beings are concerned. And why is this so? Let us first look at the parallel text in the First Book of *Enoch*.

*The Version in* 1 Enoch

In genre terms, *1 Enoch* must be defined as an apocalypse.[3] The text is attributed to Enoch, well known from Genesis 5, who because of his piety was taken directly by God. In the light of this it has followed that Enoch is considered as possessing secret knowledge, for what has he not seen and come to understand during his ecstasy? And from this it is no distance to the tradition that he returned and revealed to mankind what he had learned. It is a well-known feature of these books of revelations that the great of the past undertook special heavenly journeys, when the eternal secrets were revealed to them.

What Enoch recounts is referred to as a parable (*1 En.* 1.2). The first chapter speaks of the coming of God to redeem and to judge. The ungodly must be destroyed, but God provides peace for the righteous. But who are the righteous and who are the ungodly? The listeners are clearly not to identify themselves with the righteous too speedily; on the contrary, they are told that they have not followed God's commandments. And this is followed rather abruptly by a repetition of the story of the sons of God who perceived the beauty of the daughters of men and took of them as many as they desired and begot children by them (*1 En.* 6.1-8).

In the *Enoch* version, the sons of God are called angels or children of heaven. One senses the fear of using God's name of olden times; it is paraphrased as 'heaven'. When these angels saw the beautiful and graceful daughters of men they said to one another: 'Come, let us choose wives for ourselves from among the daughters of man and beget us children' (*1 En.* 6.2). The decision takes the form of a conspiracy, in which they enter into a mutual obligation under the leadership of Semyaz. Their leader is well aware that their plan is contrary to God's will. He therefore wishes them to undertake a mutual obligation, so that the others do not suddenly abandon the plan and leave him on his own, and 'I alone will become responsible for this great sin'. Then all 200 angels take an oath to stand together as concerns responsibility, and they descend to the summit of Mount Hermon, divided into units of ten, each with its leader, as if they were about to embark on a campaign of war.

Each of them now took a wife, went to her, had intercourse with her and taught her magic charms and incantations. And the women gave birth to the giants which were three thousand cubits high and so hungry that

3. As regards the pseudepigraphic texts, reference is made to J.H. Charlesworth (ed.), *The Old Testament Pseudepigrapha*. I. *Apocalyptic Literature and Testaments* (London: Darton, Longman & Todd, 1983).

they consumed everything the people had laboriously gathered together, so that ultimately the people did not have enough food for them (*1 En.* 7.3).

We also learn that the giants turn against the people themselves, in order to eat them. They then lay violent hand on the animal world; indeed, they even consume each other's flesh and blood. 'Then the earth brought an accusation against the oppressors' (*1 En.* 7.6). But Azazel, one of the angels named, teaches the people to forge swords and shields and to make bracelets and jewellery, to use eye make-up and to embellish the eyebrows; he shows them the most costly of all gems and all kinds of dyes. The other angels also take part in the education of the people. And of this wisdom came nothing but undoing (*1 En.* 8).

From heaven the archangels Michael, Uriel, Raphael and Gabriel see much blood being shed and all the injustice on the earth, and they go to God himself and tell him about the condition of the earth. Then the supreme God sends Uriel to Noah, and Uriel reveals to him that the earth will be destroyed by a flood. But God orders Raphael to bind Azazel hand and foot and throw him into the darkness, and to open the desert and throw him into it (*1 En.* 10.4). '... and throw on top of him rugged and sharp rocks, and cover him with darkness and there he shall live for ever, and cover his face so that he cannot see the light; and on the great day of judgment he shall be sent into the fire. And heal the world which the angels corrupted' (*1 En.* 10.5-7).

The narrative's sequence of events is simple. First the angels rebel against their father by leaving heaven and settling on earth with the daughters of men. Then they are banished to that part of the earth where desert and darkness prevail. And finally, on the day of judgment, they shall be destroyed. For the time being, therefore, they live in the desert regions of the earth or, according to *2 En.* 7.5-10, below the earth.

If we now compare the story in the *1 Enoch* with Gen. 6.1-4 there are clear differences. In the Old Testament story the author is concerned only with the punishment of mankind. It is the life of mankind which is restricted; not that of the sons of God. Also, we hear nothing of their having conspired and rebelled against the supreme God. In *1 Enoch*, both the angels and mankind are punished for the evil the angels have introduced into the world. The Old Testament text refers to the sons of God only in passing, and we are given only a somewhat imprecise rendering of the connection between them and the giants and heroes who were living at the same time. The Book of *Enoch* describes them in detail, however, and knows their names, names which are identified with Satan in other contexts;

and it is said directly that the giants are the children of these mixed marriages.

It should be added that whereas the *1 Enoch* version speaks copiously of what the connection between the heavenly and the human involves by way of new knowledge for mankind, this is toned down in the Old Testament tradition. We hear nothing, therefore, of the secret magic charms and incantations that, according to Enoch, the people take part in via the agency of the sons of God. Enoch gained access to special knowledge about heavenly matters during his journey to heaven. And his contemporaries must now be aware that the evil they encounter in everyday life arises because of these sons of God and their fall, for it was through this fall of angels that demons and satans came into existence.

Scholars do not agree on the Old Testament version's chronological relationship to the *1 Enoch* version. The whole question of the age of these texts has indeed been energetically debated in recent years. There was formerly no doubt that Genesis 6 was by far the oldest text; but since then several scholars have argued that the Old Testament editor was aware of the oldest edition of the narrative which is now to be found in *1 Enoch* 6–8, and that this very text was his model.[4]

The Jews came to know of these traditions during the Babylonian exile, but as we can see from other passages in Genesis 1–11 the editors took care to remove, or at least to amend, those features which conflicted directly with their own theology. The narratives themselves cannot be suppressed; what editing has done is to put them where they belong.

It is important, then, that the contexts in which the two versions are to be found differ. Whereas Gen. 6.1-4 is to be found as one of the four stories about *mankind's* overstepping of the boundaries established—the Fall, the fratricide, the marriages to the sons of God and the building of the Tower of Babel—the story about the sons of God in *1 Enoch* is the only one about a fall. It is also, therefore, the only story to substantiate that the creator chose to send the Flood.

Enoch locates his narrative immediately after a description of how

4. I base this primarily on Ida Kinga Fröhlich's lecture, 'Fallen Angels: Forms, Meanings and Functions of a Story in Jewish Literary Tradition (Persian and Hellenistic Ages)' given to the meeting of the Society of Biblical Literature in Vienna, 1990. Fröhlich bases her opinion on, *inter alia*, J. Milik, *The Books of Enoch: Aramaic Fragments of Qumrân Cave 4* (Oxford: Clarendon Press, 1976) and J.C. VanderKam, *Enoch and the Growth of an Apocalyptic Tradition* (CBQMS, 16; Washington: Catholic Biblical Association, 1984).

appropriately the created world is arranged and is still sustained by God. The angel-marriages are thus given the same function as the Fall in the Old Testament: to tell of the first fall and its evil consequences. But whereas the Old Testament tradition lays the blame for the Fall on disobedient mankind, *1 Enoch* tells that evil is in fact caused by these sons of God; that is, evil originates from the heavenly world.

The story of the sons of God in Genesis has been partly adapted to the theology of the Fall story, but it has not become a story about the origin of evil. Evil had already entered the world through the Fall of Adam and Eve.

Our point of reference is the image of a father and his sons, and the various traditions about how the son or sons came to leave the father. From this perspective, we may perhaps go so far as to say that the stories about the mixed marriages express the nearness between God and man by the fact that the sons of God chose voluntarily to leave their father to share their lives with humans, or in other words—and more directly—the marriage story is concerned with incarnation, but of course an incarnation that brings evil.

Both the Old Testament and *1 Enoch* distance themselves from this becoming close to people in the flesh. The sons should not have left their father and married the women; they should have stayed where they belonged. Surprisingly, this voice is at its most subdued in the Old Testament, where the sons of God are subjected to no form of punishment; but the subdued voice has a purpose. The editor wishes to ensure that the marriage story does not become the basic narrative of the relationship to evil. The less said the better about the share of the sons of God in the spread of evil in the world, for evil entered the world through man's infringement of God's commandments. According to the Old Testament the Fall occurred in the human world; not in the heavenly world.

### The Version in the Book of Jubilees
If we glance at the Book of *Jubilees*, we find there the same narrative about marriages between the angels—here referred to as the Watchers—and the daughters of humans. But what is special about the Book of *Jubilees* is that it shows them travelling down to earth several times. In the days of Jared, 'the angels of the Lord, who were called Watchers, came down to the earth in order to teach the sons of man, and perform judgment and uprightness upon the earth' (*Jub*. 4.15). Just before the Flood they appear a second time, now in order to enter into marriage with the daughters of humans (*Jub*. 5.1-5). This occurs for the third time after the

Flood, and here the purpose is to lead Noah's descendants astray. It is therefore at that time that the Watchers' own progeny, the unclean spirits, take over the scene (*Jub.* 10.1-17).

The Book of *Jubilees* was written in the second century BCE. Its author clearly uses the Genesis version as a basis, but he supplements this with passages which show that he was aware of the *1 Enoch* version. As in the Old Testament, he uses the story of the angel-marriages to form a link in a chain of narratives about mankind's overstepping its boundaries. And as in *First Enoch* the author of the Book of *Jubilees* puts great emphasis on the punishment of the angels. No one is left in any doubt that they have committed an offence and evoked God's wrath.

From a theological aspect, however, there is a change compared with the two precursors. In the Book of *Jubilees*, we learn that the marriages between the Watchers and the women led to the emergence of demons, or the unclean spirits that create the many evils under which one suffers daily, such as temptation and sickness. These unclean spirits constitute a whole army which ravages and practises evil on the earth, created as they are to corrupt (*Jub.* 10.5). After the Flood God's angels had in fact been ordered to bind them all, but their prince Mastema (the name for Satan in the Book of *Jubilees*) came to God and said: 'O Lord, Creator, leave some of them before me, and let them obey my voice. And let them do everything which I tell them, because if some of them are not left for me, I will not be able to exercise the authority of my will among the children of men because they are (intended) to corrupt and lead astray before my judgment because the evil of the sons of men is great' (*Jub.* 10.8).

Faced with this entreaty, the Lord decides to hand over to Mastema one-tenth of the evil spirits, which are to serve him until the final judgment arrives, when Mastema himself must be judged.

But what is curious is that it is the very same Watchers who in Jared's day taught mankind about righteousness, so that mankind might know the Law and thereby overcome the evil that begets the unclean spirits. The good, the Law and knowledge of the Law were indeed in the world before evil arrived; good thus has priority over evil; but it is also said that good and evil originate from the heavenly world!

The author thereby sets the scene for a dualistic view of life in which good forces and evil forces confront one another, and man must choose between the two. But he does this in such a way that one can still sense the connection back to the same father in heaven whose sons descended from the heavenly to share life with man.

The dualistic features of the Book of *Jubilees* may be one reason for the popularity of this very text within the Qumran community. For if we wished to go further into these dualistic features the natural place to turn towards would indeed be the Qumran texts.[5] It is not the nearness that is emphasized here but the distance between good and evil, and the basic metaphors here are not taken from family intercourse between a father and his sons but from war and strife.

Several passages give too close a connection with the earthly as the reason for the banishment of the sons of God from the heavenly. The sons of God came too close to man, and are therefore distanced completely from the heavenly. But another reason for the banishment is also represented: One of the sons of God tried to come too close to God.

As we saw earlier, the *Life of Adam and Eve* tells that when Michael threatened Satan with God's wrath unless he worshipped Adam Satan replied: 'If he be wrathful with me, I will set my throne above the stars of heaven and will be like the Most High' (ch. 15). It also tells in *2 Enoch* 29 that one of the archangels, Satanail, wished to set his throne higher than the clouds and to be like God in power. In this version, the rejection does not consist in his being cast down to earth, perhaps out into the desert, or in his banishment to a place below the earth. With a great sense of the dramatic, it describes how this archangel, as punishment for his pride, is to fly around in the air eternally above the bottomless pit!

According to another pseudepigraphic text, the *Apocalypse of Moses*, ch. 39, what will happen is not only that Satan will lose his throne but that Adam will take it over, to the great sorrow of Satan and his associates. The same tradition is also implied in the *Life of Adam and Eve*, ch. 47, where it tells that Adam is surrendered into the care of the archangel Michael until the day of reckoning, when God will turn Adam's sorrow into gladness. And 'then he shall sit on the throne of him who overthrew him'.

If, finally, we look at the New Testament's attitude towards the tradition of the angel-marriages, the best source is the Letter of Jude. The author addresses the community to warn against false teachers who 'deny our only Master and Lord, Jesus Christ'. As part of his warning against these ungodly people, the author reminds us that in the past also God has dealt harshly with those who did not believe. One example is 'the angels who

5. Cf., e.g., the War Scroll which describes the battle between the sons of light and of darkness, and the Rule of Community which in Section III.17–IV.18 presents the doctrine of the two spirits, the spirits of light and darkness, which are followed by the just and unjust consequences respectively.

did not take care of their high office but left their proper abode'. God keeps these people bound in darkness in eternal chains until the great day of judgment! Another example is the fate of Sodom and Gomorrah. Here also fornication and unnatural liaisons led to their suffering God's wrathful punishment.

In this version of the angel-marriages the angels who leave their proper abode are the guilty ones, but they are given the function of deterrents to mankind. The fall of the heavenly is not given an independent role as an explanation of the origin of evil. What the author has in mind is the community's redemption, and thus man's relationship with God. The community must fight against the disbelief which has stolen in, and it must therefore be aware that as God punished the ungodly time and again in the past, whether man or angels, so also will God pronounce judgment today.

### The Apocalypse of Sedrach's Description of the Fall

One of the many apocalypses from Christian times, the *Apocalypse of Sedrach*,[6] also tells of the coming into the world of the sons of God. This apocalypse deals with themes we know of from, *inter alia,* the Book of Job and *4 Ezra*, and it can be defined as a theodicy, a defence of God's justice. It is not known when it was written, but it is prudently placed in the second to fifth centuries CE. However, there is general agreement that the work contains far older Jewish traditions. In its present form it is the subject of Christian revision. This is most clearly to be seen in the introductory hymn to love, which the editor has set at the beginning in order to give his interpretation of God's relationship with man. This location of the hymn probably did not take place until the Middle Ages, but it was important to the Christian editor to stress that it was love which

6. O. Wahl (ed.), *Apocalypsis Esdrae, Apocalypsis Sedrach, Visio Beati Esdrae* (Leiden: E.J. Brill, 1977). The text is in Greek here. A German translation is to be found in P. Riessler, *Altjüdisches Schrifttum ausserhalb der Bibel* (Old Jewish Literature apart from the Bible) (Darmstadt: Wissenschaftliche Buchgesellschaft, 1966 [1928]), pp. 156-67. Cf. also Charlesworth (ed.), *The Old Testament Pseudepigrapha*, pp. 605-13. The *Apocalypse of Sedrach* is in an English translation here, with an introduction by S. Agourides. Cf. also my analysis of the text in 'If You Loved Man, Why Did You Not Kill the Devil?', in K. Jeppesen, K. Nielsen and B. Rosendal (eds.), *In the Last Days: On Jewish and Christian Apocalyptic and its Period* (Festschrift B. Otzen; Aarhus: Aarhus University Press, 1994), pp. 54-59.

brought the son of God down from heaven, 'for, as the Master said, nothing is greater than love for which a man lays down (his) life for his friends' (*Apoc. Sedr.* 1.25; cf. also Jn 15.13).

The father's love brings the son from heaven to earth, says this Christian hymn. But the *Apocalypse of Sedrach* knows more about sons of God than the hymn recounts. The text continues, somewhat abruptly, with a dialogue between Sedrach and God. Like Job, Sedrach wishes to speak to God, and he is therefore led to the third heaven by an angel. It is not God who bends down to man on earth but man who sets out on a journey to heaven to gain an understanding of the eternal secrets. Sedrach is clearly welcome in heaven. God receives him warmly, calling him 'my dear Sedrach' and asking him to say what complaint he has against his creator? Sedrach replies that he certainly wishes to complain about his father as a son should do, because 'My Lord, what did you create the earth for?' And God answers: 'For man'. Sedrach continues: 'What did you create the sea for and why did you spread every good thing upon the earth?' The reply is again: 'For man'. — 'If you have done these things, why did you destroy man?' And God answers: 'Man is my work and the creature of my hands, and I discipline him as I find it right' (ch. 3).

The dialogue continues with a series of discussions in which Sedrach presents his doubts to God, for although God is justified in disciplining his own children his punishment is in Sedrach's opinion unreasonably harsh. Sedrach expresses this as follows: 'Your discipline is punishment and fire ... It would be better for man if he were not born'. For why did God labour with his hands to create man if God had no desire to have compassion on him? Thus says Sedrach. Job expressed it in this way: 'Why is light given to one in misery, and life to the bitter in soul?' (Job 3.20). The problem is the same for Sedrach as for Job. The main question is God's lack of compassion.

God then replies by recounting his version of the Paradise story: I created the first man, Adam, and placed him in the Garden of Eden in the midst of which is the tree of life, and I told him to eat of all the fruit, only beware of the tree of life, for if he eats from it he will surely die. But Adam nevertheless ate of the tree, because the devil deceived him (ch. 4).

Sedrach does not answer directly, but comments on God's account of Adam's fall by telling a different story. This is concerned not so much with God's first creation, Adam, as with the first among the angels, the devil. According to Sedrach, it was by God's will that Adam was deceived, since it was God who at one time commanded the angels to bend down and pay homage to Adam. But the first among the angels did not obey God's commandment (cf. the tradition in the *Life of Adam and Eve*). God then chased him away because he did not obey the commandment. And it is indeed this which makes Sedrach ask an indignant question: 'If you loved man, why did you not kill the devil, the artificer of all iniquity?'

The reasoning is clear enough, although not all its stages are presented: The devil deserved death for his disobedience, but surprisingly was spared. When God chose merely to chase the devil away from heaven he at the same time gave the devil an opportunity to torment man. Adam, however, was punished for his disobedience despite having been inveigled into it by the devil, whom no man can resist for he is so strong that he fights even with God himself, says Sedrach.

Since God is in reality responsible for the devil's tempting man, the creator's justice is indeed open to question. God should therefore stop punishing man as he does. Otherwise, where is God's mercy and compassion? And as a further argument Sedrach says that if God carries on like this he can count Sedrach among the sinners (ch. 5).

Then follows God's reply, but which of Sedrach's two questions does it answer? Sedrach has asked why God did not exterminate the devil, and why God has no compassion for man?

In Paul Riessler's German translation of the text, each chapter is given a heading to assist the reader's understanding. The heading of God's reply in Chapter 6 is 'The Fall of Adam'. Similarly, in his English rendition of the Greek text, S. Agourides clarifies the first 'he' by translating it as 'man'. But the text itself does not in fact use Adam's name; we hear only of a 'he'. And in fact we await an answer to Sedrach's question: Why didn't God do away with the devil?

God says in his reply that he ordered him to do something within his reach. 'I made him wise, and the heir of heaven and earth, and I subordinated everything under him and every living thing flees from him and from his face. Having received my gifts, however, he became an alien, an adulterer and a sinner.' In the light of this, God now asks Sedrach to answer a question. The question is worded as a parable, and reads as follows:

What sort of a father would give an inheritance to his son, who having received the money goes away leaving his father and becomes an alien and in the service of aliens. The father then, seeing that the son has forsaken him and gone away, darkens his heart and going away he retrieves his wealth and banishes his son from his glory because he forsook his father. How is it that I, the wondrous and jealous God, have given everything to him, but he, having received them, became an adulterer and a sinner?

This parable of the father and the ungrateful son who is reprimanded by his father when the father becomes angry and disowns him can be read as a text contrasting with the parable of the prodigal son. According to Eckhard Rau,[7] among all the stories known about a father whose son goes abroad this parable is the closest to Luke 15. But whom does this parable best fit—Satan or Adam?

Riessler and Agourides are here in no doubt that God argues for the equity of punishing Adam and thus man because they have forsaken their father with everything he gave them. As regards the interpretation of 'he' as Adam, it should be noted that the Adam image has in this case been given some additional features which we elsewhere associate with Satan. For example, there is nothing to indicate that according to the traditions of the time Adam was an adulterer. If one were to single out someone who fitted this predication, this is of course the devil; he who seduced Eve and became the father of Cain. And what about Adam as the wise one who inherited heaven and earth? This indeed is more representative of what is told of the first among the angels; he to whom, according to the temptation narrative in Luke, all power in this world has been given over.

In the prophet Ezekiel we encounter the idea that the king of Tyre, Israel's main adversary, can be likened to a cherub in Paradise full of wisdom and understanding but who because of his pride was cast from the mountain of God (Ezek. 28). Wisdom and fall belong together in this tradition. But as regards man Sedrach establishes in ch. 7 that his disobedience results from lack of understanding.

If 'he' is then the devil and not Adam, this means that God describes himself as a father who in righteous wrath banishes his son the devil but does not destroy him. The reason for this is not given directly but is evident from the father image, for no father can go further than to disown his own son; paternal love prohibits it!

God has thereby answered Sedrach's first question; but Sedrach is apparently not satisfied. He therefore returns to the matter of God's lack of compassion for man, and insists that God is responsible for man's fate, since neither will nor wisdom distinguishes man. God has therefore punished man wrongfully. God should instead remove 'him', that is, the devil. And if God does not do this then only Sedrach remains to fill the heavens!

7. E. Rau, *Reden in Vollmacht: Hintergrund, Form und Anliegen der Gleichnisse Jesu* (Speeches in Authority: Background, Form and Message of the Parables of Jesus) (Göttingen: Vandenhoeck & Ruprecht, 1990), p. 394.

The discussion continues in ch. 7. God now points out how radiantly he created man. I created Adam and his wife and the sun, God says. And whereas Adam and the sun were of one character the wife of Adam was brighter than the moon in beauty. But that God had created the first two people as radiant as the sun and moon does not impress Sedrach, who comments dryly that this type of beauty fades in this world, and what is it worth then? The description of Adam and Eve is brief, but we are given enough information to see the proximity between the description of the first people and the heavenly beings of light whose fall is recounted in other contexts.

We must thus again conclude that traditions about heavenly beings have been associated with traditions about the first people. Whereas the framework of the Fall narrative in Genesis 3 is clearly an earthly garden, although it is a garden of God, we nevertheless observe in the later pseudepigraphic traditions a tendency to assign to the heavenly sphere the events at the beginning of time. This is what takes place in heaven, as the elect become aware through their heavenly travels which have determined the circumstances of this world. The true reasons are not to be found on earth among mankind; they are to be found in heaven where not only does God reign but also the powers of evil have their origin.

In its final version, the *Apocalypse of Sedrach* begins with a hymn to love. The purpose of the text is to show God's love for man. For the sake of man God created the world, and for the love of man God allowed him freedom of choice. This latter point is emphasized in chs. 7–8, where Sedrach marvels that God does not hold mankind back from taking the path of sin, either by causing his angels to protect him or quite simply by grasping his foot and holding him back. And God's answer is that man's freedom also emanates from God's love for him. In his love, God does not take responsibility from mankind. Love wishes there to be freedom. But from this we readers must then draw the conclusion that the possibility also exists of being lured by Satan to take the path of sin.

The following chapters, chs. 9–16, continue this reasoning in favour of God's love. God does not wish that man should die in his sin but be converted, repent and be saved. The book then ends with Sedrach himself being taken into Paradise to live there among all the saints, after he becomes convinced of God's love for sinners. Indeed, the greatest of all is love, of which the Christian editor reminds us by way of the introductory hymn. 'The most important is that this love brought the Son of God down from heaven' (*Apoc. Sedr.* 1.20).

*Excursus: The Ebionites' Interpretation of the Relationship between Jesus and Satan*

The image of the father and his sons was forcefully repeated among a group of Judaeo-Christians, the Ebionites, who lived in the Syria-Palestine region during the early centuries of the church's history. Opinion has been divided among scholars[8] on whether the Ebionites' theology was influenced by Gnosticism. A series of exhaustive investigations has shown, however, that they certainly were not Gnostics, and that they in fact tried to combat the trend towards Gnosticism of that time. Hans Joachim Schoeps goes so far as to assert that it was the Ebionites and not the much better known Fathers of the Church who in fact led the struggle against the teaching of Marcion and Valentine, and who decisively influenced the outcome of that struggle.

The Gnostics operated on the basis of a dualistic thought-model under which the Old Testament Creator-God was responsible for the evil of the world, whereas the New Testament God was the God who wished to deliver man from the world; the Ebionites, on the contrary, upheld monism. The Ebionites did not deny the existence of evil, but unlike the Gnostics they did not wish to attribute an independent status to evil. According to their doctrine, the doctrine of antitheses, God has created everything. But God has created it twofold: heaven and earth, day and night, light and fire, sun and moon, life and death. This means that the devil also was created by God, not as an evil being but as a tool for God's justice. The God who both kills and makes alive, as it reads in one of the Ebionites' favourite passages, Deut. 32.39, needs both to punish and to show mercy. The devil also therefore is a link in God's plan, and in the long term the objective of the devil's works is good.

As opposed to the Gnostics, the Ebionites have to assert, according to Schoeps, that God did not will evil in the devil; it is an expression of the devil's own will. This self-willed evil has arisen from a merging of the substances from which the devil is created: hot, cold, dry and wet. As long as these substances lay immanent in God they were not evil. But they yearned to merge and from the merging evil arose. By this means,

---

8. Cf. as regards the excursus on the Ebionites, H.J. Schoeps, *Theologie und Geschichte des Judenchristentums* (Theology and History of Judaeo-Christianity) (Tübingen: J.C.B. Mohr, 1949), and H.J. Schoeps, *Aus frühchristlicher Zeit: Religionsgeschichtliche Untersuchungen* (From Early-Christian Times: Investigations into the History of Religion) (Tübingen: J.C.B. Mohr, 1950).

the Ebionites countered the Gnostics' assertion that evil is part of the Creator-God's substance.

In different ways—often in close association with rabbinic Jewry's reference to God's two hands: one of justice and one of mercy—the doctrine regarding the devil was so fashioned that the oneness of God is upheld without making God directly responsible for having willed evil. In our context we shall be concerned with only one of the ways of describing this tension-charged relationship between God and the evil one, namely by employing the image of a father who has two sons.

To the Ebionites, Christ is not God but is in fact the son of God. It is emphasized in one of the texts that our Lord never called himself God; whereas God has in fact spoken of Christ as his son. This is a reference to the baptism, which plays a crucial part in Christology. According to the Ebionites' theology Jesus of Nazareth was a man; but by the baptism in the Jordan Jesus was chosen and appointed son of God. Through the promise of the son-relationship Jesus was adopted as son (Ps. 2.7), and by the Second Coming Jesus receives the position God intended for him in the redemption plan as lord of the world to come. (By this Christology the pre-existence of Christ and the virgin birth are both denied.)

The devil also has God as a father. As Abel and Cain have the same father, it says, so is it with the good son and the evil son. Both stem from God; the evil son in the same way as his brother the good son. Whereas Jesus is lord of the world to come, the devil is the lord of this world. The devil has not arrogated to himself power over this world against God's will; God in fact intended to use the devil to punish the evil of this world. Whereas Christ is the true son, *Christus aeternus*, who wishes to redeem man, his brother, the prince of this world, wishes to destroy man. And between them stands man with his liberty to choose either side.

The Ebionites clearly continue central ideas from the New Testament; but their solution to the theodicy problem did not become the church's solution. Whereas the Ebionites chose the monistic model, the model characterized by dualism was victorious—at least within the Western church. The narrative of a father and his two sons did not become the church's basic narrative, as some Judaeo-Christian communities might have wished. The models and narratives that succeeded, however, were characterized by combat metaphors and the preaching of Christ's final defeat of God's adversary Satan, as we learn, for example, from the Revelation to John.

A further heresy which consists of an extension of the image of God as a father with two sons, Satan and Christ, will be briefly referred to: the doctrine of apocatastasis.

In his 1967 article 'The Salvation of Satan', C.A. Patrides[9] has outlined the background and fate of the doctrine of apocatastasis. The main idea is that at the end of time all things will be mercifully restored. The theological consequence of this is, of course, rejection of the dual outcome of the judgment. If everything is to return ultimately to the original condition of purity and freedom from sin, the possibility of damnation is no longer real. The church therefore soon distanced itself from views that might be interpreted in this direction, whether formulated by a Clement of Alexandria or an Origen.

What particularly shocked the church's official representatives at the Council of Constantinople in the year 553, where the doctrine of apocatastasis was condemned, was the conclusion that it might be possible to save Satan also. It was not, however, the salvation of Satan that disturbed Clement or Origin. What was crucial for them was whether God's love had limits. But if God's love, as perfect love, was indeed limitless and irresistible then it could not even be excluded that God's mercy might be shared by Satan also.

The biblical starting point for the discussion was texts such as the Acts of the Apostles, where in 3.21 the Apostle Peter preaches that the time will come 'of universal restoration that God announced long ago through his holy prophets'. This was Paul's speech, that God shall become all in all (1 Cor. 15.28), and words such as those in 1 Jn 4.8, where God is defined as love.

The clear condemnation of the doctrine of apocatastasis subsequently caused the western church not to concern itself in practice with ideas of this nature; the matter arose in minority groups only, or was touched upon by individuals who found that Origen had been misunderstood by his contemporaries. An interesting example is the English theologian George Rust, who in 1661 took up Origen's teaching and reconsidered it, clearly intending to 'do justice to the Father'. Rust strongly emphasized that God is not only just but above all loving. The progress of the world must therefore also end in a restoration, when God became reconciled to the whole of his creation, the good as well as the evil. And if angels can turn into devils, Rust asks, would it not then please God all the more that devils become angels? Rust also did not find much sympathy for his views.

9. C.A. Patrides, 'The Salvation of Satan', *Journal of the History of Ideas* 28 (1967), pp. 467-78.

But that the official church condemned the doctrine of apocatastasis as in conflict with other Christian religious truths does not do away with the question of whether there are limits to God's love? Or, expressed in the imagery we are concerned with in this book, is it true that the father loves only one of his sons? Or is the father only a true father when both his sons are with him? Does the father suffer until the day when all can be one?

Such a day is dreamt of by the Greek author Nikos Kanzantzakis, from whom Patrides quotes the following vision of Lucifer standing at God's side as a glorious angel of light:

> One day Lucifer will be the most glorious archangel standing next to God; not Michael, Gabriel, or Raphael—but Lucifer, after he has finally transubstantiated his terrible darkness into light.

### The Fall and the Incarnation of Christ

> In the beginning was the Word, and the Word was with God, and the Word was God ... In him was life, and the life was the light of all people. The light shines in the darkness, and the darkness did not overcome it ... The light, the true light, which enlightens everyone, was coming into the world. He was in the world, and the world came into being through him; yet the world did not know him. He came to what was his own, and his own people did not accept him (Jn 1.1-11).

Thus does the Gospel according to John tell of the coming of the son of God from the heavenly world of light to the darkness of the earth. And when we read the Revelation to John we encounter in the last chapter of the book the following self-introduction, where Jesus says: 'I am of the root and the descendant of David, the bright morning-star' (Rev. 22.16). Jesus is the light that came to the world, it says in this tradition. But Jesus is not the only one who leaves the father's world of light. Satan also came to this world, and Satan can also be referred to as if one were speaking of the light.

We know from the Book of Job that the relationship between a father and his sons connotes nearness. We learn not only in the prologue that the sons are together with their father; this is also to be seen from Yahweh's great speech out of the whirlwind, for at that time God laid the bases of the earth and set the cornerstone, when the morning-stars sang together and all the heavenly beings shouted for joy (Job 38.6-7). Here, the morning-stars are referred to side by side with the sons of God. The author has not demythologized the concepts, but is clearly applying the image of

God surrounded by his sons. God is related to the heavenly lights, it says in imagery, and nevertheless one of the stars does not stay close to God.

One myth tells that one of the morning-stars fell down from heaven. The myth is not clearly rendered in the Old Testament, but the Prophet Isaiah uses the image of the falling morning-star in his satirical song about the King of Babylon. 'How you are fallen from heaven, O Day Star, son of Dawn! How are you cut down to the ground, you who laid the nations low! You said in your heart, "I will ascend to heaven; I will raise my throne above the stars of God; I will sit on the mount of assembly on the heights of Zaphon; I will ascend to the tops of the clouds, I will make myself like the Most High." But you were brought down to Sheol, to the depths of the Pit' (Isa. 14.12-15).

Scholars believe that behind this image of the fallen morning-star they can see an old Canaanite myth. Helel, a son of the auroral Shachar, tried to remove the supreme god Eljon from power; but as punishment Helel is precipitated from heaven into the kingdom of the dead. The myth can only be reconstituted, but there is little doubt that Isaiah's image draws upon concepts of this kind.[10]

Isaiah's version of the image also contained potential meanings that could be exploited in later times. The prophet Ezekiel's judgment of one of the great kings of his time, the king of Tyre, is clearly indebted to the passage from Isaiah, for according to the prophet this king of Tyre has committed the same crime as the king of Babylon; he has placed himself on a level with God. 'Your heart is proud, and you have said: "I am a god! I sit in the seat of the gods, in the heart of the seas," yet you are but a mortal, and no god, though you compare your mind with the mind of a god' (Ezek. 28.2).[11]

Ezekiel has clearly made use of the old concepts here in order to express the king's fall and the judgment on him. He describes him as a cherub who once lived in the garden of God. He was anointed and protected by God himself. Clad in the most beautiful clothes he walked on the holy mountain of God among the stones of fire, blameless in his ways from the day he was created, until iniquity was found in him. But when pride seized him, God drove him out of the garden. 'Your heart was proud

10. Cf. e.g. H. Wildberger, *Jesaja.* II. *Jesaja 13–27* (Isaiah. II. Isaiah 13–27) (BKAT; Neukirchen–Vluyn: Neukirchener Verlag, 1978), pp. 550-56.

11. Cf. as regards Ezek. 28, W. Zimmerli, *Ezechiel.* II. *Ezechiel 25–48* (Ezekiel. II. Ezekiel 25–48) (BKAT; Neukirchen–Vluyn: Neukirchener Verlag, 1969).

because of your beauty; you corrupted your wisdom for the sake of your splendour. I cast you to the ground; I exposed you before kings, to feast their eyes on you' (Ezek. 28.17). The radiant cherub was cast off just like the glorious morning-star in Isaiah.

In the Gospel according to Luke we encounter a very strange statement, which must have its origin in Isaiah's image of the fall of the morning-star. When Jesus dispatches the 70 disciples, they are commissioned to heal the sick and to proclaim that the kingdom of God is at hand. The 70 depart and return with joy, saying: 'Lord, in your name even the demons submit to us' (Lk. 10.17). Then Jesus answers them: 'I watched Satan fall from heaven like a flash of lightening. See, I have given you authority to tread on snakes and scorpions, and over all the power of the enemy; and nothing will hurt you. Nevertheless, do not rejoice at this, that the spirits submit to you, but rejoice that your names are written in heaven' (Lk. 10.18-20).

The coming of the kingdom of God means at the same time that Satan's kingdom will fall. God's adversary loses his power. In order to express this, the evangelist again uses the image of the fallen morning-star, de-scribed here as a flash of lightning from heaven. We also find the same concept of the struggle between good and evil in the Revelation to John. Here we learn of the fifth angel blowing the trumpet, and John tells that he saw a star fall from heaven down to earth, and it was given the key to the bottomless pit, and smoke rose up from the pit like smoke from a large furnace. We see that the star is no ordinary star but a heavenly being who can use a key and open the gate to the underworld.

In the Latin translation of the Bible, the Vulgate, the Isaiah passage's glorious morning-star is translated by the word Lucifer,[12] the bearer of light. This is the name the church fathers used for Satan himself, since before his fall Satan was the angel of light. Satan also appears in the *Life of Adam and Eve* 9.2, as an angel of light when he induces Eve to give up her penance in the River Tigris. Although Satan has been banished from heaven he can still clothe himself in the lustre of angels.

Satan's past history as an angel of light is included in Christian tradition, and is forcefully expressed in William Blake's well-known picture 'Satan in his Original Glory'. Satan is shown here in all his glory as the anointed cherub on the mountain of God. He is surrounded by all kinds of precious stones, as we hear of him from Ezekiel 28. But as well as this Blake adds

12. Cf. as regards the Lucifer concepts K.L. Schmidt, 'Lucifer als gefallene Engelmacht' (Lucifer as a Fallen Angelic Power), *TZ* 7 (1951), pp. 161-79.

a profusion of stars and little sprites, which are at Satan's disposal. With the globe in one hand and the sceptre in the other, Satan appears as lord of the world; but no one is in any doubt that his background is to be sought in heaven.

We sense a connection between these traditions, an impression that a heavenly one who had his existence close to God and was part of God's world of light was at some time cast out of heaven and down to earth. The coming of light to the earth does not express God's benevolent creator-presence with his creation, but that a fall has occurred among the heavenly, that an angel or son of God has tried to seize power from his father, the supreme God, and has been cast out of heaven as punishment.

We normally react with joy when we hear of light coming to the earth. For this reason it has a special impact when we come across a text which creates distance between heaven and light, between the heavenly and the angel of light. Suddenly we must extend our thought by using images that have more to do with distance and opposition than with nearness.

We have encountered various traditions about the journey of the sons of God from the paternal home to the outside world, but a common feature is the choice of the light as an image of the heavenly, and thus as characteristic of both Jesus and Lucifer.

In the Prologue to John we meet the image of the light coming to the earth with Christ. Creation repeats itself, the creative word is efficacious, and the light shines in the darkness. 'And the Word became flesh and lived among us, and we have seen his glory, the glory as of a father's only son, full of grace and truth' (Jn 1.14).

This is what the Gospel according to John has to say about the light of the world, Jesus of Nazareth. We find in Matthew and Luke the well-known stories of the Virgin Mary, who conceives by the Holy Ghost and gives birth to the son of God. Mark the Evangelist begins with the baptism and the promise, 'You are my Son, the Beloved'. All four evangelists agree that it is the son of God who comes into the world, but their way of expressing this varies.

'Let each of you look not to your own interests but to the interests of others', admonishes Paul in Phil. 2.4. And Paul continues:

> Let the same mind be in you that was in Jesus Christ, who, though he was in the form of God, did not regard equality with God as something to be exploited; but emptied himself, taking the form of a slave, being born in human likeness.

So does Paul tell of the coming of the son of God into the world (Phil.

2.5-7). The son was originally with his father, had the form of God, but renounced it and became like a human being.

The questions with which the Old Testament tradition grapples regarding the nearness and distance between God and the world is repeated in the New Testament. But the answers are often given in a way that causes us to see a surprising connection between the images.

We are aware from the Old Testament of the concept that a heavenly being who was part of God's world of light was cast out of heaven and down to earth: Satan as Lucifer. But in the Prologue to John it is Christ who comes into the world as the true light.

We are aware from Gen. 6.1-4 of the concepts that the sons of God came down to earth and entered the daughters of men and had children with them, giants and heroes who were famous. And later the evangelists tell of the virgin who became the mother of the son of God by the Holy Ghost.

But while the marriage of the sons of God to the women led to the misfortunes of the human race, according to the New Testament it also led to the redemption of the world in that the son of God voluntarily renounced equality with God and became man; indeed, he came so near to us in the flesh that he was born of woman.

Like the younger son in Luke 15, Jesus leaves his father's home. But whereas this younger son must of bitter need suffer humiliation and serve strangers Jesus chooses voluntarily to adopt the form of a servant. And common to them both is that they finally return home to their father and are reinstated in their former rights. The homecoming also forms part of the travel motif. The Letter to the Philippians reads as follows in regard to Jesus' homecoming.

> Therefore God also highly exalted him and gave him the name that is above every name, so that at the name of Jesus every knee should bend, in heaven and on earth and under the earth, and every tongue should confess that Jesus Christ is Lord, to the glory of the father (Phil. 2.9-11).

If we take a closer look at the source of Paul's images and motifs, we can immediately see that Paul uses motifs taken from Isaiah 53, the song of the suffering Servant of the Lord. But this does not exhaust the meaning of the hymn. We indeed know of the descent from the heavenly to share the fortunes of men from the traditions regarding the sons of God. But it is worth noting that the hymn in the Letter to the Philippians omits the marriage motif. Nothing is said here about Jesus' resulting from a marriage between heaven and earth, God and man. Jesus came from the heavenly to the earthly, and returned to the heavenly.

Paul also does not repeat as a matter of course what we can read about the descent of the sons of God, but he creates a contrasting text which explains that the descent is not the fall of the proud angel of light from heaven to earth. On the contrary, this son of God chose voluntarily to renounce his heavenly status. He did not cling to it, neither did he—in contrast to both angels and human beings—do anything to become equal to God. He renounced what was his own; not something he had usurped. His coming to earth was not therefore a fall but a voluntary humiliation in order to become at one with the world. This oneness reached its climax in the death on the Cross. The son of God entered into the very death which according to the ideas of the time was Satan's domain (cf., e.g., 1 Cor. 5.4-5), following which God exalted him and gave him his rightful position as the Lord.

Christ and Satan are therefore opposite cases, although both originally belonged to the heavenly. They mirror one another in their dissimilarity, and we must therefore see them in the light of one another.

In his extensive commentary on the Book of Ezekiel, Walther Zimmerli[13] refers to the hymn in the Letter to the Philippians as a Christian text contrasting with the myth of the great king's fall. The king of Tyre symbolizes mankind's unremitting attempt to become like God. In his pride and fall mankind's history repeats itself; it is the story not only of the king but of Everyman. Zimmerli then raises the question of whether there is only this one image of the reality of man: pride that ends in a fall? And in answer to this he indicates the contrasting story told by the New Testament, which proclaims what true humanity is: renunciation which leads to exaltation.

The hymn in the Letter to the Philippians struggles with a series of strong adversaries, as in the childhood narratives in Matthew and Luke. It was not unknown in the culture of the time for gods to choose wives for themselves from among humans. We have seen the important part played by the angel-marriages in the pseudepigraphic stories about the origin of evil. Such traditions belonged to the spiritual luggage of both Matthew and Luke when they had to tell of the origin of the son of God. Everyone at the time would have known that this Jesus came from Nazareth, and on suitable occasions a number of people reminded the enthusiasts that after all he was only the son of Joseph the carpenter. But the evangelists were in no doubt that Joseph's son was something different and something more. His origin was in the heavens.

13. Zimmerli, *Ezechiel*, p. 689.

When they tell of the angel's annunciation of the conception by the power of the Holy Spirit, of the angels' song on Christmas night when the heavenly world acknowledged the child in the stable, and of God's own words at the baptism in the Jordan, they are trying to convince us that Jesus was not only man but also God. The very image of the marriage between gods and humans used at the time to explain the origin of evil was given a new context to proclaim the good news. The story begins at the beginning, but in reverse.

The Gospel according to John expresses this in creation terminology: the word and the light come into the world. It is told in the childhood narratives in marriage terminology; but—it should be noted—with so many gaps in the well-known images that no one could be in any doubt that something vital is now happening differently. It is not the powers of evil making their entry to corrupt man, but the son of God bringing salvation.

As a result, Christian theology had also to employ Satan images which highlight the distance between God and the evil one and not the nearness.[14] When God came into the world as the son of God, Jesus of Nazareth, the purpose according to 1 Jn 3.8 was to overcome evil: 'The Son of God was revealed to destroy the works of the devil.' The images which refer to the struggle between good and evil therefore became theologically determinative. Where the devil is referred to as the ruler of this world in the Gospel according to John, this is indeed to emphasize the tension between God's world and this world. The coming of Jesus means that judgment is pronounced on the world and the ruler of the world is driven out (Jn 12.31), for the ruler of the world has been condemned (Jn 16.11). The synoptic gospels also see the works of Jesus as a struggle against Satan. One has only to think of the narratives about Jesus' healing of those possessed by demons (cf. for example Mk 1.21-28 par, and of Matthew's version of the dispute between Jesus and the Pharisees in Mt. 12.22-29), where the Pharisees accuse Jesus of using Beelzebul to cast out the demons.

But that these images, which insisted on the distance between God and Satan, became dominant should not cause us to overlook the fact that they are not the only images.

The biblical texts continually employ both ideas: the nearness between the two sons of God and the distance between the two sons of God. The

14. A detailed discussion of the New Testament concepts of Satan is to be found in B. Noack, *Satanás und Sotería: Untersuchungen zur neutestamentlichen Dämonologie* (Satanás and Sotería: Investigations into New Testament Demonology) (Copenhagen: Gads Forlag, 1948).

more one insists on the distance the less is heard of their common father, and the more one insists on the nearness the more important becomes the idea that they have the same father, and that this father suffers when love brings evil along with it.

We have introduced in this chapter the Ebionites' monistic heresy and the doctrine of apocatastasis. Both stress the oneness of existence, and both have clearly been rejected by the official church because they lead to the denial of other religious truths. But if we repress heresy we perhaps lose the awareness of some of those aspects which are also to be found in the biblical texts. What the Ebionites were fighting for was God's oneness as opposed to Gnosticism's dualistic thought-model. What the followers of apocatastasis were fighting for was accentuation of God's boundless love.

The biblical texts advance no dogmatic systems, but tell of God's continuous intervention in this world. And one of the ways of recounting this is by means of images of the relationship between a father and his sons. The sons are sometimes images of heavenly powers, and sometimes the image of the son is used of a person who is particularly close to God, someone like Job for example. The sons may be obedient, as Jesus showed himself to be when tempted in the wilderness; but the sons may also rebel against their father and go their own ways as when Semyaza and his brothers conspired against God and went down to earth. The father may choose to punish his disobedient sons, or he may temper justice with mercy. The freedom to choose love rather than justice is the freedom of the father; but suffering is part of love, whether this is pain because of the son's disobedience or suffering which the father shares when the son goes to his death for the sake of mankind.

The fact that the biblical texts tell stories and use images rather than developing dogmatic systems does not mean that the theology must become a purely narrative theology, or that theological study should consist only of the use and reuse of images, for theology includes not only images of God but also concepts of God. The church must be able to proclaim its message clearly and coherently, and in specific situations it must also be able to distinguish between what is true Christianity and what is heresy.

But having said this it should also be made clear that dogmatics' development of concepts has its roots in the Bible's narratives and imagery. Each generation is therefore obliged once again to take as its point of reference the use of images, and then call upon dogmatics to account for the demarcations it undertakes. Why was this or that minority view condemned as heresy?

Where does the controversy stand today? Are we again in a situation in which cosmological speculations demand an answer from the church, an answer in which the church cannot simply pretend that such speculations are by definition unchristian? This is undoubtedly true of some of those marketed today; but unless theology concerns itself with questions such as the relationship between God and Satan we can scarcely provide informed answers for those in doubt.

We live in a time characterized by uncertainty, in which clear and unambiguous answers are required. Theologians must now show their hand, set out the true position and say who represents which of the viewpoints. It can be tempting therefore to try to meet the need by choosing images which only indicate the distance between God and Satan. Theologians also recognize the pleasure and advantages of simple models. But in trying to reach a deeper understanding of such fundamental matters of existence as God and Satan we should not dismiss too glibly Niels Alstrup Dahl's[15] final admonition in his article on Satan's first-born:

> It is normally considered that the struggle against Gnosticism helped to make the Catholic church 'catholic'. But it should be seriously considered whether the heresy policy of rabbinic Judaism and the early Catholic church also contributed to making the Gnostics 'gnostic'. The old word was not without depth: orthodoxy and heresy are brothers—like Cain and Abel.

15. N.A. Dahl, 'Der erstgeborene Satans und der Vater des Teufels (Polyk. 7.1 und Joh 8.44)', pp. 70-84.

OPEN QUESTIONS

I have now read a series of texts in which the authors, each in their own way, make use of the image of a father and his sons to analyse the relationship between good and evil. They have chosen an unusually rich image. This image can be varied in a number of ways, and we are often surprised at the individual author's use of it. The image is used to answer profound existential questions; but at the same time a number of questions are raised which cannot be answered out of hand. For who in reality is the 'prodigal' son in the parable of the two sons? Is it the younger son or the elder son? Is it Jesus or Satan? And what about the fallen angel, who once moved freely in heaven but was later banished to the earth, the son of God also called Lucifer? Can this fallen angel also be described as a 'prodigal' son? And what does it really mean to speak of a 'prodigal' son when major texts emphasize that both sons are included in the father's love? What is apparently simple suddenly becomes extremely complex.

The biblical texts form part of an intertextuality open to different interpretations, and it therefore never leaves us in peace. But if we are to emphasize just one characteristic it must be the father's love for *both* his sons. This love is not without its problems; it is in fact bound up with pain and suffering, since it forms part of the image of active family life.

The relationship between good and evil is described in this image not by static concepts but by actions rooted in personal relationships. This accounts for the difficulty of including the relationships under one formula, and is the very reason why the image is suitable for expressing our experiences in words.

I shall not therefore end the book with a conclusion, but merely suggest the way in which study of the subject might be continued. The image chosen is only one among many. It is true that I regard it as a root metaphor in biblical literature, and thus fundamental to Christian theology, but this image must be supplemented by others if the richness within the tradition is to become manifest.

We cannot content ourselves with images which stem from the personal sphere. The animal world must be included; the images of the flock of sheep attacked by wild animals and of the eagle hovering caringly above its young as it teaches them to fly belong here. Fire and water, air and earth also have their place in the Bible's imagery, for all elements must be included if we are to speak truthfully of the basic conditions of life, of God and Satan. If we monopolize just one of these images and make it the limit of theology the reappraisal will end either in heresy or in narrow orthodoxy.

Images of family life are used to remind us of the complexity of life. And a closer look reveals that even the image of light and darkness, which gives a direct impression of clear opposites, contains opportunities to speak of nearness and interaction. This is to be seen most clearly in the image of Satan as the bringer of light.

The Danish hymn-writer B.S. Ingemann has written a morning hymn whose first verse reads:

> The angel of light walks in glory
> through the gates of heaven.
> Before the radiance of the angel of God
> flee all the black shadows of the night.

There is no doubt here that it is the angel of God who comes to the world and dispels all that is dark and threatening, since God is the God of light. But the old texts also recognize God as he who makes the light and creates the darkness. And these traditions are able to tell of one of the sons of God, an angel of light, who lost his place at his father's side but can still be described as Lucifer.

Nearness and distance, both must be included when the Bible speaks of the relationship between God and Satan. There was once a father who had two sons, and however different they may have been they were nevertheless sons of the same father. Or, using a different image: out of God's heaven issue both light and darkness, for from God stem both the son who the New Testament calls *the Light of the World* and the son who, on the evidence of the Old Testament, we may perhaps call *Lucifer—the shadow of God*?

# BIBLIOGRAPHY

Albertz, R., *Weltschöpfung und Menschenschöpfung: Untersucht bei Deuterojesaja, Hiob und in den Psalmen* (Creation of the World and Creation of Mankind: Investigated in Deutero-Isaiah, Job and the Psalms) (Calwer Theologische Monographien, 3; Stuttgart: Calwer Verlag, 1974).

Albright, W.F., 'Two Little Understood Amarna Letters from the Middle Jordan Valley', *BASOR* 89 (1943), pp. 7-17.

— 'North-west Semitic Names in a List of Egyptian Slaves from the Eighteenth Century BC', *JAOS* 74 (1954), pp. 222-33.

Alt, A., 'Zur Vorgeschichte des Buches Hiob' (On the Early History of the Book of Job), *ZAW* 55 (1937), pp. 265-68.

Andersen, F.I., *Job: An Introduction and Commentary* (TOTC; Leicester: Inter-Varsity Press, 1976).

Baker, J.A., *The Book of Job: Unity and Meaning* (Sheffield: JSOT Press, 1978).

Bartsch, H.W. (ed.), *Koptisch-gnostische Schriften übersetzt von (Leipoldt-) Schenke* (Coptic-gnostic texts translated by . . .) (*TF*, 20; Hamburg: Herbert Reich Evangelicher Verlag, 1960).

Beare, F.W., *The Gospel according to Matthew: A Commentary* (Oxford: Basil Blackwell, 1981).

*Biblia Pauperum, billedbibelen fra middelalderen med indledning og oversættelse af Knud Banning* (Copenhagen: Gads Forlag, 1984).

Black, M., 'Metaphor', in *Proceedings of the Aristotelian Society*, NS 55 (1954–55), pp. 273-94.

Bjørndalen, A.J., *Untersuchungen zur allegorischen Rede der Propheten Amos und Jesaja* (Allegorical Speech in the Prophets Amos and Isaiah) (BZAW, 165; Berlin: de Gruyter, 1986).

Bloom, H., *The Anxiety of Influence: A Theory of Poetry* (Oxford: Oxford University Press, 1973).

Bornkamm, G., G. Barth and H.J. Held, *Überlieferung und Auslegung im Matthäusevangelium* (Tradition and Interpretation in the Gospel according to Matthew) (Neukirchen–Vluyn: Neukirchener Verlag, 7th edn, 1975).

Bossman, M., 'Images of God in the Letters of Paul', *BTB* 18 (1988), pp. 67-76.

Boström, L., *The God of the Sages: The Portrayal of God in the Book of Proverbs* (Lund: Almqvist & Wiksell, 1990).

Brock-Utne, A., '"Der Feind": Die alttestamentliche Satansgestalt im Lichte der sozialen Verhältnisse des nahen Orients' ('"The Enemy": The Old Testament Satan Figure in the Light of Social Conditions in the Near East'), *Klio* 28 (1935), pp. 1-9.

Bultmann, R., *Kerygma and Myth* (ed. H.W. Bartsch; London: SPCK, 1953).

Capps, D., *Biblical Approaches to Pastoral Counselling* (Philadelphia: Westminster Press, 1981).

— 'The Bible's Role in Pastoral Care and Counselling: Four Basic Principles', in L. Aden and H. Ellens (eds.), *The Church and Pastoral Care* (Grand Rapids: Baker Book House, 1988).

Charlesworth, J.H. (ed.), *The Old Testament Pseudepigrapha.* I. *Apocalyptic Literature and Testaments* (London: Darton, Longman & Todd, 1983).

— *The Old Testament Pseudepigrapha.* II. *Expansion of the 'Old Testament' and Legends, Wisdom and Philosophical Literature, Prayers, Psalms, and Odes, Fragments of Lost Judeo-Hellenistic Works* (London: Darton, Longman & Todd, 1985).

Cooke, G., 'The Israelite King as Son of God', *ZAW* 73 (1961), pp. 202-25.

— 'The Sons of (the) God(s)', *ZAW* 76 (1964), pp. 22-47.

Cox, D., 'The Desire for Oblivion in Job 3', *SBFLA* 23 (1973), pp. 37-49.

Dahl, N.A., 'Der erstgeborene Satans und der Vater des Teufels (Polyk. 7.1 und Joh 8.44)', in Walther Eltester (ed.), *Apophoreta, Festschrift für Ernst Haenchen zu seinem siebzigsten Geburtstag am 10. Dezember 1964* ('Satan's First-born and the Devil's Father [Polyk. 7.1 and John 8.44]', in Walther Eltester (ed.), *Apophoreta, Festschrift for Ernst Haenchen on his seventieth birthday on 10 December 1964*) (Berlin: Töpelmann, 1964), pp. 70-84.

Day, P.L., *An Adversary in Heaven: śāṭān in the Hebrew Bible* (Atlanta: Scholars Press, 1988).

Drower, E.S., and R. Macuch, *A Mandaic Dictionary* (Oxford: Clarendon Press, 1963).

Duhm, H., *Die bösen Geister im Alten Testament* (Evil Spirits in the Old Testament) (Tübingen: J.C.B. Mohr, 1904).

Eagleton, T., *Literary Theory: An Introduction* (Oxford: Basil Blackwell, 1983).

Fascher, E., *Jesus und der Satan: Eine Studie zur Auslegung der Versuchungsgeschichte* (Jesus and Satan: A Study of the Interpretation of the Temptation Narrative) (Halle: Niemeyer, 1949).

Fish, S., *Is There a Text in This Class? The Authority of Interpretative Communities* (Cambridge, MA: Harvard University Press, 1980).

Fishbane, M., 'Jer. 4 and Job 3: A Recovered Use of the Creation Pattern', *VT* 21 (1971), pp. 151-67.

Fohrer, G., 'Zur Vorgeschichte und Komposition des Buches Hiob' (On the Early History and Composition of the Book of Job), *VT* 6 (1956), pp. 249-67.

Franzoni, G., *Der Teufel—mein Bruder: Der Abschied von der ewigen*

*Verdamnis* (The Devil—My Brother: Farewell to Eternal Damnation) (Munich: Kösel, 1990; publ. in Italian in 1986).

Frye, N., *The Great Code: The Bible and Literature* (London: Ark Edition, 1983).

Gerhardsson, B., *The Testing of God's Son (Mt. 4:1-11 & Par): An Analysis of an Early Christian Midrash* (Lund: C.W.K. Gleerup, 1966).

— 'Gottes Sohn als Diener Gottes: Messias, Agape und Himmelsherrschaft nach dem Matthäusevangelium' (God's Son as the Servant of God: Messiah, Agape and Dominion of Heaven according to Matthew's Gospel), *ST* 27 (1973), pp. 73-106.

Gesenius, W., E. Kautzsch and G. Bergsträsser, *Hebräische Grammatik* (Hebrew Grammar) (Hildesheim: Georg Olms, 1963).

Gibson, J.C.L., 'On Evil in the Book of Job', in L. Eslinger and G. Taylor (eds.), *Ascribe to the Lord: Biblical and Other Studies in Memory of Peter C. Craigie* (JSOTSup, 67; Sheffield: JSOT Press, 1988), pp. 399-419.

Ginzberg, L., *The Legends of the Jews I* (Philadelphia: Jewish Publication Society of America, 5728–1968).

— *The Legends of the Jews II* (Philadelphia: Jewish Publication Society of America, 5730–1969).

Girard, R., *La Route antique des hommes pervers* (Paris: Grasset & Fascelle, 1985).

Gordis, R., *The Book of Job: Commentary. New Translation, and Special Studies* (New York: Jewish Theological Seminary of America, 1978).

Green, M., *I Believe in Satan's Downfall* (London: Hodder & Stoughton, 1981, republished in 1988).

Haag, H., 'Abschied vom Teufel' (Farewell to the Devil) in H. Küng (ed.), *Theologische Meditationen* (Zürich/Einsiedeln/Köln: Benziger, 1969).

— *Teufelsglaube: Mit Beiträgen von Katharina Elliger, Bernhard Lang und Meinrad Limbeck* (Belief in the Devil: With contributions from Katharina Elliger, Bernhard Lang and Meinrad Limbeck) (Tübingen: Katzmann, 1974).

Habel, N.C., *The Book of Job: A Commentary* (OTL; London: SCM Press, 1985).

Handelman, S.A., *The Slayers of Moses: The Emergence of Rabbinic Interpretation in Modern Literary Theory* (Albany: State University of New York Press, 1982).

Hansen, K., *—og glædelig er hver en dag* (—and full of joy is every day. Sermons) (Hadsten: Forlaget Mimer, 1990).

Heinz-Mohr, G., *Plädoyer für den Hymnus* (Speech in Defence of the Hymn) (Kassel: Johannes Stauda, 1981).

Hoffmann, Y., 'The Relation Between the Prologue and the Speech Cycles in Job: A Reconsideration', *VT* 31 (1981), pp. 160-70.

Hofius, O., 'Alttestamentliche Motive im Gleichnis vom verlorenen Sohn'

(Old Testament Motifs in the Parable of the Prodigal Son), *NTS* 24 (1978), pp. 240-48.

Horst, F., *Hiob Kapitel 1–19* (Job, Chapters 1–19) (BKAT, XVI.1; Neukirchen–Vluyn: Neukirchener Verlag, 1974).

Jacobsen, T., *The Treasures of Darkness: A History of Mesopotamian Religion* (New Haven: Yale University Press, 1976).

Jasper, D., *The Study of Literature and Religion: An Introduction* (London: Macmillan, 1989).

Jeanrond, W.G., *Text and Interpretation as Categories of Theological Thinking* (Dublin: Gill and Macmillan, 1988).

Jirku, A., *Die Dämonen und ihre Abwehr im Alten Testament* (Demons and their Defence in the Old Testament) (Leipzig: A. Deichert, 1912).

Jülicher, A., *Die Gleichnisreden Jesu. I. Die Gleichnisreden im Allgemeinen* (Jesus' Parables. I. The Parables in General) (repr.; Tübingen: J.C.B. Mohr, 2nd edn, 1910).

Kaupel, H., *Die Dämonen im Alten Testament* (Demons in the Old Testament) (Augsburg: Dr B. Filser, 1930).

Keel, O., *Jahwes Entgegnung an Ijob: Eine Deutung von Ijob 38–41 vor dem Hintergrund der zeitgenössischen Bildkunst* (Yahweh's Reply to Job: An Interpretation of Job 38–41 against the Background of Contemporary Imagery) (Göttingen: Vandenhoeck & Ruprecht, 1978).

Kluger, R., *see* Schärf Kluger, R.

Knudtzon, J.A., *Die El-Amarna-Tafeln I-II* (The El-Amarna Tablets I-II) (Leipzig: J. C. Hinrichs, 1915).

Kort, W.A., *Story, Text, and Scripture: Literary Interests in Biblical Narrative* (University Park: Pennsylvania State University Press, 1988).

Kraus, H.-J., *Psalmen* (BKAT XV.1; Neukirchen–Vluyn: Neukirchener Verlag, 4th edn, 1972).

Lewis, C.S., *The Screwtape Letters* (Glasgow: Collins, Fount Paperbacks, 1942).

Lindström, F., *God and the Origin of Evil* (Lund: Almqvist & Wiksell, 1983).

Lods, A., 'Les Origines de la figure de Satan, ses fonctions à la cour céleste', in *Mélanges syriens offerts à M.R. Dussaud* (Bibliothèque archeologique et historique, 30; Paris: 1939), II, pp. 649-60.

Maag, V., *Hiob: Wandlung und Verarbeitung des Problems in Novelle, Dialogdichtung und Spätfassungen* (Job: Conversion and Assimilation of the Problem into Short Story, Dialogue Poetry and Late Editions) (Göttingen: Vandenhoeck & Ruprecht, 1982).

McFague, S., *Metaphorical Theology: Models of God in Religious Language* (Philadelphia: Fortress Press, 1982).

Malina, B.J., *The New Testament World: Insights from Cultural Anthropology* (London: SCM Press, 1983).

Mettinger, T.N.D., *In Search of God: The Meaning and Message of the Everlasting Names* (Philadephia: Fortress Press, 1988).

— 'The Study of the Gottesbild—Problems and Suggestions', *SEÅ* 54 (1989), pp. 135-45.

Milik, J., *The Books of Enoch: Aramaic Fragments of Qumrân Cave 4* (Oxford: Clarendon Press, 1976).

Müller, H.-P., *Das Hiobproblem* (The Job Problem) (Erträge der Forschung, 84; Darmstadt: Wissenschaftliche Buchgesellschaft, 1978).

Nielsen, K., *Yahweh as Prosecutor and Judge: An Investigation of the Prophetic Lawsuit (Rîb-Pattern)* (JSOTSup, 9; Sheffield: JSOT Press, 1978).

— *There is Hope for a Tree: The Tree as Metaphor in Isaiah* (JSOTSup, 65; Sheffield: JSOT Press, 1989).

— 'If You Loved Man, Why Did You Not Kill the Devil?', in K. Jeppesen, K. Nielsen and B. Rosendal (eds.), *In the Last Days: On Jewish and Christian Apocalyptic and its Period* (Festschrift B. Otzen; Aarhus: Aarhus University Press, 1994), pp. 54-59.

Noack, B., *Satanás und Sotería: Untersuchungen zur neutestamentlichen Dämonologie* (Satanás and Sotería: Investigations into New Testament Demonology) (Copenhagen: Gads Forlag, 1948).

Norris, C., *Deconstruction and the Interests of Theory* (London: Routledge, rev. edn, 1991).

North, R., 'Angel-Prophet or Satan-Prophet?', *ZAW* 82 (1970), pp. 31-67.

Pagel, E., *The Origin of Satan* (Harmondsworth: Penguin Books, 1996).

Patrides, C.A., 'The Salvation of Satan', *Journal of the History of Ideas* 28 (1967), pp. 467-78.

Petersen, D.L., *Haggai and Zechariah 1–8* (OTL; Philadelphia: Westminster Press, 1984).

Pöhlmann, W., 'Die Abschichtung des verlorenen Sohnes (Lk. 15.12f.)' (The Distribution to the Prodigal Son), *ZNW* 70 (1979), pp. 194-213.

Poland, L.M., *Literary Criticism and Biblical Hermeneutics: A Critique of Formalist Approaches* (Chico, CA: Scholars Press, 1985).

Pope, M.H., *Job: Introduction, Translation, and Notes* (AB; Garden City, NY: Doubleday, 1973).

Porter, P.A., *Metaphors and Monsters: A Literary-Critical Study of Daniel 7 and 8* (Toronto: Dr Paul A. Porter, 1985).

Prickett, S., *Words and the Word: Language, Poetics and Biblical Interpretation* (Cambridge: Cambridge University Press, 1988).

Rau, E., *Reden in Vollmacht: Hintergrund, Form und Anliegen der Gleichnisse Jesu* (Speeches in Authority: Background, Form and Message of the Parables of Jesus) (Göttingen: Vandenhoeck & Ruprecht, 1990).

Rengstorf, K.H., *Die Re-Investitur des verlorenen Sohnes in der Gleichniserzählung Jesu Luke 15, 11-32* (The Re-Investiture of the Prodigal Son in Jesus' Parables) (Arbeitsgemeinschaft für Forschung des Landes Nordrhein-Westfalen, Geisteswissenschaft, 137; Cologne/ Opladen: Westdeutscher Verlag, 1967).

Ricoeur, P., *Interpretation Theory: Discourse and the Surplus of Meaning* (Fort Worth: Texas Christian University Press, 1976).

— 'The Metaphorical Process as Cognition, Imagination, and Feeling', in S. Sacks (ed.), *On Metaphor* (Chicago: University of Chicago Press, 1979).

Robinson, J.M. (ed.), *The Nag Hammadi Library in English* (Leiden: E.J. Brill, 3rd edn, 1988).

Roskoff, G., *Geschichte des Teufels* (The History of the Devil) (Leipzig: Brockhaus, 1869).

Scharbert, J., 'Traditions- und Redaktionsgeschichte von Gen 6, 1–4' (Traditional and Editorial History of Gen. 6.1-4), *BZ* 11 (1967), pp. 66-78.

Schärf Kluger, R., *Die Gestalt des Satans im Alten Testament* (ed. C.G. Jung; *Symbolik des Geistes* 3; Zürich: Rascher & Cie. A.-G. Verlag, 1948. ET *Satan in the Old Testament*; Evanston: Northwestern University Press, 1967).

Schlisske, W., *Gottessöhne und Gottessohn im Alten Testament: Phasen der Entmythisierung im Alten Testament* (Sons of God and Son of God in the Old Testament: Phases of Demythologization in the Old Testament) (Stuttgart: Kohlhammer, 1973).

Schmidt, H., *Das Gebet der Angeklagten im Alten Testament* (The Prayer of the Accused in the Old Testament) (BZAW, 49; Giessen: Töpelmann, 1928).

Schmidt, K.L., 'Lucifer als gefallene Engelmacht' (Lucifer as a Fallen Angelic Power), *TZ* 7 (1951), pp. 161-79.

Schoeps, H.J., *Theologie und Geschichte des Judenchristentums* (Theology and History of Judaeo-Christianity) (Tübingen: J.C.B. Mohr, 1949).

— *Aus frühchristlicher Zeit: Religionsgeschichtliche Untersuchungen* (From Early-Christian Times: Investigations into the History of Religion) (Tübingen: J.C.B. Mohr, 1950).

Schramm, T., 'Bibliodrama und Exegese: Anmerkungen zum Gleichnis vom gütigen Vater (Lk. 15, 11–32)' (Bibliodrama and Exegesis: Commentary on the Parable of the Indulgent Father), *Kieler Entwürfe für Schule und Kirche* 11 (Kiel: Pädagogisch-Theologisches Institut Nordelbien, 1990), pp. 21-51.

Sløk, J., *Det absurde Teater og Jesu Forkyndelse* (The Absurd Theatre and Jesus' Preaching) (Copenhagen: Gyldendal, 1968).

Sternberg, M., *The Poetics of Biblical Narrative: Ideological Literature and the Drama of Reading* (Bloomington: Indiana University Press, 1985).

Tallqvist, K.L., *Akkadische Götterepitheta* (Accadian God-Epithets) (Helsinki: Firsted, 1938; New York: Georg Olms, 1974).

Thiselton, A.C., 'Reader-Response Hermeneutics', in R. Lundin, A.C. Thiselton and C. Walhout, *The Responsibility of Hermeneutics* (Exeter: Paternoster Press, 1985).

Torczyner, H., 'How Satan came into the World', *ExpTim* (1936–37), pp. 563-65.

— 'Wie Satan in die Welt kam' (How Satan Came into the World), *Mitteilungsblätter der hebräischen Universität Jerusalem* (Information Sheets, IV; Jerusalem: Hebrew University, 1938), pp. 15-21.

Tracy, D., *Plurality and Ambiguity: Hermeneutics, Religion, Hope* (San Francisco: Harper & Row, 1987).

VanderKam, J.C., *Enoch and the Growth of an Apocalyptic Tradition* (CBQMS, 16; Washington: Catholic Biblical Association, 1984).

Volz, P., *Das dämonische in Jahwe* (The Demoniac in Yahweh) (Tübingen: J.C.B. Mohr, 1924).

Wahl, O. (ed.), *Apocalypsis Esdrae, Apocalypsis Sedrach, Visio Beati Esdrae* (Leiden: E.J. Brill, 1977 [Greek]). A German translation is to be found in P. Riessler, *Altjüdisches Schrifttum ausserhalb der Bibel* (Old Jewish Literature apart from the Bible) (Darmstadt: Wissenschaftliche Buchgesellschaft, 1966 [1928]), pp. 156-67.

Walhout, C., 'Texts and Actions', in R. Lundin, A.C. Thiselton and C. Walhout, *The Responsibility of Hermeneutics* (Exeter: Paternoster Press, 1985).

Wellek R., and A. Warren, *Theory of Literature* (New York & London: A Harvest/HJB₁ Book, 3rd edn, 1977).

Wildberger, H., *Jesaja. II. Jesaja 13–27* (Isaiah. II. Isaiah 13–27) (BKAT; Neukirchen–Vluyn: Neukirchener Verlag, 1978).

Wimsatt, W.K. Jr, and M.C. Beardsley, 'The Intentional Fallacy', in *The Verbal Icon: Studies in the Meaning of Poetry* (Lexington, KY: University of Kentucky Press, 1954).

Wright, N.G., *The Fair Face of Evil: Putting the Power of Darkness in its Place* (London: Marshall Pickering, 1989).

Wright, T.R., *Theology and Literature* (Oxford: Basil Blackwell, 1988).

Würthwein, E., 'Gott und Mensch in Dialog und Gottesreden des Buches Hiob', in *Wort und Existenz: Studien zum Alten Testament* ('God and Man in Dialogue and Speeches of the Lord in the Book of Job', in *Word and Existence: Studies on the Old Testament*) (Göttingen: Vandenhoeck & Ruprecht, 1970), pp. 217-92.

Young, R. (ed.), *Untying the Text: A Post-Structuralist Reader* (London: Routledge & Kegan Paul, 1987).

Zimmerli, W., *Ezechiel. II. Ezechiel 25–48* (Ezekiel. II. Ezekiel 25–48) (BKAT; Neukirchen–Vluyn: Neukirchener Verlag, 1969).

# INDEXES

## INDEX OF REFERENCES

### OLD TESTAMENT

## OTHER ANCIENT REFERENCES

# Index of Authors